GRACE INTERLACED

A MEMOIR

VIRGINIA HESLINGA

3clocks
publications

GRACE INTERLACED

This book is dedicated to
Elizabeth Lynne Alexander Finnigan Drake,
August 1952-December 2022,
who told me in 1971 that one
day I would be able to write the full story.

RESPONSES TO GRACE INTERLACED

"*Grace Interlaced* is truly an inspirational story for anyone who is seeking God's grace in their own life journey. Virginia Heslinga has so eloquently expressed her innermost thoughts as she shares her own personal narrative of overcoming tragedy. A wonderful read that is heartening to the soul!"

Randi Marcinkiewicz, Licensed Mental Health Counselor

"As a former fire chief and 30-plus-year veteran of emergency services, reading Grace Interlaced drew me into the deeply emotional story of a family tragedy many in the emergency services community rarely see. As a former colleague of Professor Heslinga's, the raw description of some of her life's most intimate details highlights her courage and sensitivity regarding a story that needs to be told. As one who has been exposed to more than my share of psychosocial trauma, the arch of this story leaves you with an appreciation for the life-long and diverse nature of the effort to heal and develop as a human being. Get ready for not only a dramatic read but a poignant ride."

I. David Daniels, Ph.D., CSD, VPS

"Readers will come away with a greater sense of who Virginia is as a person due to the events that shaped her. Her faith and caring ways have always been evident, but the book also shows her strength, humor, family loyalty, and fears, all in a way that will resonate both with those who know her well and with strangers who are struggling with their own grief or traumatic experience but who may find the strength to persevere with the help of her book."

Carolyn Allard, Freelance Editor

"While walking my dog, I had a chance encounter with an exceptional stranger. This encounter was a gift from God because the stranger's words were a remarkable encouragement I have never forgotten. Like my experience, Dr. Heslinga has experienced the same type of mysterious gifts from God revealed in *Grace Interlaced*. They are real and impact for life."

Dale C. Bradley, Master Printmaker, Bradley Studio in North Adams, MA

"A pure and honest telling of a remarkable life story. Virginia's ability to have the reader relate, feel the emotions, and take the perspective of the main character (at each stage of her development) is noteworthy. The memoir is a beautiful telling of an individual's resiliency, and faith."

Christine L. Holmes, Ed.D.
NECHE/Project Consultant
Vice President for Academic Affairs (retired)

publications

Published by 3clocks Publications, LLC.

Grace Interlaced: A Memoir
Copyright © 2023 by Virginia Heslinga
Ebook ISBN: 979-8-9883543-0-7
Paperback ISBN: 979-8-9883543-1-4
Audiobook ISBN: 979-8-9883543-2-1

Cover and Interior Design by Gordon Saunders

Selection, coordination, and arrangement of cover photographs and text were created by the illustrator. The image of a young girl leaning against a house was generated by AI.

Publisher's Note:

This is a work of creative non-fiction. The author has presented the events to the best of her abilities. While all the incidents in the book are based on fact, some names and identifying details have been changed to protect privacy.

In addition to telling a story, the book aims to provide information and to stimulate action. The author and publisher make no claim to provide any type of professional advice. The author and publisher hope the contents of this volume will be helpful to readers. But readers must take responsibility for their own choices, actions, and results.

CONTENTS

1

FIRE, FLIGHT, FEAR

Our house was on fire. I was outside sitting against the wall of the neighbor's house. Flames like evil orange tongues took long licks at the window frames on the second floor. Then the tongues stuck out of the roof and licked higher, bulging, spitting sparks over everything. I could see the top of the house above the heads of the adults who crowded the edge of the grass next to our property. Smoke and ashes floated as slowly as an evil monster searching for someone to grab.

Some people came to watch out of distress and concern, but they didn't approach the house. Others, simply gawkers, arrived to stare and stand between me and the cement driveway. The thick, gritty, sour-smelling smoke peppered the whole corner of our block.

I'd seen a *National Geographic* special on carrion-eating birds. I'd heard the sounds those awful birds made—gravelly squawks, gagging caws, deep hisses—and they seemed to have no feelings as they picked at the dying and the dead. Their scary faces, noises, and bodies blended into the sights, sounds, and expressions of the people straining their necks to see the fire devouring my house.

Flames soared up from the back roof, and I shivered. People had arrived even before the fire trucks and police cars. But no one approached the house. They could see the danger of the fierce fire.

No one had come to help—no one except a young man who had just shown up on our front porch. He tried to help me get the little boys out of the house. But then he had disappeared. In the instant I turned to lift Daniel and grab Mark's hand to get them off the porch, the young man had left. I didn't see where he went. He was just gone, and we had to get away from the house.

How long ago was that? Thirty minutes? An hour? I thought it must have been at least an hour. It had taken two calls, one from my house and one from the neighbor's, and then more minutes before the fire trucks arrived.

After the trucks and firefighters appeared, I pressed back harder against the wall of the neighbor's house and tried not to think. I wanted to stop the most awful, frightening thought from forming. I stared at the firemen. They worked like a well-prepared team, moving hoses, ladders, and their bodies toward the house.

My parents arrived home. The police had stopped the cars on our street, a major avenue, but my father drove around the angled cruisers and right into our front yard, parking next to a fire truck. Both of my parents leaped out of the car. My mother staggered just a couple of steps, her hands over her mouth. My father ran to the ladder leaning against the front of the house. It stopped at the second floor window that was my brothers' bedroom.

A police officer took hold of my mother and pulled her back behind our car. A firefighter tried to grab my father, but he broke away and was up the ladder in seconds. With his fists he smashed the window to my brothers' bedroom. Dark smoke poured out like a hangman's hood over my father, and he started to fall backward.

A firefighter who had rushed up the ladder after my father prevented him from taking a long fall. Smoke kept rushing out of the broken window. The firefighter guided my father down the ladder. I missed seeing them touch the ground because people in the growing crowd moved closer together in front of me.

My parents had gone out to help the town determine a plan to raise money for the Red Cross. It was a school night, and they decided it would be fine for me to babysit my two younger brothers and our pastor's toddler son. The pastor and his wife were away at a convention.

I heard my mother screaming. Dad kept yelling; it sounded like a roar and had no words.

The crowd shifted. I saw my parents being escorted to an ambulance. I thought I saw the EMTs put the boys in the same ambulance too. Was it just Mark and Daniel, or had Andy been rescued from the house? The ambulance drove away, lights flashing and sirens blaring.

The crowd moved as slowly as a snake as they angled for a better view of the fire and the efforts of the firefighters. I sat still, feeling invisible, and prayed.

I often heard my parents say with pride that I was in church when I was fewer than two weeks old and had rarely missed a Sunday in my whole life. That was true for my brothers too. Church, God, the Bible, and praying were a daily part of our lives.

We learned that God answers prayers. God especially loves children. So I sat on the ground with my back against the cold siding and begged God to have the firefighters rescue my youngest brother. I had not been able to bring Andy out of the house.

I pulled my knees in close to my chest, and while I hugged them tight, I watched my house burn down, my life crash and break. Firefighters fought through steam, flames, smoke, and jets of water. So far, the fire had not been smothered. Smoke, like the long arms of a monster, had come out of the roof and through the window my father had broken.

My parents loved each other and each of us, but anyone with eyes and ears understood that Andrew was the favorite, not just of my parents but of almost anyone who knew our family. Andrew was my youngest brother. He was a sound sleeper once he finally quit acting silly and settled down.

My neighbors, the ones who owned the house on this side of our driveway against which I now sat and who were as old as my grandparents, were good people. Ever since they left the house to talk to the nearest police officer, I had not moved from my position.

The May night felt almost cold. In my green cotton pajamas, I shivered while watching the fire. I looked toward the flames still surging out of the rooms and the roof. I knew the world was not a safe place, but my house had been safe.

I didn't see anyone my age or younger among the people around me. I noticed some older teenagers, but only a few. They were the ones who hung out at the little shopping mall just a block from our house. Who would take their children to watch a house burn down on a May evening?

Could it really be Monday evening? Sunday, the day before, had been Mother's Day, and we had all given Mom treats. From breakfast in bed to gifts in the evening, she smiled a lot throughout the day.

Today we had gone to school. We came home and did our homework, and I helped Mom fix supper. The boys played.

Mom and Dad gave me reminders for my babysitting hours. They told the boys to listen to me and to be extra good playing with our pastor's toddler son. Then they left for the meeting where they would help to figure out how to raise the most money for the Red Cross.

Kids would have to go to school tomorrow, but I likely would not. I had no house, no clothes, and no one from my family near me.

My family had left in the ambulance without me. People put them in the ambulance without me. Would they need to put the fire out before anyone came looking for me?

I tried to think about what would happen if Andy had not been in the ambulance. Firefighters were strong, brave heroes. If they could go into the burning house, through the smoke, and put out the fire, then they could find Andy. If he'd breathed in the smoke, they could revive him.

Just when it seemed the water from the hoses was finally drowning the power of the fire, a chunk of the back roof and wall caved in with a whoosh and a growl. People shouted in surprise. The fire leaped, revived, and rose around the house as if chomping pieces out of it, chewing and laughing.

The conversation around me grew louder. I heard the crowd's guesses and gossip. People spoke like they knew what happened.

"I heard the babysitter was smoking."

"I heard the little boys were playing with matches."

"It was popcorn. They were making popcorn, and the butter caught fire."

"The parents just went out and left the children alone!"

"Imagine leaving a houseful of little children alone to go out for an evening!"

"Awful leaving children alone just to go out! Who does that?"

"I heard they had candles set up around a Ouija board."

"The babysitter was leading a séance."

"That house is a total loss now."

"Imagine going out and coming home to this!"

"Did the babysitter survive?"

"Did all the kids get out?"

I could have let all the voices and words around me become a wall of noise to tune out what everyone said, but I didn't. I listened. The babysitter was me. Most people thought the babysitter was the reason for the fire. I thought they were right, even if it wasn't from candles or a séance.

When I looked at the flames and the holes in the roof and walls, I knew we could never live there again. Firefighters had sent such huge streams of liquid over the house that I guessed our basement would be full of water, maybe to its ceiling.

Near me an old man hugged a woman and said, "It's a total loss."

Total loss. Everything was burning or covered with smoke and water. Total loss? I had nothing except the cotton pajamas I wore. The boys and my parents would have only the clothes they were wearing.

I'd been taught that God would take care of us. What was God doing now? Why did God allow this? I'd heard two sermons a week for most of my life, and I remembered now the ones about Job, who had lost everything and had asked God why. I knew what God had said to Job: "Who are you to ask me such questions?"

Job had suffered every kind of loss and still trusted God. Could I really trust a God who would take everything away? Job's wife had said, "Curse God and die." Job didn't do that.

In my house, we had a story from the Bible every night before bed. Mom would read them to us, but Dad made them come alive. He made the Bible stories exciting with acting and sound effects, and sometimes he assigned parts to us.

When Dad was in the army, he had learned to drop straight forward and yet not smash his face. With the David and Goliath story, we took turns being David. If we didn't get David's part, we could be Saul or the soldiers behind David. When we acted like David facing down Goliath and whirled a stone out of a slingshot, Dad's expression as Goliath would go from a frown to a wide-eyed stare. Down he would fall, straight forward, to land at David's feet. No matter which one of us was David, we enjoyed watching Goliath fall.

I wanted the fire to fall. It was bigger and more horrible than any Goliath. Did God hear my prayers now? What if Andy didn't survive? What if praying wasted time because God didn't care? Didn't exist? Did He choose not to stop the fire, or did He just let it burn because I had done something wrong?

Maybe if God wouldn't answer my pleading, I could offer my life to Him. So I did that. I told God I would do anything He wanted me to do. I would be a missionary in some faraway awful place for my whole life if Andy would be safe.

I had begged God over and over to rescue Andy. I had offered him everything by promising to give him my whole life —to send me wherever He wanted, to do whatever He wanted. Could that be enough to let Andy survive? What if it wasn't enough? What else could I do?

Would God care if I threatened? Could I say, "Rescue Andy or I can never trust You again. I'll turn away from You." Could I even do that? Would I make everything worse just by thinking about turning away from God?

The firefighters moved ladders and hoses. They climbed, chopped, and sprayed, constantly trying to put out the fire. I sat not knowing what had happened to Andrew, but I guessed.

I wondered how my parents would react if Andy died in the fire. How would they deal with Andy being gone? How would I?

Blame would come my way. I was the babysitter. Protecting the children in my care had been my main responsibility.

I might have only been twelve, but I'd been babysitting my brothers and other children for two years. Whatever happened would come down on me. It had to be my fault. I guessed it would be easier for people to blame a babysitter than to blame God.

Very slowly, keeping a hand on the house's smooth siding, I stood up. I thought I should go to the police officer I could see. I wished I had gone in the ambulance with my parents.

The officer was talking to our kind elderly neighbors. I couldn't walk to him, so instead I stared. Then I saw him look in my direction. The old man pointed and spoke to the policeman. The woman hurried toward me. Her husband and the officer followed.

What could they do to help? What would they say? Would any of them be able to tell me if Andy was alive or dead?

RIPOSTA FAMILY TREE

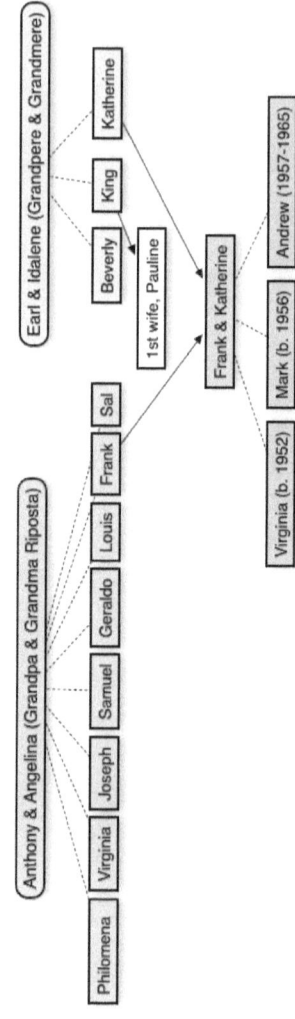

2

A SHARING HOUSE

My father set the rules in our house. We never questioned him about anything. He had his reasons, and he was the dad. We learned in church that the man was the head of the household, and Dad seemed suited to that role.

Dad grew up in Kearny, New Jersey, a mostly immigrant Italian neighborhood where children didn't learn to speak English until they went to school. His mother had eleven babies, but only eight survived to adulthood. While they were growing up, they rarely had the full amount of anything they needed: food, coal, furniture, or clothing.

Dad reminded us every time we sat down to eat that we were lucky. He reminded us when schedules or travel caused us to miss a meal that we really didn't know hunger. He reminded us each night that we were lucky to have our own beds, warm blankets, a house with plenty of heat, two parents who loved us, and a God who would always be with us.

I respected my dad, but that was partly from fear. Probably this was because I didn't get to know him until I was almost three. He had been away in Korea. Mom and I lived with her older sister, Beverly, in an apartment. Sometimes when Beverly could babysit, Mom would go to learn cooking and other household tasks from Dad's sisters. They taught her Italian meal preparation and how to keep a house.

In one of Dad's first days back from the service, when we weren't with his family at dinnertime, Aunt Beverly made a meal. I was in a high chair. Dad put a little of everything on my plate—fruit, vegetables, mashed potatoes, and meat. I ate everything but the meat, and Dad said, "Eat that; it's good."

"She doesn't eat meat," Mom and Beverly said, almost in unison.

"What do you mean, she doesn't eat meat?"

"She's never liked it. We've had her try it, but she always spits it out."

"We hardly ever had meat when I was growing up. My daughter will eat meat." Dad always expected what he said to happen. He picked up the baby-size fork, put some meat on it, and lifted it to my mouth.

I kept my mouth shut.

"Virginia, open your mouth and eat this. It's good for you."

I kept my mouth shut.

"Eat this." Dad lifted the fork again. I did not do what this man, a stranger to me, told me to.

"Eat this now," he said in a lower voice.

I still kept my mouth shut.

He put the fork down on the plate, scooped me out of the high chair, took me to the bathroom, and spanked me. I don't remember if the spanking was really as bad as Mom and Aunt Beverly said it was. They never spanked me. Mom said Beverly wondered if they should call the police, but they didn't.

I do remember the spanking. It was my first clash with this man who was my father. He brought me out of the bathroom and back to the high chair. He put some meat on the fork and offered it to me. This time I ate it. I ate every bit of meat on my plate.

Dad reminded us every day about something we should be thankful for. There was no complaining allowed because we had more than most people in the world. He always stressed sharing with others. I thought that Dad made us look at people poorer than we were.

Mom looked up to people who had more than we did and wished we could have a life like rich people. Dad didn't argue with her, but he reminded us that he had grown up poor in a big family. Mom had been the spoiled baby of her family who got almost everything she wanted. She had a romantic attitude and a vivid imagination.

The rule Dad stressed most in our house required each of us to always look out for the needs of other people. If we got up from the table to refill our water glass, we had to fill any other glasses that were not full. If we served ourselves some food without checking on what other people at the table needed, we had to leave right away and go to our rooms.

This command to share and look out for the needs of others guided our household, especially when Dad was at home. None of us wanted to face the punishment for not sharing. At the least, any selfish action would mean a scolding and being sent to our rooms. At the worst, selfishness would earn a spanking and no television for a week.

Mainly, Mark and Andy required me to share my attention. I had to share my time to help them learn to play games, to construct projects, to read to them, to supervise them, and to help them with their silly little kid homework. I also helped them memorize the Bible verses Dad required us to learn. I would do this by reading the verses to them over and over.

When I helped or played with Mark and Andy, Mom

could work on something without interruption or sometimes relax and watch her soap operas undisturbed. She would tell me I was a good big sister. She said that maybe when I was older, I could get a summer job for a rich family as a nanny. Then I could see how wealthy people lived because I would live with them and travel with them to take care of the children.

I didn't know why Mom thought I'd want a job taking care of other kids, but I didn't ask any questions. Dad expected respect. From Dad, Mom, and church, we knew we'd better be respectful of our parents and any elders.

With Mark and Andy, it was different. My expressions and tone of voice let them know when I was aggravated because I had to play with them. Mark looked hurt or sad by my tone of voice or abrupt actions. Andy laughed, shrugged, and did whatever he wanted to do, except when it came to pleasing Dad.

Frank and Andrew, 1958

Andy had special radar about sharing, especially if adults were nearby. "This is a sharing house," he would remind Mark or me. If Dad was within hearing distance and Andy and Mark fought over a toy, Andy would quickly push the toy toward Mark. He'd say, "You can have it. This is a sharing house."

Inevitably Dad would appear and say, "That's what I like to

hear," and he would beam with pride at his sons, especially Andy.

I thought about all this while I stared at our house. The house we had lived in for just three years was destroyed. There was nothing left to treasure or share. I doubted Dad would ever beam with pride at me again.

$$\backsim$$

THE POLICE OFFICER and the kind neighbors came to me.

"Oh! My dear, you must be cold!" The wife rushed into her house as fast as her little old legs could carry her. When she reappeared, she put a crocheted shawl around me.

"Thank you," I said as she hugged me. I had kept my arms around my chest. I'd needed a bra now, but I didn't wear one under my pajamas. I knew everything poked out when I was cold. The shawl felt great and let me relax my arms.

The policeman asked, "You're Virginia Riposta?"

"Yes."

"They took your parents and the boys to the hospital in the ambulances. Did you see the ambulances?"

"A little. People blocked my view. Did they get my brother Andrew out of the house?"

The officer continued as if he hadn't heard me.

"Your parents asked us to find you. Your brother Mark said you were outside. Are you hurt?"

"No."

"Your mother told us that if you weren't hurt, we should take you to friends. The Clauss family. Your parents will come there soon, after the hospital releases them from the emergency area. You know the Clausses?"

"Yes. Ed and Lucille. They have two sons."

"I'll take you there now. Your parents and the boys should be leaving the hospital soon and will join you there."

"The boys?"

"That's all they told me."

The officer held out his arm like ushers do. I reached out to take it, but before I could, both the neighbors gave me another hug.

The officer talked to me only briefly on the way to Lucille and Ed's house. My ears felt stuffed. I knew I was sitting up front in a police car. Even though I had an uncle who was a police detective, I'd never ridden in a cruiser. The officer finally stopped talking. I wondered if anyone taught them how to talk to kids after their family's house had burned down.

When did my parents know I was outside and not somewhere in that smoke? Daniel, the pastor's son, wasn't two yet. He hardly said any words. When had Mark told Mom or Dad or anyone else that I was outside? Had the firefighters spent time and risked their lives looking for me before Mark told them I wasn't inside the house?

Of the three of us, Andy did not have one bit of shyness. People noticed that. Dad and Mom seemed proud of their brown-eyed boy's personality.

I got out of the police car without any help. The officer walked carefully next to me toward the Clausses' home. Lucille Clauss opened the front door.

Andy would go through any open door. As Lucille hugged me, I felt the force of a memory of Andy sharing his enthusiasm naked in a crowd.

ANDY EXISTED like a roly-poly sprite when we lived in Carteret, even after he was old enough to go to school. Every house in our suburban neighborhood was a modern split-level according to 1961 standards. Young first-time homeowners filled our neighborhood. Mom said many people had bought their houses with veterans benefits after serving in World War II or in Korea.

67 Tennyson Street, Carteret, New Jersey

SUMMERS CONSISTED OF COOKOUTS, pool parties, even block parties because the neighborhood had a sharing spirit. In hot weather people wanted to spend evenings outside because few of the homes in the development had any air-conditioning other than a window unit in a bedroom or living room. On the hottest days, windows, front doors, and back doors with screens would be wide open.

One late May afternoon that was as hot as a summer day, my brothers played upstairs in a tub that had been filled so full of bubble bath that they could cover each other and their toys in thick capes of frothy bubbles. Mom was fixing supper in the kitchen. I was on the floor in the family room creating clothes for some paper dolls. The windows and doors were wide open.

Suddenly I heard the Mister Softee music. Mister Softee trucks usually went through our neighborhood late afternoons or early evenings on weekdays and midafternoons on Saturdays and Sundays. The loudspeaker on top of the truck projected the recording of bell-like music with the Mister Softee jingle that most kids in our neighborhood could sing.

> *The creamiest, dreamiest soft ice cream*
> *You get from Mister Softee*
> *For a refreshing delight supreme*
> *Look for Mister Softee*

Mark and Andy would hear the music even in the bath. Mom and Dad always let us get ice cream when the truck came down our street. Since we were in the middle of the block, Mister Softee often stopped right in front of our house. I decided to go ask for money to buy ice cream for the boys and me.

I walked to the second floor of our split-level house. When I reached the bottom of the stairs, I looked up and saw Mark and Andy running out onto the third-floor landing. They were naked except for capes and caps of bubbles. Mark stopped at the top of the stairs but not Andy.

Covered in a hood, cape, sleeves, and leggings of bubbles, Andy ran down the stairs, almost tumbling over himself.

"Andy! Stop!" I yelled. I reached out to grab him and got ahold of his arm, but the bubbles made him more slippery than a tadpole. He wriggled out of my grasp and laughed as he ran down the few steps to the first floor, then across the family room and out the open front door.

Should I chase my naked little brother out into a gathering crowd of parents and children? Not me!

"Mom!" I hollered as I saw more bubbles disappearing as Andy ran into the heat and sunshine. "Mom! Andy is outside naked!"

I didn't move any closer to the front door. I could not imagine ever showing my face in public again. Everyone at school would know about my little brother running outside to get an ice cream wearing only soap bubbles. Such a brother now surely would be talked about beyond our neighborhood.

Mom was smiling as she walked outside. I even heard her laugh. Laugh over this? How could she? Careful not to go outside myself, I went close to the front door just to hear what everyone was saying.

Parents laughed and called out to her. "Andy is up front!"

"Andy looks shiny clean, Katherine."

"Andy is getting a large free ice-cream cone."

"Mister Softee said he wants a picture of his special customer."

The driver did laugh. He practically shouted to his audience, "If I had a camera, I'd take a picture. I could make a poster. This kid drops everything for Mister Softee ice cream!"

Crazy, spontaneous, impulsive, determined, fast, and loving life—from people to ice cream—all these descriptions fit Andy. People loved him. No matter what he did, Mom and Dad loved Andy and laughed when he did something that would have gotten me in trouble.

3

SAFER IN HER CARE

My mind was dizzy with thoughts of Andy as Lucille led me into her house. So many memories swirled like a mixed-up movie. My head hurt. My eyes hurt. I stumbled, and the policeman reached out to keep me from falling.

It was the middle of the night. In all the houses and apartments that we had passed, people slept. Lucille and Ed rarely used their front door, but the policeman couldn't have known that.

Lucille and Ed Clauss had been watching for us. I heard them tell the police officer that my mom had called from the hospital. Mom told them that I would arrive before the rest of them, because I hadn't gone to the hospital.

Lucille smelled good and felt good as she hugged me tightly. Mom said Lucille was an Alabama belle transported to the north who lived for her family, friends, and public service. Mom envied Lucille's college degree in business from one of the oldest universities in Alabama. Lucille chose to be a stay-at-home mom. She participated in many of the town committees.

Mom admired Lucille, but my father said Lucille did too much.

The police officer stepped into the house behind me. Lucille led me through their small foyer and large living room, medium-size dining room, and into the kitchen. She pulled out a chair at the table for me and hugged me around the shoulders again as soon as I was seated.

"The family will probably be here soon," I heard the officer tell Ed. Then they both left the kitchen and walked back toward the front door.

"Virginia, honey." The word *honey* sounded slow, sweet, golden when Lucille said it. She hugged me again. "What is this? A shawl?"

"The neighbors gave it to me. I was cold."

"Are you warm enough now? Can I take it away?"

"Yes."

"What can I get you? Hot tea? Hot chocolate?"

"Nothing."

"I have some good sweet tea. You could have some of that." Ignoring my response, Lucille went to get a glass of her sweet southern-style tea. Our family put very little sugar in tea; we used more lemon, but doing something made Lucille feel better.

I guessed Ed would stay talking to the policeman out by the front door. Grown-ups tried to discuss serious things without kids hearing.

"Here you go. Are you hungry?"

"No. No, thank you."

She hugged me again and said, "I'll be right back." The officer had left, and Ed had closed the door. Now I knew they would talk there rather than in front of me. Lucille and Ed had always seemed to have more conversation with each other than my parents did.

I had the feeling it was Lucille who ran their household so smoothly. It would be Lucille who would cope with even this disaster coming into their home and family life. Ed would be the support for whatever she decided. I felt that was why my dad didn't like Lucille as much as Mom did.

In our house, the man made all the major decisions and many of the smaller ones. Lucille ran her house, and Ed seemed comfortable with that arrangement. Lucille could be a role model and a help to Mom and me. Even though Mom had an older sister, she needed a friend like Lucille. I had given Lucille a nickname right after we got to know her, Mother Helpful. Lucille liked the name. I felt safer in her care.

Mom was good at hospitality, visiting old people, playing the piano, and decorating. She made people feel special. I thought she probably practiced that a lot just to make Dad happy each day. He had moods. Andy did too. He was the most like Dad of the three of us.

I sipped the tea and tried not to think about the fire. I thought about Carteret, where we had lived when I was in the first to the fifth grade. Most women in our neighborhood were stay-at-home moms. They had coffee klatches, made crafts together, talked, traded coupons, shared recipes, and gardened.

The neighbors to the south of us, Helen and Manny, were fun. Helen loved movies, plays, soap operas, paintings on velvet, Frank Sinatra, Tony Curtis, Elvis Presley, Tom Jones, and shopping. She also held coffee klatches and invited women to bring their children.

Helen had a drawerful of different kinds of treats. A child visitor could always choose one. I knew only one other person who had this, my aunt Virginia. Helen and my Aunt Virginia were both Italian, daughters of immigrants.

Helen talked about her disappointment in not being able to have children of her own. Whenever anyone came to her house with a child, Helen talked about wanting children. My mom and others heard Helen's wishes, but they didn't seem to think she suffered. They envied Helen her free time and money.

Manny, Helen's husband, worked for a big movie theater, so entertainment news and the Academy Awards were Helen's main interests. She could talk about award-winning movies or the personal lives of famous actors and actresses like she knew them herself. I liked her facts about animal stars that Mark and Andy and I saw frequently: Lassie, Rin Tin Tin, Trigger, and Buttermilk. Movie stories to her were like Bible stories to Dad.

Walt Disney held a favored status with Helen. One day the women were talking about the latest Disney movie, and Mom was asked to comment on the ones we liked.

She looked embarrassed for a moment but then explained that we went to a very conservative church. As members, we had agreed not to go to movies. Total silence followed her statement. I thought that was good because I hoped they could convince Mom that going to Disney movies would be fine.

"What? Why not?"

"Disney movies are good, clean entertainment!"

"No movies? Are you serious?"

"Why can't you go to movies?"

Mom explained that money spent going to movies supported the values of a Hollywood lifestyle. The way people connected with the film industry did not support God's values. So our church asked members not to support Hollywood.

Everyone stopped talking and just stared at Mom like she was an alien. Finally, Helen said, "You agreed with that?"

"Frank did first, then I did. But it's just while we're members. It's part of what members promise. We'll follow those rules while we're members."

When any of our friends talked about 20,000 *Leagues Under the Sea, Treasure Island, Lady and the Tramp, Alice in*

Wonderland, Old Yeller, The Story of Robin Hood, Cinderella, Peter Pan, Sleeping Beauty, Snow White, or *The Shaggy Dog,* we just listened or talked about the books. We had the books of all those stories but hadn't seen the movies.

Dad took rules seriously. Mom went along with him because they were married. She knew Dad should be the head of the household. For Helen, depriving children of the experience of clean family movies seemed wrong. She said so and shared a solution that would let us see movies and not give Hollywood any money.

From that afternoon on, whenever a new children's movie came to Manny's theater, he would bring home the reels and a projector. Helen showed Mom the best location to hang a pale sheet in our house. Then Manny would bring the movies and projector to our family room and show the movies against the sheet on the wall.

We understood this arrangement was not to be spread around the neighborhood. Helen and Manny did not want the theater to lose business, but since our family didn't give them any business, Helen said this was okay. I guessed it was an acceptable way to get around the church rule. Mom went along with Helen and Manny's generous solution about the movies, and if Dad disagreed with her, we didn't hear them argue.

On movie nights, Mom made popcorn. We also had soda and sometimes even the kind of boxed candy they sold at the theaters. We three kids were on our best behavior in front of Helen, Manny, and Mom. Somehow Andy managed to eat as much of Mark's and my popcorn as he did of his own. Since we had a sharing house, we let him eat it.

THE MEMORIES MADE me feel like crying, but I didn't. I thought I should have already cried. I squeezed my eyes shut and opened them, but there were no tears. The fire had not made me cry. The worry over Andy and anyone who had gone in the ambulance had not made me cry. The memories had not made me cry. The nice neighbors and Lucille and Ed's kindness had not made me cry. What was wrong with me?

~

LATER LESSONS LEARNED: **Fire, Fear, Feelings**

More than half a century past my twelve-year-old self, I want to go back and sit beside her, close but not forcing a hug. My twelve-year-old self wouldn't have wanted a hug. She had a prickly sensation and a pressure behind her eyes for days but could not cry.

Traumas that threaten one's life, a one-time event or something chronic like any kind of abuse, have an effect that causes some people to cry constantly while other people don't have the ability to cry. Struggling against guilt or shame, thinking that you should have done something different, can shut off some emotional reactions.

Although my twelve-year-old self didn't cry, worse effects come from walling off deep connections to others. Posttraumatic stress disorder can cause concerns, fears, and reactions (or lack of reactions) long after the trauma. A common problem is irregular sleep patterns and being extra anxious at night.

No one in my family went to a counselor or support group. We didn't return to our regular routines until months after the fire. A calm atmosphere did not exist when the adults were on edge. We didn't talk about the fire or about our fears or feelings. Even if an adult had tried to speak with me, my instinct was to put it all behind the walls that had sprung up around my heart.

4

CRYING WHEN THE LIGHTS WENT OUT

I t was nearly two o'clock in the morning, and Lucille told Ed to go to bed because he would have to get their two boys to school. Ed did not agree. He insisted he would stay up until the rest of my family arrived. He gave me a few gentle pats on my back before he went to his office.

Suddenly, Lucille just stopped moving and looked at me. She focused on my wretched appearance in my pajamas. "Virginia, honey, why don't you go in the little bathroom there by the hall. I'll bring you some clean clothes and slippers. You can take a shower and put on a nice warm set of my pajamas. My underwear will be big on you, but it will be soft and clean."

I thought that sounded like a good idea because I felt grit on my feet, and the cold had gone through my pajamas and skin. The first thing I did was use the toilet. I saw blood.

Menstruation. Mom had told me the facts of life and about girls getting a period as a sign they were changing to be a woman. We'd seen a movie on menstruation in health class at school. Now? Now had to be the time I got my first period? I tried to remember if the movie said that something awful could make a girl get her period.

Would Lucille have any of the stuff a girl needed? She was older than my mom. Was I still a girl? I was twelve. Now I had my period. Did that mean I was a woman now? I didn't feel like a woman. I didn't even want to be a woman. I wanted to cry, but I didn't.

Lucille knocked on the door. "May I come in?"

"Yes," I answered but didn't move from sitting on the toilet.

"Virginia—are you all right?"

"I got my period for the first time. I don't have any stuff for it."

Lucille's hand went to cover her mouth like women do when they want to hide a gasp or a shocked expression. Then she blinked, took her hand down, and opened the cabinet below the sink. "You should just use a pad for now. Your period will be light for now, for the first few times. Sometimes you don't have it every month for a while."

"I saw that in a movie at school."

Lucille took out towels and a washcloth. "You take your time in the shower, honey. Being warm and clean will make you feel better. I'll give you a cup of hot tea when you come out."

It was 2:00 a.m. when I sat at the kitchen sipping hot tea with milk and sugar in it. Physically I felt clean and warm, but inside I shivered. I squeezed the hot mug of tea tight and tried to think of anything but the fire. I failed.

"Your parents will be here soon. I got a call, and some men from the fire department need to ask you a few questions. They'll come by later today when you've had some rest. You know they have to investigate."

Someone knocked on their back door, and Lucille opened

it. I could see two men in uniform. It was not the police. They were officers in the fire department.

Just the sight of them made me shiver more. I looked at my arms and hands to see if my shaking was visible. It wasn't.

Lucille looked concerned as she led the men to the table where I sat. I wondered if these firefighters had heard all the wild stories that had circulated among the crowd of gawkers who had come to watch the house burn down. What would they ask? Surely, they would wonder why I survived without getting all the children out of the house.

From the expressions on the firemen's faces, I guessed Andy had not survived. Lucille led the men to the kitchen table. Their expressions were serious.

The one with the special badge said, "Hello, Virginia, I'm Chief Denk. This is my fire marshal. We thought your parents would be here by now. We heard they were on the way."

"We thought so too," Lucille agreed. Ed came into the kitchen. He stood near Lucille, who stood near me. They hovered as if to protect me. I blurted out my main question.

"Did my brother Andrew get out of the house? Is Andy dead?"

The men exchanged a quick glance, and the chief said, "Virginia, we are very sorry to tell you that Andrew inhaled too much smoke."

"While he was sleeping?" As I asked the question, I felt a deep numbing inner cold.

"Yes. He inhaled smoke while he was asleep."

"Because he was in the top bunk?"

"Yes. The smoke was thickest near the ceiling. The smoke had grown thicker and had been rising for some time before the fire burst out and the electricity went off."

"He died from inhaling too much smoke?"

"Yes." He paused and looked at me.

When I didn't cry or act upset, he said, "Do you think you can answer some questions? We need to ask some questions before we can give a final report. We must collect information from people who were in the house while we complete our investigation of everything that happened. The little boys can't help us."

"Are Mark and Daniel all right?"

"Yes, with a few minor problems. The hospital will check them carefully. Do you feel like you can talk to us now?"

"Yes."

"And answer some questions?"

"Yes."

Lucille pulled out a chair and sat close to me. Ed stood behind her with his hands on her shoulders. The fire marshal took out a pad and pencil.

"I need to write down all the information you give us," he said. I nodded.

"Will you tell us anything you can remember about what happened last night since you're the oldest person who was in the house?" the chief asked.

"I was the babysitter. I babysit a lot, not just for my brothers but for other people too. My parents went to a committee meeting about raising money for the Red Cross."

"Do you remember what time they left?"

"About seven. The boys were ready for bed. We had a visitor, our pastor's son, Daniel. I put Daniel to bed right after my parents left. We had a crib set up in my room. I don't sleep with a night-light, but we had one on for Daniel since he doesn't know our house, and his mom said he sleeps better with a night-light."

"Where was the night-light?"

"In the back of my room. I read him a story, sang a couple of songs to him, prayed with him, and went back downstairs to watch TV with Mark and Andy. I had to get them into bed by eight."

"Did they go to bed by eight?"

"Yes."

"Upstairs in the room with the bunk beds?"

"Yes, the one at the front of the house. Andy has the top bunk."

"Did they go right to sleep?"

"No. They never do. They talked and were silly. I yelled at them. I scolded them before they got quiet." For a moment I couldn't say anything. Andy was dead, and the last thing I did was yell at him to stop being a brat and go to sleep.

The firemen waited quietly until I could say more. A tiredness seemed to melt my insides. I had to lean on the table.

"The third time I went upstairs to tell them to be quiet, Daniel started crying because their noise had woken him. I went in to see him, and I sang to him again. He wanted stuffed animals and pointed to some. I have a lot of stuffed animals because I collect them. My room was full of them. I put a bunch in his crib, and he seemed happy. He laid right down with them. The boys got quiet then, so I went downstairs. Around eight thirty Daniel started crying again."

"You know the time?"

"There's a clock right by our television. It's an old clock, but it runs on electricity now. I always pay attention to the time when I'm babysitting. People usually ask when their kids did something or went to bed."

"When Daniel started crying again, at eight thirty, what did you do?"

"I went back upstairs. I tried singing to him. I rubbed his

back and gave him another stuffed animal, but he was still sobbing. So I went into Mark and Andy's room and woke Mark. I told him he had to sleep in my bed. Daniel settled down as soon as he saw Mark in the bed near the crib. Mark fell right back to sleep as soon as he got into the bed."

"And Andrew was still asleep in the top bunk, in that front bedroom, the room over the living room?"

"Yes, and Mark and Daniel were sleeping in my room."

"Everything seemed fine then?"

I didn't get to answer the question because the house phone on the wall beside us rang. We all stopped talking as Lucille reached to answer it, but I didn't stop thinking. While Lucille was on the phone, we sat quietly, and I remembered another time when Andy could have died.

ANDY WAS JUST eleven months younger than Mark and five years younger than me. When Mom came home after having Andy, she leaned down to show the new baby to Mark and me. Mark moved in close to touch him. He even kissed Andy's forehead.

I remembered I had stayed back. With a second son in the house, my father would be even more proud of having boys. Dad's voice deepened to a special tone every time he said the word *son*.

Brother sounded like a normal word when my mother said it, but when Dad said *your brother*, his voice went deeper and rose in volume, like a flag raised at a special ceremony. Whenever we went anywhere, my father made the introductions for our family: "This is my son, Mark; my wife, Katherine; and my daughter, Virginia."

So now there was another brother. I could just hear the introductions: "These are my sons, Mark and Andrew; my wife, Katherine; and my daughter, Virginia." In his view sons were in a higher category than Mom and me.

My father was full of plans for them right away. I never heard him talk about set plans for me unless it was about going to church events. For Mark and Andy, I'd heard him talking about Little League, Cub Scouts, and Royal Rangers. Sometimes Dad would hold both boys, one in each arm, and talk to them about what they'd do in the future. His voice sounded like a big cat purring. Mark would look right at his face like a serious little man. Andy gurgled, smiled, laughed, or patted Dad's face.

But one day Andrew's happy baby personality changed. It happened right when he started to be able to hold and drink a bottle by himself. Mom had been relieved when she could leave Andy with a bottle to drink on his own.

Mom never nursed any of us. Some women on the Italian side of the family nursed their children. But Mom told me putting a baby to the breast was for people too poor to buy bottles and formula, too old fashioned, too primitive, or just too ignorant. No woman in our Carteret neighborhood nursed their babies. None of the relatives on Mom's side of the family in New England did either. They all wanted to use the latest scientific formulas.

Just days into being given a bottle to hold and drink on his own, Andy's attitude toward all of us, toward every day, changed. His natural smiley happiness evaporated. He cried more and loudly. Sometimes he would just scream. It wasn't a scream of pain. He sounded angry. Even when Mom picked him up, he still looked furious.

One day into that week when Andrew became extra loud with screaming cries, Mom and I rushed into the boys' room and saw Andy staring at Mark through the bars of his crib. Mark was guzzling down the full bottle that Mom had given Andy.

When did Mark first take a bottle from Andy? Whenever he had, Andy must have expected Mark would take a drink and give it back. We watched Mark drink the whole bottle fast, then give it back to Andy, empty. We had discovered why Andy was whining, crying, screaming, and angry.

Mom rarely yelled, but she did now. "Mark!"

He jumped and turned to look at us. His face was a deeper red than his auburn curls.

"Take Mark downstairs," Mom growled like a lioness. "Mark, you sit on a chair in the kitchen. Virginia, bring me another bottle for Andy."

I took Mark by the hand, and we went down to the kitchen. Mark didn't look at me when I left the kitchen with another prepared bottle. He just sat on a chair, swinging his legs. He was so little that his feet were a long way from the floor.

Although I was surprised that Mark was drinking Andy's bottle, I didn't have the angry waves that rolled out of Mom. I guess she thought Andy really could have died from not drinking his bottles. She'd wait until she was calmer before she talked to Mark.

I knew that she'd say she was going to tell Dad. Mom didn't spank. That was Dad's responsibility. Dad always talked to us before he spanked us, and he was calm when he gave the spanking, whether he used his hand, a belt, or a wooden spoon.

Studying Mark, I guessed Dad wouldn't spank him much, maybe not at all. Mark seemed barely more than a toddler, and he was the first son. What would Mark understand from this? Probably not much except that he better not take Andy's bottles anymore.

Mark and Andy, 1958

ANDY HAD a temper but didn't hold grudges. I didn't even think babies could hold grudges. To me, they were like puppies.

It didn't matter that Mark had stolen most of Andrew's bottles for days; Andy still smiled every time he saw Mark. He'd survived days with little food. We couldn't know if he'd even had one full bottle during that time.

I wondered, *Had Mark really wanted Andy to go without food? Had Mark been jealous of Andy? Would Mark have wanted Andy gone?*

LUCILLE PUT THE PHONE DOWN. "They'll be here soon."

We all were silent for a few moments. Then the chief said, "So it was after eight thirty. Mark and Daniel were in your room. Andy was asleep in the top bunk."

"Yes. I went downstairs and watched *Dr. Kildare*, and everything was quiet. Then *Ben Casey* came on. That show starts at ten. Usually, I have to go to bed at ten, but not if I'm babysitting. Daniel started crying again about ten fifteen. He was so loud, I thought he would wake Mark and Andy.

"I ran upstairs, but I was only halfway up when the television shut off and all the lights went out. I stopped. The flashlight was downstairs, on a shelf between the kitchen and the basement.

"But Daniel kept crying a screaming kind of cry, so I ran upstairs. At the top, I could see a big light from my room. Daniel was standing up in the crib, crying. Mark was still asleep.

"The whole wall by the head of my bed was covered by fire. I have long drapes, ceiling to floor. The drapes—" I had been trying to tell these men everything that had happened that evening, but it felt almost impossible to describe the drapes. I pictured that sight again and forced the words out. "The drapes were like a wall of fire."

I stopped talking. The numbness that had covered me for the past hours melted. I could see and feel the wall of fiery drapes again. It had sucked the air out of the room. The sight of it punched me in my brain, lungs, and heart.

I couldn't talk. I felt like I had breathed in fire. I didn't move or speak.

The fire marshal cleared his throat. Lucille rubbed my back in circles from between my shoulder blades down to the low part of my spine.

Then the chief said, "We can stop for now." The man who was writing looked up at me with an expression that held no pressure to demand that I say more. He agreed with a nod.

I swallowed, blinked, and said, "I want to keep going." I did want to finish telling them everything I remembered, but just then the door they had used to come into Lucille and Ed's house opened again.

A policeman stepped inside. He turned to help someone behind him into the house. The firemen stood up together and to see who was arriving.

Mom came in first. She was holding Mark by his hand. He clutched her clothing with his other hand, clinging like the baby orangutans we'd seen at the zoo cling to their mothers.

Dad came into the kitchen after them. He walked like each foot had a giant weight on it. I had never seen him look so confused. His suit jacket and shirt were gone; he wore just his T-shirt. He had bandages on his hands and partway up his arms to cover the injuries he'd sustained when he broke the window to the boys' bedroom. Like a sleepwalker, he turned his head toward Lucille and Ed. He blinked and stared like he was trying to remember their names.

Then he saw me. His eyes fastened on my face. Waves of confusion caused his expression to twist and twitch. His eyes became laser-focused on me. He spoke in a hoarse voice.

"If you could get two out, why couldn't you get three out?"

Mom and Lucille gasped loudly enough for me to hear them. The men from the fire department exchanged glances.

Dad stared right at me. He looked around the room, then back at me. His eyes locked on me like he wouldn't turn away until I gave him an answer.

What could I say? I felt like my insides were being crushed to a pulp just by hearing the question. *If you could get two out, why couldn't you get three out?* Should I tell him how hard I tried? It wouldn't matter to him. I hadn't rescued his favorite son.

As if he thought I had not heard him, he repeated his question more loudly. "If you could get two out, why couldn't you get three out?"

The chief stood up quickly, with the fire marshal directly following. They turned to face my father, standing shoulder to shoulder. They created an instant uniformed wall between my dad and me.

Mom cried, "Oh Frank!" She gave clingy Mark a push toward Lucille. Mark started to cry. Lucille reached for him, and he held tight to her.

Dad spoke again. He wasn't looking at me anymore, but he still wanted an answer. With a groan in his voice and his words slurred, he asked again, "If she could get two out, why couldn't she get three out?"

"Shhh, shhhhh," Mom said to him. She cried. Mom and the policeman guided Dad into the little sitting room beyond the kitchen. Lucille called it a parlor. It was *L* shaped, so I couldn't see my parents anymore, but the policeman came back into view.

I could hear both my parents crying. Mark didn't make any noise. Lucille put her hand on my shoulder, then turned and said something softly to Ed. He went into the parlor.

"Just sit, Frank. Just sit there," I heard Ed say. Then we all heard Dad cry, ragged, gulping sobs—sounds I'd never heard before.

Mom reappeared. She said to me, "He didn't mean that. Virginia, he didn't mean that." Then she began to sob while tears streamed down her face.

Why do adults tell such clear lies when they try to help someone who has heard awful words? I knew he meant it. He would always mean it. I would always know he meant it. *If you could get two out, why couldn't you get three out?*

Lucille put her arms around my mother and guided her back to the parlor. Mark went along too. He would not let go of Lucille. The firemen looked at each other and then at me but didn't say anything until Lucille reappeared with Mark.

Mark seemed like a slow-motion ball in a pinball machine, moving one way and then another. Lucille led him past everyone and out of the kitchen. We could hear her talking to

Mark as she took him upstairs. "I have a sleeping bag and a Jetsons pillow for you. My boys are asleep in twin beds in that room. You just get into the sleeping bag and go to sleep."

The policeman who had led my parents into the house talked softly with the two fire department officers. Then he nodded to them and left the house.

The fireman who had been taking notes said to me, "Young lady, you did an amazing job tonight, one many grown-ups could not have done. We're going to leave now, but we'll come back later today, after you and your parents have had some rest. We need to get any additional information that you can give us. But you need to rest now." The chief nodded in agreement.

They walked to the door, but the chief turned and said, "Your father is very sad and upset. People say things when they're upset that they don't mean." Then he nodded to me, and they left the house.

People say things they don't mean when they're upset? I did not believe that. In my heart and thoughts, when people were upset, they said things they did really think. When people aren't upset, they can control what they say. People can hide what they're really thinking when they aren't upset.

My dad had fought in the Korean War. He was bossy in our house, but I did not think he was mean. He always stressed the value of helping people, of sharing. He gave a lot to others, especially those who didn't have much of anything. God wanted us to help people. That's why he and Mom had been out working with the Republican, Union, and Red Cross Committees. They were hoping the town campaign would raise a lot of money for the Red Cross.

The question Dad had asked me came from his real thoughts. I knew that. No matter what the firemen said, or Mom said, or anyone said. Dad had asked what other people would wonder about.

I knew he had asked his heart-and-mind question. I asked that same question of myself. I just never thought anyone else would ask it of me, out loud, in front of other people. I had no answer. I didn't know if I ever would. I didn't know if he really expected a response. I just hoped he wouldn't ask it again, especially not in front of more people.

WHEN DAD TOLD us to do something, we'd get in trouble in an instant for not doing it—right then, no waiting. I joked with my friends that my dad had a dictator attitude, but he wasn't mean. He spanked us or punished us in some other way if we did something wrong, but it was a penalty, not meanness.

I was different from my dad. I knew that I had a mean streak. I had felt it and had used its power. Before I fell asleep on the couch in Ed's office in those early hours of May 11, I remembered times when I should have been a better big sister to my little brothers.

Whenever Mom and Dad were busy, the boys became my responsibility. By the time I had reached fourth grade, I felt like an experienced babysitter. Anytime during the day, I could be put in charge of supervising the boys in their simple-minded silliness. Once I asked if I could be paid for babysitting. Dad said, "You live here, don't you? Use water, heat, electricity, food, clothes, trips, and toys? That's enough pay, I think."

We had one car. If Mom wanted it, she had to drive Dad to work. Since he had three jobs, there never seemed to be a time when the car sat in our driveway. I knew babysitting was in store for me one Saturday morning when Mom woke me early. "I'm taking Dad to work so I can have the car for shopping today. The boys will be up soon."

I don't remember if I said anything before I got out of

bed, but Mom knew I would be wide awake when Mark and Andy got up. They would run downstairs for breakfast and television in the family room. On Saturday mornings they liked to watch *Howdy Doody* and *Bozo the Clown*. I preferred *Sky King* and *Fury*, but we had only one television. The babysitter needed to let the boys watch their favorites until an adult was home to supervise sharing.

Through the picture window in our family room, I watched Mom and Dad drive away. Dad had his early Saturday jobs at a factory. It was so close that Mom could drive him there and be back in fifteen minutes.

Soon after they left, Mark and Andy made their typical jumble-tumble noise coming down the stairs. Today of all days, they had gotten up extra early. I wished they'd stayed asleep until Mom got back.

They jumped, pushed, and laughed as they came down to the first level, to our big family room, and stopped. Then they looked around and ran into the kitchen, where they found no one and no food on the table. They came back through to the family room and saw me by the window.

"Where's Mom and Dad?" Andy asked.

In an instant, I chose to put on a serious expression. I liked drama and making up stories. I didn't know if they would believe me, but I'd try to convince them.

"They're gone."

"What do you mean, gone?" Mark asked. He was always more sensitive and quicker to believe me than Andy.

"They said they're sick of us, especially you two. You're so loud and silly. You make messes. You make Mrs. L come over here, complaining about you taking her flowers and eating her tomatoes. So they're gone. Mom and Dad left us."

Mark looked right at me when I said these lies with the best serious acting that I could muster. His eyes instantly filled with tears. He walked to the window and looked out.

Andy stood where he was, looking at me and then at Mark. He still didn't get it.

"Where's Mom and Dad?" he asked again.

I looked him in the eye and said, "You're so much trouble; they're sick of you and Mark and me, and they left us."

"No," Andy disagreed and frowned at me.

I said nothing.

"They're coming back?" Andy asked Mark.

Mark, still crying quietly, said, "No."

Then Andy began to cry. There they were, the two little people who drove me crazy. They had changed my life by showing up in it. I couldn't believe how easily Mark had believed me, and Andy had too, only a minute later. Now that I had convinced them, I felt bad about making them cry. I knew they'd better not be crying when Mom got back.

"Do you want some cereal? I'll fix you breakfast." I knew I needed to calm them down before Mom got home. So why didn't I tell them right then that I had made it up?

Andy hugged Mark. They sat down on the floor, hugging each other and crying. I stood watching them and wondered how I could get them to stop fast. I didn't want them to even have tears on their faces when Mom got back.

Just then Mom turned into the driveway. Mark and Andy didn't realize this because they were still sitting on the floor, hugging and crying on each other.

"Look! Mom's back!" I shouted. They stopped sobbing and stood up just as Mom came into the house.

"What's going on?" she asked as they rushed to her and hugged her legs.

When Mark told her what I had said, she looked horrified, then close to tears herself. "Virginia, how could you be so mean? Go to your room. Just wait till your father gets home! I'm so disappointed in you."

She took the boys to the kitchen and gave them cupcakes for breakfast. When she went grocery shopping, she took both boys with her, something she normally did not do. Mom told me to stay in my room. I watched them leave and stayed in my room with my books and toys.

I wondered how long Mom and Dad would continue to think sending me to my room was a punishment. For what I'd done that day, it wouldn't be my only punishment. What else would happen? I would have to wait until Dad got home.

Dad had the role of disciplinarian and took pride in strict control over all of us, except Andy. He was always easier on Andy.

Spankings and punishments were doled out calmly. We couldn't know whether he would just go through the motions because he didn't want to spare the rod and spoil the child. He quoted Proverbs 13:24 to us. Even when he exploded verbally, he always stayed calm when he spanked us.

When he got home from work, Mom had me stand next to her while she told him what I had done. Dad had looked at me like I was someone or something he had never seen before. Then he said in most serious, quiet voice, "Don't you know how much your brothers love and trust you? You lied to them. You scared them."

I was wearing jeans and a T-shirt. He had me bend over, and he spanked me with his leather belt. He did this calmly, like he spanked any of us. Before he sent me to my room, he said, "I'm very disappointed in you, Virginia."

Now, on this day, May 11, Dad definitely blamed me. That thought and the feelings of loss and fear kept me awake long after I had settled into the sheets and blankets Lucille made into a bed on the couch in Ed's office. I couldn't imagine what he would say or do later this morning.

5

SHOWING UP

D ad's older brother, Uncle Gerry, who was a detective, got information first about the fire and Andy from someone at his station. He called all the other brothers and sisters. The family arrived just after Ed left to take his boys to school.

Showing up means a lot to Italian families. Showing up means love. If there is a special reason for family to gather, only a serious problem or illness can prevent them from showing up.

At every family event, people noticed who showed up, who gave kisses to whom, and who hugged with good big hugs. If I went into a room filled with family and kissed only half the people, those who did not get a kiss would wonder if I was in a bad mood or mad at them. If there was something to celebrate, it was a joy to get together. If there was a sad reason, showing up shared a clear message of caring. Like food, showing up and affection represented love for my Italian relatives.

Just like we always needed to have more food than necessary at any gathering, we also needed to give abundantly of affection. Loudness and the emotions suited to the gathering also were expected. Andy did well with all of it. He'd run to people with hugs and kisses. He loved getting and giving hugs and kisses. Andy seemed naturally loud. We teased that he had swallowed a microphone.

Mark and I did what was expected, but it felt awkward to me to know we had to kiss and hug everyone in the room. Andy loved attention. He was a natural actor, and he easily ran around a room, kissing and hugging family.

On Tuesday, May 11, at 8:00 a.m., my Italian uncles entered with respectful quietness when Lucille opened the door. I had just come out of the study and watched them surge through Lucille and Ed's house. Mom was in the kitchen, fixing coffee to take up to Dad.

The brothers changed that plan. Uncle Sammy and Uncle Sal went upstairs without the coffee. Louis, Joe, and Gerry hugged Mom and led her to a chair at the kitchen table, where they also placed platters of food. That was another family rule. Never show up empty-handed. Bring food—delicious, varied, and a lot.

Uncle Sal was the youngest brother, the baby of the family. Dad and Sal had both been in Korea. Dad stayed a private in the trenches. Sal became a driver for a general. Uncle Louis liked to have Sal as a driver when they were going someplace out of their town.

Uncle Louis was a big man physically. He called on his youngest brother, slim, trim Uncle Sal, for a variety of jobs. Uncle Sal looked like a movie star and moved like a prize fighter. He had worked dealing cards for special private games in New York City and as a bodyguard.

I didn't move closer to the kitchen. I looked up the stairs and wondered if any one of them could bring back the father I had before the fire. Mom was wilted, stunned like a bird that had crashed into a picture window. She was hurt and confused, but I could still see and feel she was the mom we knew.

Uncle Gerry looked like a detective, strong, solid, and serious. He stood by Mom's chair speaking softly to her, with his hand on her back, not alarmed that she cried. Dad's family cried when they were happy or sad. Dad's four older brothers had all fought in World War II but had returned to New Jersey to achieve success through hard work and by helping one another. Uncle Louis was the one to make millionaire status.

Uncle Joey was the eldest brother, slim, neat, and organized. He seemed tense and intense to me. I wondered if that came from being the oldest brother of a big bunch.

Uncle Sammy usually smiled and joked, but I'd been at his house enough to see that he had the temperament I'd come to expect of Italian men. Temper—it could blow up in an instant but disappear minutes later. The man was happy again and expected everyone else to forget about the temper blast too. Uncle Sammy, like everyone else in the family, was generous. He owned a popular bar and restaurant.

My father's older sisters, Aunt Philomena and Aunt Virginia, did not come along this early morning. I knew why, just like I knew why the wives of Joey, Sammy, Gerry, Louis, and Sal had not come. They had children to look after, to get off to school. They wanted to protect their children from sadness and thoughts of death, especially the death of a child. Dad and Mom wanted to protect us too. It hadn't worked.

I leaned against the wall where I could look up the stairs. Uncle Sammy and Uncle Sal were bringing Dad down. They talked and hugged him as they walked into the kitchen. But they didn't stop there. They continued to the parlor.

Lucille came to stand behind Mom's chair as the men left her to surround Dad in the little parlor, where sad cries of disbelief were heard loudly. The brothers all freely stated that

Frank was the good one. I knew that in high school he had considered becoming a priest. Dad's family believed a religious family member, priest or nun, could help them with prayers for getting into heaven after probably a time in purgatory. I thought their wives would rate a lot less time in purgatory for having persevered in marriage to these domineering uncles of mine.

Once I asked Mom why we didn't live closer to Dad's family. She said she didn't want to live where most of the people didn't speak English as their main language. I knew she wondered what everyone was saying when they talked in Italian. I wondered too. They spoke in Italian now in Lucille's parlor.

Uncle Louis suddenly declared in English, "This shouldn't have happened to Frank. God should not have let this happen." I wondered what God thought of Uncle Louis's pronouncement.

Everyone in Dad's family believed in God, but only Uncle Louis would actually say what God should and shouldn't do. If Dad had been in his right mind, he might have cautioned Louis, but Dad wasn't in his right mind. There was no way to know what he would say, especially if it was in Italian.

Lucille stood close and seemed protective of Mom. Dad had all his brothers. I had one brother and thought I should go see what he was doing.

I NEVER KNEW how a memory could fill a slow walk up a flight of stairs. This memory was of my most outstanding time of being a mean big sister. I'd gone upstairs then too with a plan for terrifying my brothers.

Every summer from the time I was a toddler, I went to

Maine to stay with Mom's parents, who we called Grandmere and Grandpere. They rented a pony for me in the summers after I turned ten. My friends in Maine had horses the way my friends in New Jersey had bikes. Once the pony's owner saw that we took care of the animal well, we could have the same one the next year. For a couple of summers, I had a pony named King.

Summer in Waldoboro, 1964

KING WAS reddish-brown in color and was an Indian pony, so he looked like a pinto. King had the energy of a firecracker. He threw me a few times at the start of every summer, but when I persisted in getting back on, he eventually settled down.

The boys couldn't ride him alone. Mom and Dad had me lead them around the yard on King. I watched the pony carefully and held the reins firmly. As much as Mark and Andy drove me crazy, I didn't want them to get hurt.

King did not like noises, but Mark chose to act like his

favorite cowboy, hollering out words he heard on *Bonanza* and *Gunsmoke*. Andy whooped, then said he was an Indian chief. King flicked his ears forward and back at the noises Mark and Andy made. King had my sympathy.

Every time I led them around the barn or over the nearest mowed field, the boys smiled and laughed. My parents and grandparents looked happy because I kept the boys smiling right up till suppertime. Then all anyone had to do was mention dinner, and Mark and Andy slid off the saddle.

Supper was delayed when the owner came with his horse trailer to pick up King. This provided more amusement for the boys because King did not want to go into the trailer. He showed his resistance by prancing, stomping, and pulling, which provided entertainment that the boys loved.

At supper, Mark asked if I felt sad that King had been taken away. I said I did feel sad, but just a little. Grandmere and Grandpere didn't want a pony year-round, and there was no way we could have an animal like King in our yard in New Jersey.

The next day was worse. There was no pony to distract Mark and Andy from following me and demanding my attention. Anything I tried to do, the boys interrupted with noise, needs, or whining. Mom and Dad said I should play with them.

I took the boys outside. They had no single idea about what to play. They rolled down hills, dug in a sand pit, climbed apple trees, and threw apples at each other.

All summer I enjoyed the apple trees. I would take a pile of books that I had chosen at the Waldoboro Library, climb into one of the trees, and read the day away. When I got hungry, I would reach out and have a fresh apple. I could spend all day by myself traveling to other places and times through books.

Now I had to follow the boys around and watch their silliness. I didn't remember ever acting like they did. I liked being on my own and reading.

As the sun went down, and they still ran around yelling and laughing, I started to think about the secret room I had discovered under the eaves the previous summer. Behind a bookcase that looked like it was built into the wall was a long attic room that Mark and Andy had never seen. They didn't know it existed.

Tucked under the eaves with a built-in bookcase front, the room was invisible to anyone who didn't know about it. In the early 1800s, when the farm had been built, people still feared attacks from local tribes. There was a full fieldstone walled cellar to hide in, but some houses, like this long old farmhouse, also had a shelter on another floor.

Every shelf of the bookcase that covered the entrance was filled with books. I'd read half of them. The room outside the secret room had twin beds. I slept in one of those beds when I was alone in the house with my grandparents through the summer. When my parents arrived with Mark and Andy, the boys got the room with the twin beds. My parents had the double bed in the guest room, and Grandmere made the divan in her sewing room into a bed for me.

Most evenings after supper, the adults watched television or read books, or Mom and Grandmere took turns playing the piano. They could both play by ear. We children could play games or do crafts until an adult said, "Time to go to bed." Mark and Andy had to go to bed earlier than I did.

I could go upstairs and get ready for bed while they got their bedtime snack, a drink of milk, a cookie, or a piece of pie. Then they would go up to their room. They'd use the large upstairs bathroom between the room with the twin beds and Grandmere and Grandpere's bedroom. They'd brush their teeth, get their pajamas on, get into bed, and wait for an adult to come up and pray with them. The only time this routine changed was if the boys were so dirty that they needed a bath. They got as much water on the floor in their playing as they did over their bodies, but they never had to clean it up. Mom and I did that.

I went upstairs as soon as the boys went to the kitchen for their snack. I had time to grab Grandpere's big black leather gloves and black balaclava and then get into my own pajamas and into the secret room before the boys came upstairs. I knew where to reach between the books to unlatch the bookcase door. There was a window in the far end of the secret room, so on this summer evening, I had plenty of light.

A trunk that had belonged to my mother's brother was the right height for a seat near the bookcase door. I could sit on the trunk while I listened and watched for the boys get into bed. On one bookshelf, an opening as tall as a book and an inch wide allowed people in the secret room to look out.

Mark and Andy didn't have to go to sleep right away in the summer, and they never did. They talked, made fart sounds with their armpits, had a contest on who could burp louder, told silly knock-knock jokes, and sang goofy songs until a grown-up appeared. After that, if they could stay quiet for just five minutes, they'd fall asleep.

As evening fell, rain clouds rolled in, fully covering the sky. The clouds outside the windows gave the room a gray dusky color, dim and ghostly, which was perfect for my plans.

I wanted the bookcase to remain silent except for the one scratchy squeak I knew it could make if I pressed down on the inside handle while I opened the door. Waiting, I sat on the trunk and listened to my brothers yapping like silly puppies. Then I heard the toilet flush and the water run. Finally, after wrestling and bumping into walls, they were ready to enter the bedroom.

Mark flung the bathroom door wide open and rushed to his bed. He dove onto the twin bed right next to the bookcase. When Mark was alone with Andy, he acted almost as silly as Andy. He twisted like a human pretzel on the bed, laughing and talking to Andy. He alternately kicked out a rhythm against the books. Mark often treated books with roughness. He did not like to read.

Andy ran into the room and leaped onto his bed. He bounced on it like an acrobat on a trampoline. Both boys laughed at each other and at nothing. They talked about what they'd do the next day and slowly put their feet under the covers. But they remained sitting up. Mark had his back to the bookcase as he faced Andy, and Andy sat on his bed looking at Mark.

I had put on the black balaclava before the big black leather gloves. Those I pulled on and up my arms almost to the elbow. The light from the moody evening sunset was gone. Dusk filled the windows, so everything was bathed in shades of gray. Slowly, like a vampire rising from a crypt, I moved the bookcase door.

The first eeeeeking squeak of the antique hinges caught Andy's attention. He was facing the bookcase and saw the wall slowly move. Mark probably heard it, but he paid more attention to the change in his brother's switch from playful to frozen.

I kept moving the bookcase door slowly because it made more noise that way. As soon as the space was wide enough, I moved my right hand into view in slow motion. I had curved my gloved hand into a claw shape. Then I had to give up the view of Andy's wide eyes because I moved to the edge of the opening to stick my head out.

Andy's brown eyes stayed on me, and they could not have opened wider or become any rounder. He raised a hand and pointed at the bookcase like a Shakespeare character pointing out a ghost. His index finger and hand wavered toward my raised claw. Eyes wide, mouth wider, Andy didn't make a sound.

Mark turned quicker than a hummingbird. Wearing the balaclava, only my eyes were visible. He saw the claw hand raised above my head. Mark turned into a redheaded rocket that flew out of the room right behind the little brother who screamed all the way down the stairs. I heard them hollering through the corridor, into the dining room, and then into the living room, where they cried to the adults about a monster coming out of the wall.

The adult voices raised in startled confusion, but I couldn't understand what they were saying. Tones and words combined in surprise and anger. I heard them coming to the stairs. I laughed, even though I knew I shouldn't because I would be in trouble. Still, I laughed. My plan had worked.

If we were home, I'd be spanked and cut off from any family fun for at least a couple of weeks. Here in Maine, Dad's reaction would be milder. He wouldn't want to upset Grandmere and Grandpere, even though he thought they spoiled me. It wasn't his choice that I spend every summer in Maine with Mom's parents, but he'd been letting it happen since I was a toddler.

Grandmere and Grandpere had never spanked any of their children. Dad said anyone could guess that fact. I wasn't sure how he knew they had never spanked any of their three children, but he seemed to think anyone could tell.

Some other punishment would come my way. I had known that when I chose to scare the boys. The whole plan, the whole effect, the simple pieces of costume and action, had totally panicked my brothers. I saw it as a mean but successful joke.

Dad gave me a spanking. He used his belt, the soft part, since he held it by the buckle end. He also said I would go to bed early that night, and for the last two days we were in Maine, I was not allowed to watch television or to read.

Mom and Grandmere seemed surprised and sad. They found it hard to believe I would try to terrify two little boys who loved me and looked up to me. Grandpere didn't give any opinion, but the next morning he took me with him into town at eight o'clock for coffee and freshly made doughnuts at his favorite Waldoboro general store. Since he'd been a deputy sheriff, I thought he might have the most to say about my behavior, but he didn't talk about it at all. I felt like he had some sympathy for me, even though everyone else seemed disappointed by and angry at my behavior.

From that night onward, Andy chose a shield of music, like he believed singing loudly would give protection against anything scary. When he and Mark were told to go up to bed, Andy would sing Christian songs full volume. His favorite was "We Shall See the King."

Andy sang loudly as he and Mark went through the hallway and up the stairs. He kept singing while he brushed his teeth, got into his pajamas, and dove into bed and pulled the blankets over his head. That's how the rest of us knew the boys were not only in bed but also under the covers waiting for the adult who would come upstairs to say nighttime prayers with them.

THESE MEMORIES HURT my heart now. They were what I had been thinking of before I opened the door to the Clauss boys' room to see what my remaining brother was doing.

LATER LESSONS LEARNED: Jealousy and Resentment

Why are siblings who love each other and who share life's experiences mean to one another? I wondered that at twelve. Probably by college I understood that I experienced jealousy toward the boys who seemed more valued by Dad. Conflict resolution in our house was a threat from Mom to tell Dad or a stern quick punishment of some kind from Dad. Frustration or anger that could not be shown to adults can come out as meanness to siblings.

Counselors in the twenty-first century advise showing empathy to the older sibling who is mean to younger siblings. It is also recommended that a parent communicate separately with each child. Building individual connections with each child can create a sense of security and support. No one ever explained to us that some fighting or arguing is normal among siblings and that it is a way for children to sort out problems or figure out strategies to move through conflict.

6

HELPERS AND HATERS

Mark played with Ray and Ed's toys. I wondered if he really felt happy and free of bad memories while he played with toys that were all new to him. He had not been clingy since Lucille had taken him to her sons' room to sleep.

I knew Mark wouldn't miss going to school. He liked his teacher and had friends, but he didn't like schoolwork and hardly ever talked about school at home.

He looked up when I came into the room.

"Hi. I came up to see how you're doing."

"Hi. I'm playing."

I could see that. I could also tell he didn't really want to talk. He had not spoken much at all since I woke him to pull him out of bed, away from the fire.

"Ray and Eddie have a lot of toys."

"They said I could play with any of them."

"They told you that before they went to school?"

"Yes."

I couldn't remember the last time Mark had a roomful of

good toys to play with alone. Ray and Eddie had toys that appeared in commercials frequently, but they also had toys their dad had made for them. Ed had made his boys a home-made version of Lincoln Logs, and this handcrafted set had a lot more logs and connectors than the store-bought version.

What did Mark think about? Was he able to ignore everything and play?

Mark didn't yet understand how much we'd lost. He knew Andy was gone, dead, but he hadn't asked any questions about it.

Mark looked up at me and smiled. He could still smile. I didn't know if I could. No one expected us to smile. When I looked down at his head, I could see that all the hair on the top of his head looked bleached, but it wasn't. It was singed from being so close to the wall of fire. How could he have been so close to the flames that his hair had been singed by the heat and not woken up until I pulled him out of my bed?

"Uncles Joey, Sammy, Gerry, Louis, and Sal are downstairs."

Mark didn't say anything.

"Do you want to come down and have some breakfast?"

"No."

"Would you like me to play up here with you for a while?"

"Sure." He turned and smiled at me like I was giving him a treat.

"You're being a really good kid playing up here. Did any of the uncles come in to talk to you? Uncle Sammy and Uncle Sal came upstairs to bring Dad down for some breakfast."

"Nobody came in here."

"They probably didn't even know you were in here playing. Everyone downstairs is sad."

"'Cause Andy is dead."

"Yes." I reached out for some of the logs to fit together. I thought I could build a cabin or a fence to go with what Mark had already constructed.

"Andy's in heaven." He spoke without looking at me. I sat down beside him.

"Yes."

"Probably the angel took him there."

"The angel?"

"The one who helped us."

"An angel helped us?"

"Uh-huh."

"Where was the angel?"

"Inside, then outside."

"What angel?"

"The guy."

"Who? The guy who showed up on the porch?"

"I guess."

"What do you mean, you guess?"

"He looked different on the porch."

"Different from what?"

"Different from how he looked inside the house."

"You saw him in the house before we saw him on the porch?"

"Uh-huh. Upstairs. His clothes were different upstairs when he picked me up and took me downstairs."

"What? The same guy?"

"Yes."

"He was upstairs? He brought you downstairs?"

"Yes, in the bedroom. I was yelling to Andy. The guy was behind me. Then he was next to me."

"When you were in your bedroom?"

"Yes. The smoke hurt my eyes. He picked me up."

"You just let him pick you up?"

"He was strong. He hugged me. He smelled good."

"He smelled good? Didn't you smell smoke?"

"Not when my face was by him. He carried me downstairs."

"Mark, you think the same guy who talked to me on the porch was in our house?"

"Yes. He was."

"He brought you downstairs when you were trying to wake Andy?"

"Yes."

"You didn't tell me that before. Are you sure?"

Mark looked directly at me. "The guy on the porch looked the same in his face but his clothes were different."

"Is that why you think the guy was an angel?" I put down the log pieces I'd been holding and stared at Mark.

Mark set down two handfuls of Lincoln Logs. He looked at me and answered so carefully that it seemed like he thought I must be stupid to not understand what he had told me. "The angel brought me down the stairs. He didn't smell like smoke. He was an angel, and upstairs he had white clothes. He had white clothes when he left me at the bottom of the stairs. When you grabbed me by the stairs, I didn't see him. He was gone. Just gone."

"You're sure it was the same guy as the one on the porch?"

"Yes. I saw his face up close when he carried me."

"In the house?"

"Yes, in white clothes and on the stairs and when he left me at the bottom of the stairs."

"You didn't say anything about him."

"You pushed me outside. You put me on the porch and gave me Daniel to hold. Then I saw the angel guy on the porch. He had different clothes."

"But upstairs in the house he had on white clothes?"

"Yes. I yelled to Andy. I yelled to Andy to wake up, like you told me. I was crying. My eyes hurt. My nose hurt. I went to the bed. I was going to climb up and shake Andy. Then the angel picked me up and took me into the hall. I could see him. His clothes were white. He smelled good. I saw his face. I saw him up close when he carried me."

"Did he say anything to you?"

"No. I didn't hear him talk until he spoke to you."

"The same man?"

"Yes, in different clothes on the porch."

"So—an angel?"

"Angels can change how they look. Angels rescue people."

"Yes."

"He rescued us." There was no confusion in Mark's voice.

I started building with the logs again. I pictured that young man on the porch. I'd never seen him before, but he looked like a normal guy. Mark seemed positive about seeing this same man in the house, upstairs, an angel in white. He had brought Mark downstairs? What could I say?

I should feel thankful. If it really was an angel, I should feel amazed. The Bible had plenty of stories about angels helping people and giving messages. But now I didn't feel grateful.

My mind swirled with confusion and anger.

If Mark was older, I would have asked him why, if he'd come to help us, the angel didn't rescue Andy? Why could an angel be right there and not save all the children? Why could he bring Mark downstairs and not grab Andy too?

Mark didn't seem to have any questions. He was sure it was an angel and didn't question why the angel would not have also rescued Andy. It wouldn't help to say any of my angry questions to Mark, so I didn't.

I had read stories about other people who had been helped by angels, but I never expected to see one. Could he really have appeared in white clothes to Mark in the house and then showed up on the porch dressed like a regular guy?

Mark sounded positive that the man on the porch was the same man who was in the house, just in different clothes. No wings visible in either place—but not all the angels in the Bible appeared with wings.

Now I had something odd and unbelievable to think about in this whole mess. Something else that created more questions that were impossible to answer. My head hurt as much as my heart. For a while longer, Mark and I quietly built log houses, fences, and a barn. I wondered if I should tell any of the grown-ups about the guy Mark thought was an angel. Before I could decide, the doorbell rang.

I jumped up, sure that more of Dad's family had arrived. Providing for la famiglia includes every kind of support. Exclamations, hugs, food, working together, money, stuff—anything that could help someone in the family. Uncle Gerry had gone out to his car to talk to his department, and the front door had locked behind him.

Mark and I stood at the bottom of the stairs and watched our uncles coming through to the front room. Uncle Sammy had Dad by the arm.

"I'm taking Frank back up to bed," he said.

Mark and I moved quickly into the hall area. All the uncles clustered near the stairs, but they parted like the Red Sea for Moses when Lucille brought Mom from the kitchen to the living room.

Lucille and Mom sat on the couch. Mark and I moved to sit near them. Mark leaned against Mom. I sat on a leather hassock near the couch. Uncle Louis stood in front of the other brothers.

"Sal's going to take you kids out to get some clothes, stuff we didn't bring, clothes for the funeral, and shoes." Uncle Sal stepped forward.

Uncle Louis continued, "Gerry and me and Joe will contact the insurance. Sammy will take care of planning the wake after calling hours on Friday. That's right, Katherine? You want calling hours on Thursday and Friday?"

"Yes." Mom spoke so softly we really couldn't hear her, but we could read her lips.

Mom's sister, my aunt Beverly, might not have even heard the news yet. Aunt Pauline, Mom's sister-in-law, wouldn't know either. They would be at work. Someone would need to call them as well as Grandmere and Grandpere in Maine. I wondered if any of my uncles had told their mother, Grandma Riposta, about the fire and Andy's death.

The network of sharing news was so much faster with Dad's family. They always seemed ready to support one another with whatever was needed. They were warmhearted.

It crossed my mind that living in Maine made people seem cold in comparison to these New Jersey relatives. But I knew it wasn't just the place. Time with Dad's family compared to time in Maine was like being in two different countries.

Uncle Louis led the way over to Mom to give her a kiss and to order, "Get some rest."

Joe, Gerry, and Sal followed, kissing and hugging Mom and Lucille. Lucille stood straight and still as a slim tree while receiving these displays of affection. Uncle Sammy arrived downstairs, and they left, all except for Uncle Sal.

Uncle Sal stood waiting for Mark and me. He said, "You two put on some of the clothes we brought. No shoes in that stuff, so you'll have to wear your slippers, but we'll get shoes."

"The bags of clothes are in the kitchen. You can change in the little bathroom," Lucille said as she stood up to go with us. Mom stayed on the couch. Uncle Sal sat down next to her.

"It will be okay, Katherine. We'll get you through this."

Mark and I did as we were told. While I changed out of the pajamas borrowed from Lucille into clothes sent by my cousins, I knew Dad's family would help us. I believed Uncle Sal's words and knew Mom did too. In Dad's family, men protected their family.

Uncle Sal didn't rush us. He was better at waiting than Dad. Uncle Sal took us to the largest department store in Union. He always looked good in whatever he wore. So did his wife, Aunt Rosalie. Everyone said she looked like a young Elizabeth Taylor. She and Sal were a gorgeous couple, and Aunt Rosalie was Jewish. Uncle Sal said after Frank married a Protestant girl, he knew the way was open for him to propose to Rosalie.

Sal had a new car with St. Anthony on the dashboard and fuzzy dice hanging from the mirror. When he turned on the radio, it was rock and roll, something our dad never played and that he told us was the devil's heartbeat.

My mind went to another source of guilt. Maybe the fire was my fault for being a disobedient daughter. God had awful punishments for disobedient children. I'd read those in the Old Testament and had heard sermons about what should be done to disobedient children. In the Old Testament, disobedient children could be killed by their parents or the community.

I listened to the music Dad forbid in our house. I heard it at my friends' houses and on the radio at our house when Mom and Dad weren't home. I'd received Beatles albums as gifts, and I hid them on the floor under my bed. If Mom ever discovered them when vacuuming, she didn't say anything.

Once Mom told me Elvis was her favorite singer in her teenage years. In our long rides to Maine with Mom driving, she played rock and roll on the radio. I also heard her play some of the most famous Elvis songs on our piano when Dad wasn't home. She sang them too, and I would sing with her.

Would God burn down a house because a disobedient and rebellious daughter hid forbidden Beatles albums under her bed? The fire had started in my room. Was it my fault?

The department store had just opened, so we saw no other customers yet. Sal told us to pick out what we needed—underwear, socks, slippers, gym shoes, regular shoes—and also that we would need two nice dark-colored outfits for Andy's calling hours and the funeral.

My mind went blank when he mentioned Andy's funeral.

"You need me to say the list again?" Uncle Sal asked.

I shook my head and turned to look at the girls' section. Then I looked at Mark. At eight and half, Mark seemed smaller in height and weight than Andy had been. People usually thought Andy was the oldest son. Mark leaned against Uncle Sal.

"Mark needs help," I said to Uncle Sal.

"Sure." He bent down to give Mark a hug, then put his hand on Mark's back and guided him into the boys' section. I watched them for a few moments, then began to gather everything Uncle Sal had said we needed. It seemed weird going back to Lucille and Ed's looking like we'd been on a shopping spree. Who did that after a death in the family?

Uncle Sal did not drive back to Lucille and Ed's by the most direct route, the one that would go past our burned-down house on Magie Avenue. He wanted to protect us from seeing the charred and now waterlogged ruin. The house had been near an intersection of three towns.

To one side were a couple of houses with normal neighbors. To the other side, one house was owned by a couple who were gone most days and who had a scary old woman living with them. Beyond this house was a gas station and then another main road, Galloping Hill Road. I wondered how the crazy old woman would act when looking at the disastrous ruin of our house. By avoiding our street, Uncle Sal caused me to think more about the neighbor who one day threatened to attack Mark, Andy, and me.

She was built like a stalagmite topped with a thick gray and white helmet of hair. It was Andy who came up with the stalagmite comparison. He'd seen some pictures of stalactites and stalagmites in my science book. With one glance he had pointed at an especially lumpy stalagmite and said the name of our irrational neighbor.

In the fall, when the old grouchy neighbor came into her yard, she'd pick up leaves that had blown into the yard and throw them one by one toward the street or our yard. "Thesa notta mine!" she shouted to no one and everyone. We had seen passersby move off the sidewalk and to the shoulder of the road while she yelled at them.

Her face had the square carved look of a totem. Her skin, olive tan, had visible hairs even though we never got close to her. They could be spotted from a distance on her chin and on the side of her face. With her large dark-frame glasses and angry expressions, she looked like an evil cartoon creation.

She often paced across her backyard, talking to herself in Italian. Dad knew what she said, but none of the rest of us did. I had seen Dad frown when she was out talking to herself. He just told us to stay away from her and to go inside and play if she seemed like she was going to stay out in the yard.

Dad didn't want us in our yard even if she just sat on the back porch steps and stared at us while we played. He had spoken to her in Italian. I thought he sounded respectful and friendly, but she shouted in anger if anyone talked to her. She shouted at Dad, but since it was in Italian, we didn't know what she said.

I tried to ignore the old woman and felt sorry for the couple who lived with her. If I was alone, I'd never have to interact with her. Reading or listening to music in the house seemed much more attractive to me than playing in the yard, but Mark and Andy preferred being outside. I had the assignment to watch them and to guide them inside whenever the crazy stalagmite neighbor appeared outside, pacing and grumbling to herself.

One spring day that felt like midsummer, Mark and Andy played catch in our backyard. The old lady came outside and stood as still as a statue by her back steps. I could see she was mumbling to herself, but unlike her normal behavior, she was not loud.

She seemed to stare more intently at the boys than usual. Mumbling, she moved toward the driveway of her house, which marked the line between her property and ours. Mark and Andy were definitely in our backyard, but they were near her driveway.

If she had super powers, lasers could have shot out of her eyes to destroy the boys. Solid as a fire hydrant, she stood with her hands on her hips. Suddenly she surprised the boys and me by shouting, "You tink I dunna know whata you do? You tink I dunna know? I'm a gonna turna da hose on you! I'm a gonna turna da hose on you!"

She rushed as fast as her tree trunk legs would carry her toward the spigot that stuck out of the cement blocks under her back porch steps. A hose was attached to that spigot. Mark moved quickly to stand behind me but didn't say anything.

Andy rushed toward our garage. Why? What was Andy doing?

Then I saw the neatly coiled hose beneath the spigot on the side of our garage. Andy turned the spigot on with one forceful yank and picked up the hose with the quick ease of a teenager. I couldn't believe my eyes as he turned his sturdy six-year-old self around, hose nozzle in hand.

"I'm going to turn the hose on you!" he shouted back at her. Quick as a flashbulb, he rushed to the edge of the driveway. The old lady had only picked up the nozzle of her hose.

They faced each other like roosters trained to fight! I ran to grab the hose from Andy and pulled hard on it, so hard that Andy was knocked back. Then I rushed to turn off the spigot. Mark waited where we had been standing.

Dropping the rubberized weapon, I got ahold of Andy. "Go inside," I called to Mark. He listened right away. In our house, with our dad, you listened immediately to the authority or you'd be in trouble.

Andy did not move easily from the driveway. He kept his big brown eyes on the old woman who still held the hose. She had not thought to turn on the water, but she continued to splutter her crazy words as well as some curses at us.

"I'm a gonna tella you parents how rotten you kidsa are!" Still more words from her in English. The surprises from her continued. "Turna da hose on me? You gonna turna da hose on me? You tink you gonna turna da hose on me?"

I yanked on Andy as hard as I could and pulled him with me out of the backyard. I took him around the corner into the driveway. We paused. We heard the stalagmite woman yelling for a few more moments. When she could no longer see us, her yelling usually stopped, just like someone had turned off her volume.

"We're going inside," I said like the boss my brothers thought I was. Mark, ahead of me, opened the door. He held it open for Andy and me.

The side door of our house opened into a hallway. To the right, up five steps, was the kitchen. To the left, down ten steps, was the basement, which Mom and Dad had made into a family room. Mark went inside and up toward the kitchen. He was out of reach but turned back to look at me as if to say, *What now?*

I stood on the landing and turned Andy toward me. No anger appeared on his face at all.

"What did you think you were doing, Andy? You can't turn a hose on a crazy old woman."

"Yes, I can. She said she'd turn the hose on us! Why couldn't I spray her?"

WHY COULDN'T HE? Did I wish that I had let Andy use the hose on our Italian stalagmite neighbor? I did now. It wasn't kind or Christian. Even though I felt sorry for her family and I was afraid of her, I would have let him do that and more if only he would be alive again.

7

THE TELLING

When Uncle Sal dropped us off, he checked on Dad, kissed Mom and Lucille, and said he'd be back in the morning. He had barely driven away when a vehicle from the fire department parked in front of the Clausses' house.

"Oh dear, your poor mom is so tired," Lucille said softly.

I doubted Mom had gotten much sleep because of the dark shadows under her eyes, but medicine seemed to work better for her than for Dad. I looked back outside. Walking toward the door were the same two officers who had come to the house in the middle of the night, the chief and the fire marshal.

Lucille invited them inside. I knew they were good men doing a tough job, but I wished we didn't have to talk about it again. I wanted to tell as much as I could remember, but at the same time, it hurt to think about the fire.

The officers apologized for having to come and ask questions at this time. Lucille escorted us all into Ed's office. Mom stood up, and I waited for her to come to my side before we went to the office. I was glad I had folded up the sheet and blanket Lucille had used to make a bed on the couch for me. The man who had taken notes the night before took out his pad and a pencil.

"Virginia, would you please tell us again what you can remember about Monday night? Take your time We don't have to rush. Begin wherever you'd like." Both officers looked kind to me.

I started again from putting the boys to bed. I tried to remember everything, especially from the time that the power went off in the house. I needed to say it all for myself again, for Mom, even for Lucille. I told them about trying to get the boys to go to sleep, about the number of times I went upstairs to tell them to be quiet.

I told about yelling at Mark and Andy to end their silliness, about giving Daniel more stuffed animals and making sure he could have the night-light. It was just a light bulb in a little tube stick of a lamp. I could plug it into the back wall, the one covered with the long drapes. The outlet was under the drapes.

Mark had moved like a sleepwalker when I got him to go from his bottom bunk to my bed. The light, the extra stuffed animals, and having Mark sleeping in the bed nearby finally calmed Daniel down. By the time I went upstairs and discovered the fire, Daniel's cries were almost screams.

"The light from the fire made my room from the back wall bright. Smoke was dark gray and hung down low off the ceiling. It smelled like burned nylon. Daniel stood crying in the crib. Mark was still asleep under the covers, with the top of his head toward the wall of fire.

"I grabbed Daniel from the crib and threw him over my shoulder like a sack of potatoes. He kept crying while I had one arm tight around him. I shook Mark hard. Holding Daniel as tightly as I could, I pushed and poked Mark to wake him. I had to yank him out of the bed. Finally, he stood up on his own.

"'What? What?' he said as I pushed him ahead of me into the hall. He didn't even look back at the flaming drapes or the ceiling that had disappeared beneath the dark smoke. With Daniel over my shoulder and holding Mark by the arm, I went to the doorway of the room he and Andy shared.

"'Wake up! Andy! Get up! Andy!' I yelled. I had to hurry to call for help. The phone was downstairs on a wall practically under my bedroom. Since I had to call the operator to get the fire department, I told Mark to wake Andy and come downstairs. Mark was just stepping into his bedroom when I got my last glimpse of him. I rushed in the dark down the stairs to call for help from the kitchen. Daniel was heavy, but he had stopped crying.

"The wall phone had a ten-foot-long cord. Mom wanted to be able to talk on the phone from different rooms. The cord was so long that anyone could talk on it in the back hall, the kitchen, my parents' bedroom, even the edge of the living room.

"The operator answered. The yellow hard plastic phone felt warm. It attached on the kitchen wall right under my bedroom wall. I told the operator we had a big fire in the house and gave the address. She asked me twice to repeat the address.

"Then I hung up and rushed back to the living room. Mark stood alone at the foot of the stairs. He seemed confused. Mark looked from me to the stairs, back and forth, like he didn't know where he was or what he should do.

"He cried, 'Andy wouldn't wake up. There's too much smoke. I hollered but then . . . ' He stopped talking and looked up the stairs again like he expected to see Andy."

I stopped. I wondered if now would be the time to tell them what Mark had told me about seeing the man in white upstairs, the man who had brought him down the stairs. Everyone was waiting for me to go on.

Could I tell them about an angel—if that was what the guy

was? They wouldn't believe me. I wanted to believe it, but wouldn't an angel have rescued all the children? I wouldn't tell them now.

"I grabbed Mark and said, 'We're going out on the front porch. Mark! Listen! You and Daniel sit in the corner near the hedges. I'll get Andy.' When I opened the front door, I carried Daniel and pulled Mark to the far corner of our cement and stone front porch. No one could see them from the street because the tall hedges gave the porch privacy. 'Hug Daniel, and don't move!' I told Mark. Then I turned to go back inside. A young man stood by our front door. He looked a lot like my cousins who were in their twenties, but I didn't know him. He said, 'You're going back inside?' I said, 'I have a brother upstairs.' I pushed past him, went inside, and ran up the stairs. The young man stayed right behind me. I coughed in the hallway at the top of the stairs. It was hard to breathe.

"Gritty, bitter, almost stinging smoke filled the hallway. I remembered a favorite television show, *Fury*. A fire raged in the horse barn where Fury lived. People wrapped wet cloths around their noses and mouths to get into the barn. Those wet cloths helped them to get farther into the barn and to grab the horses and get them out.

"I thought, *I could do that!* My skin had ash and grit all over it. I went into the bathroom and wet a washcloth till it was sopping wet. Then I held the cold wet cloth over my face to cross the hall into the boys' bedroom. I only got to the bedroom doorway when the washcloth dried out. Smoke made my eyes burn. It was hard to breathe.

"I looked to the right. My room was a box of flames. I tried to look into the boys' bedroom, but I couldn't even see the bunk beds. I rushed back to the bathroom and soaked the washcloth again. I wanted to holler out Andy's name, but I couldn't. I made it a few steps into the boys' bedroom before I started choking. The heat and smoke made me dizzy. The cloth over my face wasn't helping at all.

"Then the young guy took hold of my arm. He pulled me from the boys' bedroom and said, 'You have to leave now.' He took me down the stairs. He was strong enough to carry me, but he didn't. He held on to me and brought me downstairs. I didn't want to go. I would have kept trying to get Andy, but I couldn't pull away from the guy.

"At the bottom of the stairs, I yelled, 'I have to call the fire department again! They should be here!' He let go of me. I ran back to the kitchen to the wall phone and reached for it, but before I touched it, the young man pushed my arm down. The phone was a melted blob of yellow plastic. He took hold of me again and pulled me to the front door, outside, and onto the porch.

"I looked at the corner where I had left Mark and Daniel. Mark had Daniel on his lap and was hugging him tightly. Daniel didn't cry or resist. 'Leave the porch,' the young man commanded us. He put his hand on my back to push me to the boys. I didn't look at him but at Mark and Daniel. I took Daniel into my arms. Mark grabbed hold of me. We hurried down the front porch steps between the high hedges. I thought the young man would be right there behind me, but he wasn't. I didn't know if he went back inside. He was just gone.

"Where was the fire department? Where was the guy? I said my address to the operator a total of three times when I first called. How long had it been?

"We had a large tree between our house and Magie Avenue. I put Mark and Daniel down at the base of that tree. Mark could sit on a large root and hold Daniel like he had on the porch. I worried the young man had gone back inside. I wondered where the fire trucks were. 'Stay here! Right by this tree. Just like on the porch! Don't move,' I told them. Mark nodded and held Daniel."

I stopped talking. I thought about how I had to leave Mark holding Daniel again while I tried to get help. Did the people in the room all believe me? Each person sat like manikins except for the tears on Mom and Lucille's faces.

In that moment, I asked the question I felt everyone should be wondering about.

"I called for help again from our neighbor's house. When the fire trucks did arrive, there were so many of them. They filled the street. The fire was showing across the back roof, flames shooting up. What took the fire trucks so long to arrive?"

The fire department officers looked at each other. It didn't seem like they wanted to answer. Had I done something else wrong in the way I tried to get us out of the house or in calling the operator?

I was afraid to hear their answer, because it might be my fault. Still, I wanted to know why the fire trucks were so slow to arrive. No one spoke.

It took only a second of waiting in silence for my mind to remember when speed drew the attention of a man in uniform. That man in uniform had scared Andy to tears.

SPEED MATTERED. In 1963, when Mom drove us to Maine, the boys slept soundly in the far back of the station wagon. Mom played a rock and roll station softly, which featured a lot of songs by Elvis, Mom's favorite. We zoomed along and made great time into Connecticut.

Near three that morning, Mark and Andy both snored lightly. I don't know who spotted the flashing lights behind us first. Mom probably saw them in the rearview mirror. I caught their flashing in the left side of my peripheral vision since I sat slightly turned toward Mom.

Mom had been speeding. There were hardly any cars on the road. Dad went over the speed limit sometimes, but he had not gotten a ticket. I wondered if Mom worried about telling Dad she got a ticket 'cause he'd be angry.

A state trooper car with its roof light flashing and spinning guided us to the side of the road. Mom pulled off far to the right on the shoulder of Interstate 95. The combination of change in speed, bumping over the rough shoulder, and the trooper's lights woke the boys.

They sat up in the flat back where Mom had made a bed of pillows and blankets. Mark and Andy glanced toward the car with the flashing lights behind us. They rubbed their eyes and looked around. The trooper's car had stopped right behind ours, and the lights on top continued revolving and flashing.

The trooper was tall. He adjusted his wide-brimmed official hat before he walked toward our car. We could all see his outline clearly in the headlights of his car as he walked toward us.

Before he stopped beside the car, Andy did a dive and tumble from the way back into the middle seat. Even though suitcases filled the middle seat, there was enough room for him to stand right behind the driver. He peered outward and was at the right height to see the large black leather gun belt on the trooper's right hip.

Mom rolled down her window. I don't know what the trooper was looking at, but for a few seconds, he just stared into the car. His gun belt against the grayish uniform looked scarier than any I'd seen in television shows. Then he stooped down to peer farther into the car.

At that moment Andy pushed himself between Mom and

her lowered window. Andy said in a voice so loud it was a shout, "Are you going to shoot my mother?"

He started to cry. All of us, including the trooper, felt Andy's fear. The trooper took off his hat and scooched so that he could look right at Andy.

He spoke in a deep, reassuring voice. "I just stopped your car to tell your mother she needs to drive more slowly. It's dangerous to drive too fast."

Andy took deep breaths, some kind of sobs. He stopped crying. The trooper looked less scary without his hat and down at our eye level. He talked longer in a calming voice about speed limits. He told us a story about people who drove too fast who hit a deer that leaped out to cross the highway. He said he wanted us to be safe.

Then he asked Mom where we were from and where we were going. He asked for her license and the car registration. She gave him her license, and I grabbed the registration from the glove compartment and handed it to her.

The trooper took the items, looked them over, and gave them back. Andy stayed right there at Mom's left shoulder, looking at the trooper. I sat still. Mark stayed in the blankets in the back of the station wagon.

Then the trooper repeated his warning. "Keep to a safe speed, ma'am. Have a safe trip." Then he backed away from the car, put his hat back on, and nodded to all of us.

We watched him return to his car. Mom's eyes were on the rearview mirror. We kids turned and stared after him. Then Andy hugged Mom around her neck. I thought it looked like a choke hold, but she sighed and smiled. Andy turned to climb back to the area where Mark was sitting up with the best view of the police car.

As Mom slowly pulled out onto the empty highway, she

called Andy's name. He had just reached the flat back part of the wagon.

"What, Mom?" he asked.

I thought she would tell him and Mark to settle down and go back to sleep. I was wrong. Mom surprised me sometimes because she wasn't a by-the-rules person like Dad was.

"Andy, if I'm ever stopped by another policeman, I want you to come up to my window as fast as you can and ask the policeman that same question."

THE EVENTS of that night flashed through my mind, but looking at the firefighters, I still wanted the answer to my question. Didn't everyone in the room want to know why the fire trucks took so long to arrive? Had it even been a minute since I asked them? What would they tell me?

8

NECESSARY DETAILS

"Virginia, Magie Avenue is long, and the area by your house touches three different towns, Elizabeth, Roselle Park, and Union. The operator wasn't sure which fire department to call. You gave an address, but the operator didn't know the town. She didn't want to call the wrong department.

"By the time the operator realized the delay for calling a department was too long, she called all the departments that might cover your address. That's why so many trucks and cars showed up—fire, ambulance, and police. They found Mark and Daniel right away by the tree where you left them. They didn't see you, but Mark said you were outside."

"I was by the side wall of our neighbor's house," I said to the chief, who had answered my question. "I didn't see the boys or even all of our house. People stood in the way. I listened to them. I couldn't see what was happening. I prayed for the fire-fighters to rescue Andy."

Every adult looked at me until the fire marshal said, "You didn't know people were looking for you?"

"I didn't know. I just kept praying Andy would get out."

"And you just stayed sitting by the neighbor's house?"

"Yes."

"Did you see the young man again, the one who helped you try to get to Andy and then who brought you out?" the chief asked.

"No."

"Can you describe him more than just saying he looked like some of your cousins?"

Could I describe him? I closed my eyes to try to see him on the porch. "He had dark curly hair and brown eyes. Just a normal face, maybe his nose was a little big. He had on a dark sweatshirt and jeans—I don't know what kind of shoes. That's all I remember about him."

"When you wet the washcloth and put it over your face to try to get into the boys' bedroom, did the young man do the same?"

"I don't think so. No. He didn't go into the bathroom. I could hear him clearly when he spoke to me."

"He stayed right by you?"

"Yes. I felt him close to me the whole time."

"He didn't try to go by you to the bunk beds?"

"No. I couldn't ask him to. I couldn't talk. There was too much smoke."

"But he talked to you? He told you when you had to leave."

"Yes."

"And he didn't have anything over his face?"

"No."

"You heard him clearly?"

"Yes."

"Then he took you down the stairs?"

"Yes."

"And he stopped you from burning your hand on the melting phone?"

"Yes."

"You definitely heard him say that you had to leave?"

"Yes."

"And he helped you to leave the house? He told you to get the boys off the porch?"

"Yes. He pulled me out of the house. And I did what he said. I was going to ask him to stay with the boys while I went to make another call about the fire, but he was just gone."

The two firemen looked at each other. The chief sighed. The notetaker glanced at me as if I might have more to say. We all sat still.

Then the fire marshal shut his notebook and put his pen away. They stood up.

"We're very sorry for your loss and that we had to bother you with so many questions today." The chief spoke with clear sincerity.

Lucille stood up too, but not Mom or me, not right away.

The chief said, "I'm sorry you had to go over all of this, Virginia, but what you told us helps us figure out more details about the fire. Mrs. Riposta, we'll send you and Mr. Riposta two copies of our report. Give one to your insurance company. They'll send their own investigator, but not quickly. I hope you know our whole department feels the sadness of your loss."

Mom stood up. She didn't say anything, but they shook hands. Then Mom and I watched Lucille lead them to the front door. We both stayed in Ed's study. We didn't talk. She didn't hug me either. Mom looked exhausted.

When Lucille came back, she hugged Mom right away. "Katherine, you need to go upstairs and rest. I know more of your family is coming over. They could get here any time. Please try to rest until they arrive. Your sister, Beverly, called, and your sister-in-law, Pauline. Ethel called too. Please go have a rest. Mark is playing happily with Eddie and Raymond's toys. Virginia can keep me company."

Mom nodded and let Lucille lead her upstairs. I wondered if there would be more trouble from the official fire report. Would the insurance company blame me? If the report said it was my fault in some way, maybe the insurance company wouldn't give Mom and Dad anything.

Should I have told them Mark thought the guy was an angel? I didn't know what to believe about that young man. Mark sure sounded like he was telling the truth about him. I sat thinking of how much I had hurt my family by failing to get Andy out of the house.

When had my family most hurt me? I didn't think of arguments, spankings, being sent to my room, or having other privileges taken away. I tried to think if there was a truly serious time when I was deeply hurt by the people I loved and trusted. I thought of one that included a death.

THE SUMMER before Mark and Andy and I would all be in school, me in fifth grade, Mark in first, and Andy in kindergarten, started out with a special surprise. When my birthday came in June, Grandmere and Grandpere had a special present delivered to their farm in Waldoboro, a lamb. He was cute but had manure stains, matted wool, and ticks.

Grandpere and I spent hours cleaning him. We picked off all the ticks and used buckets of hot water and strong soap, plus we had to cut away the worst of the matted wool. We did a final whitening rinse and used a dog brush and metal comb to fluff out the beautifully clean white wool. Grandmere brought out a strip of blue ribbon for us to put around the lamb's neck.

"Now he looks like a birthday present." Grandmere smiled and patted the lamb. He didn't seem to mind a bit. "What kind of lamb is he, Earl?"

"A Dorset. It's a breed that came from England. This little guy will be a good pet for the summer. When Virginia leaves at the end of the summer, this lamb can go to a farm." Grandpere winked at Grandmere. She frowned at him and turned to me.

She asked, "Have you named him yet?"

I looked at the little lamb with the wool on his head, body, and legs and the energy that made him seem very bouncy. He was cute, but it had taken a lot of trouble to clean him up.

"Trouble. Can we name him Troubles?"

"Sure, you can. He's yours. You can fix the front stall in the barn for him," Grandpere replied, sounding happy.

"But he's so little, and he was with other sheep before we brought him here. Won't he be scared?"

"He's an animal, Virginia, and your pet for the summer. He'll adjust." Grandpere spoke calmly, and Grandmere nodded agreement.

Troubles responded to attention. He even followed me around like the lamb in the children's song. I couldn't take him off the property, but our family farm had plenty of acres for running, walking, and playing.

Dad never agreed to having a pet bigger than hamsters or gerbils, and he didn't really like those. Mom prevailed by telling him why kids needed pets. He agreed but added that we couldn't afford any big vet bills, so the critters had better stay healthy.

No one was surprised when my parents and the boys arrived at the end of the summer and Andy asked to ride Troubles. Grandpere discouraged it, but when the grown-ups were out of sight, the boys did try riding Troubles. They learned that an almost full-grown lamb could act like a bronco. After a few hard ground hits, their efforts to ride Troubles stopped.

During one of our last summer evenings, when we all had ice cream to enjoy, Mom and Dad came out with big news. When we went back to New Jersey, it would be to Union and into a new house. Union was nearer to the towns where Dad's family lived, and it had good schools.

"When you leave to go to your new home, Troubles will be leaving too," Grandpere said. "Just like you're going to a new home, so will Troubles. You'll need to say goodbye to him tomorrow because the weekend will be very busy, with lots of family coming. It wouldn't be good to say goodbye to Troubles with so many people around."

"Where will Troubles go?" Andy asked.

"We got him from a farm near here." I looked to my grandfather to give details.

Grandpere added, "I'll take Troubles to a place that has lots of sheep. Don't worry about him. He's had a great summer here."

Mark and Andy and I did not argue about delaying Troubles's departure. Since we lived in a metropolitan suburb, we could only experience time with farm animals like Troubles in petting zoos or in Maine. On the last night Troubles was with us, we took sleeping bags out to the barn and slept on hay near him.

The next day, Grandpere opened the back door of his big old Cadillac and put Troubles on the floor in the back seat.

"Can we go too?" I asked.

"Better let it be goodbye here," Grandpere answered.

We watched the car until it went down the long driveway and turned left onto Bremen Road. I was surprised that my brothers could stand still as long as I did to watch the car take

Troubles away. When we couldn't see it any longer, Andy said, "Let's play croquet."

Cousins, aunts, and uncles from towns in Maine and Massachusetts started arriving the next morning to spend time with us before we left for New Jersey. Grandmere had done a lot of baking. Mom helped by following Grandmere's directions. Mom was not a very good baker.

Some of the relatives would stay at the farm, so every sleeping area was full. Others would stay down the road at Aunt Winnie and Uncle Neville's house or at Aunt Caroline and Uncle Bob's house in Damariscotta. People would visit back and forth through Saturday. On Sunday everyone would gather back at Grandpere and Grandmere's farm for a big dinner.

Grandmere used her finest ironstone china from England, and she had me set goblets and silverware at each place. Lots of flowers grew on the farm, some wild and some cultivated. Mom cut and arranged them as if painting a picture. Then she placed vases full of orange, white, and yellow bouquets around the dining room.

At one o'clock on Sunday, everyone gathered in the dining room. We were crowded, bumping elbows, but no one seemed to mind. Just lifting my fork or passing dishes required careful motions so that I didn't poke the people on either side of me at the long table. We kids had narrow old cane bottom chairs squeezed between the larger dining room chairs for the adults. Mark and Andy sat across the table from me.

After Grandmere said a prayer of thankfulness, everyone started taking food and passing dishes around the table. Talking and laughing sounded and felt happy. Then the oldest person at the table, Aunt Winnie, spoke up to compliment her younger sister, my grandmother.

"Idalene," Aunt Winnie said, speaking loudly like many old

people who are hard of hearing do, "this is a wonderful meal. It's the best roast lamb I've ever had. It couldn't be more tender."

I looked at my plate, then at Great-Aunt Winnie, then at my grandmother, and I knew. I put down my fork and resisted the urge to throw up right there at the table. I felt like I'd been tricked into cannibalism. Tears filled my eyes.

I could see my plate: vegetables, mint jelly, mashed potatoes, Jell-O salad, and a slice of roast lamb. The slice was missing the chunk I had already eaten. I had not even thought about what the meat was when Dad put it on my plate. We knew we were supposed to eat what Dad put on our plate.

Everyone started agreeing and complimenting Grandmere on the lamb. I glanced at her and saw more distress than delight. What had Grandpere said? "Troubles will go to a place that has lots of sheep. Don't worry about him. He's had a good summer."

I put my hands in my lap. When I looked at my grandmother and grandfather, I wanted to yell, scream, and cry, but all I did was sit still. I could not stop the tears from sliding down my face. I only moved to wipe them away. People kept talking about the delicious meal.

If I made upsetting comments or yelled about Troubles, Dad would punish me. It would ruin the dinner for everyone. It would be a bad ending to a wonderful summer, so I sat there looking at my plate, trying not to cry anymore.

"What? What is it?" Mark stage whispered across the table to me. Mark usually wanted to know what I thought or did.

I leaned forward as far as I could toward Mark and said, "It's Troubles. The lamb roast is Troubles. They didn't take him to another farm. They took him to a butcher." Mark understood me. Seeing the tears that immediately filled his eyes, I loved and appreciated him more than I ever had.

Mark put down his fork. We both looked around the table at the adults who were eating, talking, taking more of the many dishes, including the roasted lamb. Passing the plate of Troubles around, they chatted and smiled.

Andy hadn't noticed. He was about to eat a forkful of lamb when Mark used his right elbow to hit Andy in the ribs.

"What?" Andy asked, and he was loud enough that anyone at the table might have thought Andy was talking to them.

Conversation dropped away as the family looked toward the boys just as Mark said, "It's Troubles."

"What's Troubles?" Andy asked with his microphone-loud voice. Now the table became quiet. Grandmere looked like she might cry.

"The meat is Troubles. They took Troubles to a butcher, not a farm. Right?" Mark looked at me while he wiped away the tears on his face. Andy glanced toward me for confirmation.

I nodded and said, "It's Troubles. The meat is Troubles." No adult contradicted me. They all knew Grandpere and Grandmere had given me a pet lamb for the summer. Aunt Winnie and Uncle Neville and many other relatives had even seen me playing with him that summer.

Andy looked at the meat on his fork, at Mark, at me, and then around the table. He did not seem horrified. He asked everyone and no one, "It's really Troubles?"

Nobody answered right away, but Grandpere finally said, in a clear voice, "Yes."

Andy looked from Grandpere, who was seated at the far end of the table, to me. He liked having everyone looking at him. He had everyone's attention as he lifted the fork toward his nose. He sniffed the meat. Then he put the forkful of meat in his mouth and chewed with enthusiasm.

I made a noise like a dying seagull. Mark gasped. We watched Andy enjoy having an audience watch him chew,

chew, chew, and swallow. Then he announced, "Troubles tastes good."

Now I WONDERED when the next troubles would arrive. My stomach and feet felt like they were made of iron. I followed Lucille into the kitchen when Mom went upstairs to take a nap. We barely had mixed one batch of the sweet tea she and her family preferred when the doorbell rang. I looked at Lucille. Her expression said she had no clue who she'd find at the front door.

9

CLOSEST FRIEND AND SWEET
SICK DAY

It was not a family member at the door; it was Ethel, the mother of Mark and Andrew's best friends, Harvey and Barry. Ethel was one of Mom's best friends too. She didn't top five feet, but she conveyed power in her voice and actions. She hugged me for a long time, her embrace strong enough to make breathing difficult.

As soon as she let me go, she started crying and reached out to take Lucille by both hands. Lucille's expression showed that Ethel must be squeezing her hands as hard as she had hugged me.

"Is Katherine here?"

"Yes. But she's sleeping, so—"

"I'm up," Mom said as she came down the stairs. She didn't smile, but I felt sure Ethel's presence would help her. Ethel made people feel better whether she was serious or joking around, except for her husband, Herman. She laughed at his puns, but she also scolded him.

Lucille backed away, and Ethel, a blonde-frosted dynamo, put her arms around Mom and hugged her all the way to the living room couch. Ethel was shorter than Mom, but she moved Mom as easily as a feather in the wind. They sat-fell onto the couch. Ethel pressed her face against my mother's shoulder and cried, "Oh Katherine, Oh Katherine." They both just sat and wept on each other.

I realized that I could sit or stand silently in the room and feel invisible. I sat again, still on the small straight chair near the door to the kitchen.

Lucille wiped her own eyes and went back to the kitchen. The couch faced the front wall with a picture window and the front door. Ethel and Mom took no notice of me as they grabbed tissues from the Kleenex box on the nearest end table and sat clutching each other's hands.

"Katherine, Katherine, I have to tell you what happened."

Usually, Ethel called my mom Kathy. Since she said Katherine, I knew she felt extremely upset. What was so urgent that she had to tell Mom? Ethel wasn't the one who had lost a son, a home, and everything in it. What could Ethel think was bigger or even as important as the fire that took Andrew from us?

"What?" my mom asked. "What happened, Ethel?" She said it as if she expected Ethel already knew about everything that had happened at our house, as if Ethel's news had equal importance. Ethel kept tight hold of Mom's hands.

"Last night the boys went to bed at eight. You know, ever since we got the bigger apartment, and they have their own rooms, they go to sleep well. They sleep soundly after they read for a little while, but sometimes they just play. Herman has to tell them to turn the lights out, and they go right to sleep."

Ethel's two boys often came over to our house to play with Mark and Andy. Harvey was the same age as Mark, and Barry was the same age as Andy. Harvey and Mark had fun together, but Harvey liked to read more than Mark and took homework more seriously, so sometimes he didn't come over to play. Barry seemed shy to most people, but he showed no quietness with Andy. They could play well together for hours.

Andy and Barry were like chocolate and butterscotch chips. Andy had dark hair and big brown eyes in his round, solid body. Barry had blond hair and blue eyes in his slim body. Andy laughed often, and Barry laughed as much as Andy. They were the closest little kid friends I ever had seen.

I had decided my life would be easier if I had Harvey and Mark as brothers or Andy and Barry as brothers. Each pair played well together, never fighting, hardly ever arguing. I watched all four boys and listened to them. Harvey and Mark got along, but with Barry and Andy, it seemed like they communicated without even speaking. Barry and Andy differed as much as lasagna and Gefilte fish, but they had a constant connection.

"Kathy, we heard fire trucks last night. It was after ten o'clock. Herman and me, we were watching TV. The fire trucks were loud, you know, because our apartment is close to the avenue. I heard Barry holler, a loud cry. Herman went with me to the boys' bedroom. Harvey was still sound asleep. Barry was sitting up, crying and crying. 'What is it?,' we asked him over and over. He couldn't talk. He just cried." Ethel held my mother's hands and moved closer to her.

"Kathy, it took minutes, but Barry said, 'There's a fire at Andy's house. The fire trucks are going to Andy's house.' I said, 'No, no. You had a bad dream. The fire trucks aren't going to Andy's house.' I hugged Barry and whispered this to him. We didn't want to wake Harvey."

Mom looked as white as the sheer curtains between Lucille's living room drapes. Ethel just went on. It seemed like she couldn't pause to even take another breath before she continued.

"I said, 'Barry, you're wrong. Put your slippers on. I'll take you to Andy's house.' Barry just shook his head and kept crying. He said, 'No, the fire trucks are at Andy's house. They are.' Herman said, 'Fine. Good idea. Go.' He would stay home with Harvey, who had slept through all of this. Barry got up and put on his slippers. We went to the coat closet, got Barry's light jacket, and went to the car. Barry slid over in the front seat so that he was right against me. We drove out of the apartment complex. There was no traffic at that time of night. It took just a couple of minutes before we caught sight of your house on Magie Avenue. The closer I got, the more fire trucks, ambulances, and police cars I saw—and I realized they were in front of your house.

"I pulled into the nearest driveway to turn around. I told Barry we had to go home because there were too many trucks and cars blocking Magie Avenue and we couldn't even get through to Andy's house. I told him, 'You'll just have to see Andy in school, and you can talk about the fire trucks.' He shook his head, Kathy. He told me, 'No. Andy is gone.' He cried all the way home. I took him into the apartment. Herman was waiting for us. He saw my face. He knew.

"Barry's eyes were swollen, like he'd lost a boxing match. Herman and I sat with him in his bed until he fell sleep. It's a good thing he fell asleep because as soon as he did, we cried too. I told Herman what Barry said about Andy. We didn't send the boys to school today."

Now she slid her hands up over Mom's forearms. Ethel held Mom like someone trying to keep a grip on this life and cried.

Lucille looked pale. "Your little boy must have really loved Andy." Then Lucille left the room. I stayed where I was to see if Ethel said more.

"Herman was in the kitchen early. You know we have a

little TV out there. He saw it on the early-morning local news. He saw the report. He dropped his mug of coffee. It broke. I heard that and went to the kitchen. He told me what he saw on the news.

"We told Harvey and Barry together. Herman didn't go to work today. He never misses work. You know him. He's home with the boys so I could come tell you this. Harvey didn't want to go to school, and I don't think Barry ever could leave us today. Oh my God, Kathy!"

Ethel and my mom hugged like they were souls on the *Titanic*. I looked at them embracing and crying and thought that Barry and Andy really did have a special connection. Could Barry have loved Andy more than Mark or I loved Andy? How could he be so sure the fire trucks were going to Andy's house? How did he know Andy was gone from this world?

Ethel might have stayed longer, but the doorbell rang. Aunt Beverly and Aunt Pauline came into the living room. No one said anything. Lucille, Beverly, and Pauline stood looking at Mom and Ethel.

I sat still knowing Bevy and Pauline had to see Ethel's swollen tear-stained face. Ethel had never appeared with makeup in the years they'd known her. What they might have said or done did not happen because Dad surprised us all by coming down the stairs into the living room.

Mom and Lucille jumped up right away to guide Dad into the kitchen. They fussed over him and served him food the way adults often tried to tempt kids to eat something. This version of Dad did not seem real. He had always been in charge. When he didn't have to work on weekends, he always took us some-place interesting for fun.

Just this past Saturday, we had one of the most unusual days out that we had ever had. It was supposed to be a special family day, but Andy getting sick changed that. May 8, Saturday, had long been planned by my parents to be one of our best family days.

THE WORLD'S Fair had been in New York for over a year. Finally, we could go see the famous international event as a family. We had been looking forward to it for months because we couldn't go the previous year, and it would end in October.

Mom and Dad didn't spend much money on family vacations, but the trip to the World's Fair would be an event in history that our family could enjoy together. It seemed even more special because it would be part of Mother's Day weekend.

Saturday morning of our big trip, Andy woke up before the sun. He vomited over the side of the top bunk. The spill fell short of the plastic garbage can near the bed.

Since my bedroom was diagonal to my brothers and the doors to their room and mine were open, I heard Andy. I rushed into the room and found Mark was still sound asleep in the bottom bunk. Neither the noise nor the smell woke him. Andy was holding the guardrail on the top bunk with both hands, his chin resting on it, looking like he could throw up again.

I ran to the bathroom and brought the larger plastic trash can to Andy. I held it in front of him just as he spewed for the second time. The gross smell and look didn't bother me as much as the fact that I knew my parents wouldn't want a family trip now.

When I got a wet washcloth for Andy, I also reached under the sink. Rags plus the spray cleaner would help me get started on the mess that sat on the rug. Maybe now that he had vomited, Andy would feel better and we would still be able to go to the World's Fair.

"Sorry," Andy said as I handed him the warm washcloth for his face.

"It's okay. You didn't get sick on purpose."

I never knew what my parents heard that woke them, but suddenly they stood in the doorway behind me. Dad walked to the bunks and lifted Andy down. Mark rolled over, looked up at everyone, and wrinkled his nose at the scent of Pine-Sol mixed with vomit.

"What?" he asked.

Mom moved to the lower bunk and sat next to Mark. "Andy's sick."

"Are we still going to the World's Fair?" Mark asked as I thought it.

Dad and Mom exchanged a message with their eyes. Then Dad said, "Andy and Mom will stay home. You and Virginia and I will still go. We should leave in an hour so that we get there right when it opens. Okay?"

Andy shed tears but didn't make a sound as Dad carried him out of the room and downstairs.

"You get up and get dressed now, Mark. Your things are all laid out there on the chair. Virginia, thanks for getting the worst of the mess up. I'll finish this. You two go downstairs as soon as you're dressed."

By just minutes after eight, Andy was sleeping soundly, and Mom was waving us goodbye. Mark sat in the front seat with Dad. The seat arrangement was not designed to allow the youngest, shortest child in the car to see better. Mark got to sit in the front because he was the only son on the trip. We didn't have seat belts or bucket seats, so Mark just slid over and leaned on Dad. I could tell he enjoyed the closeness.

In one of his part-time jobs, Dad worked as a chauffeur. He

told us about places on our route. He said people should know about the roads they took and the areas they drove through to get to work, to go on a vacation, or to have a special day like we would have. He sounded cheerful, but I had heard him talking about disappointment with Mom before we left.

Dad knew his way around our state and through the cities. He drove the limo clients many times. Mark liked going through the Lincoln Tunnel. Andy would have liked that too because, to him, tunnels were mini adventures.

After the minutes in the tunnel, we cut through New York City. Finally, we could see Corona Park, the Flushing Meadows. Standing high above the normal local architecture were amazing arches, outer space sci-fi tops of buildings, and the tower just like the one where the Jetsons lived. We watched *The Jetsons* cartoon every week. When we were with Dad, Mark and I did not express the excitement we felt. Silly actions showed a lack of appreciation, according to him.

I thought of Mom and Andy throughout the whole day. They would have enjoyed everything: It's a Small World, Moments with Mr. Lincoln from Disney, a sculpture made of steel showing the world in rings, the Jetsons' house at the top of a tall needle with its incredible household items for the future, like a little round robot that could vacuum on its own.

1964/65 World's Fair postcard

WE SAW a person fly with a jet pack—a real live full-grown man zooming into the air with just the power of a jet pack! We'd seen this on television and in movies, but to watch it in person, a man just flying up and around with a pack on his back, made anything seem possible.

Mark and I knew astronauts could use jet packs and lots of other new exciting equipment. As a family, we'd watched television reports of Astronauts Shepard and Glenn's trips into space.

Dad chose the places we'd visit. Since his family took great pride in Italian ancestry and the Catholic church, we visited the Vatican's contribution, which had guards and even bullet-proof glass around it. It was the *Pieta* carved by Michelangelo. The wait to see it was long, so Dad made the time interesting by talking about someday going to Italy, to Rome, and seeing the other art contained in the Vatican, especially the Sistine Chapel.

Finally, we could go to one of the areas selling food. Dad bought Belgian waffles. He'd had them, but we'd never had. They were big waffles with whipped cream, strawberries, and chocolate. I knew Mom and Andy would have enjoyed them.

Even though Dad didn't want to carry anything around with us, he looked for a souvenir for Andy. He bought him a tiny model of a Ford Mustang. Dad and his brothers liked cars and knew how to fix most of the common needs and problems.

Dad picked out a red mustang for Andy and a little yellow model for Mark. Then he told me to select something, so I chose a medium-size flag with images of World's Fair sights.

We didn't have the time or energy to walk around the whole fairgrounds, but we did go in the RCA pavilion to see color televisions and Futurama. We had a ride into the future. We saw a picture phone. I couldn't imagine when normal people would have the ability to see the person they talked to on the phone, but Futurama said it would be common in the future.

The opposite of the future appeared in the pavilion featuring dinosaurs. They moved their bodies and jaws. Even Dad thought they looked so incredible that he bought three little dinosaurs made of hard rubber, one for each of us. Mark wanted the triceratops. I chose the apatosaurus, and Dad bought a tyrannosaurus rex for Andy.

In the Africa pavilion, we saw gorillas, giraffes, and lions. Florida had creatures too, but they were sea creatures, dolphins and seals. We looked at the place where helicopters arrived from the Port Authority heliport and stayed there until we actually saw one take off and one land. Andy would have loved that display.

There were many more paths to walk, but our footsteps had slowed. Dad picked Mark up in one smooth strong move and carried him on his shoulders. Mark smiled with delight down at me. This was something Mark hadn't enjoyed in a long time. Dad usually carried the youngest child around on his shoulders. Andy was bigger and stronger than Mark, but Dad still carried the youngest child on any trip. Sometimes it was one of our cousins.

Mark and I fell asleep on the ride home. We woke up when Dad stopped at White Castle. We gave him our orders, and he bought Andy's typical order of five hamburgers to take home. Dad said he didn't know if Andy would be hungry yet, but Mom would be glad not to cook. Plus, we could all share Andy's hamburgers if he didn't want to eat them.

We did have hamburgers when we got home because Andy was asleep. Mom said he felt better, but he never could have eaten all those hamburgers. Chicken noodle soup and crackers had been enough for Andy's supper. Mom said when she'd tucked him into bed, he'd wanted to snuggle against her while she read to him. Even though he had been sick, she said it had been good to have a day with him resting and snuggling. She said, "It turned out to be a sweet day."

"Really?" Dad asked as he rubbed her back.

"Yes, it was different from what we planned, but it felt good to have a day just cuddling with Andy. It fits well with Mother's Day. Don't you think so?"

I LOOKED at my parents sitting now at Lucille and Ed's table. They looked old. They didn't look old last Saturday, Sunday, or even Monday when they left to go to the Republican Committee meeting. They were attractive and lively adults when they left the house last Monday night.

Mark moved next to me where I leaned against the side of the refrigerator. I wondered what he thought about Dad and Mom acting so differently, staying with the Clauss family, having no house, no school, and family coming in and out in bunches. Did Mark think about Andy? Did he think about the fire or the guy he felt sure was an angel?

Mark took my hand but didn't say anything. I looked down at his thick red hair, singed orange-blond on top. He could have burned up. We all could have. I tried to keep my face and body from showing the sadness, worry, and anger that came and went all day. I held Mark's hand tightly while I wondered if the next day would be better or worse.

10

GANGSTER OR EVANGELIST AND FUNERAL PLANS

W ould the pastor's help make Dad better? I doubted it. Mom and Dad taught us to trust and respect God and to respect people in the role of pastor. Dad encouraged people to respect ministers and priests, but he said all people were flawed. We should look only to Jesus for perfection. Dad said if a person trusted in a pastor or priest instead of in God, they would be let down.

Our current pastor's first name began with a *J*, but his middle name was the old-fashioned name of Oliver. He didn't seem old-fashioned because of his habits and interests, like staying out late on a Saturday night with friends and showing up some Sundays without a sermon. Then he would tell everyone that the Lord told him to have a prayer and praise service. He'd gained the nickname Jolly Olly from the happy way he announced the news of no sermon. The nickname Jolly Olly didn't sound very respectful.

Sure enough, midmorning on Wednesday, the pastor arrived. Lucille opened the door for him. He saw my mother at once along with my aunts Beverly, Pauline, and Marie. Marie wasn't an aunt by blood relation, but she sure seemed like one. There was a coffee table between them. He looked around as if wondering whether my father was going to join us, but he didn't say it. Everyone sat quietly knowing that Dad rarely showed up downstairs.

Aunt Marie had arrived early. She was Catholic, but she never seemed intimidated by or fearful of anyone. I thought that was because only a few administrative people separated her from Jimmy Hoffa at the Teamsters' Union office. Aunt Marie even frowned at the pastor as if to say, *You better not make this funeral planning hard.* Aunt Marie was fast at reading people.

The pastor looked at Mom the whole time he talked, not at the aunts or at me. He told Mom how much he appreciated having his son and how sorry he was that she had the grief of losing Andrew. Then he launched into comforting talk about knowing where Andy was and how we could look forward to seeing him again one day when we all arrived in heaven.

I sat on the little straight chair by the kitchen doorway. As he spoke, I wondered, *How could he know that? How could we know that? Why was he so sure Andy was in heaven? Could I trust everything I'd been taught?* Doubts had been in my mind since I realized Andy had not survived.

The pastor saw the need for more comfort on the faces looking at him, so he decided to explain exactly why he was sure Andy was in heaven. If it was all true, that was certainly where Andy was. Andy had even double-guaranteed getting into heaven.

∾

ON SUNDAY, May 2, at the close of the evening sermon, the pastor gave an altar call. Anyone who wanted to have their sins forgiven and give their life to the Lord Jesus could come forward. Anyone who had backslid away from what they knew was right could come forward. Anyone who needed prayer for healing or for some personal concern could come forward. The pastor and deacons would pray with them.

When Andy pushed by Mom and Dad, out into the center aisle, and then walked toward the pastor and the altar, a change occurred in the words and prayers being said aloud. At only seven years old, Andy, as well as our family, was known by the whole congregation. We helped in Children's Hour, Missionettes, Boys' Brigade, visitation, pastoral committees, Vacation Bible School, evangelism, nursery care, Sunday school, youth group events, and church holiday special plans and suppers. My parents thought kids learned best from working alongside adults.

In our Assembly of God church, Andy's walk down the aisle elicited rapturous shouts. "Hallelujah, Jesus. One of your lambs has heard your voice! Praise you, Jesus! Love this boy, Lord! Praise be to God!"

When Andy got to the front, the pastor put his hand on Andy's shoulder and bent down to talk to him. He also signaled the deacons to approach. They all put a hand on Andy's head, shoulders, or back, and they prayed with him about this life decision. They prayed out loud so that everyone could hear their joy and requests for God to fill this young man's heart with love, life, and power. They didn't emphasize forgiveness of sins. I guess they figured at age seven that Andy couldn't have committed too many serious sins.

Sister Dickinson said to Andy, "I'm glad to see you've given your life to Jesus, Andy. You could be a great evangelist one day."

Cliff, a friend of my father's, leaned in close to him and said, "Frank, I know you must be happy this night. Relieved too, huh? Your boy Andy, he's a live wire. I figured he was going to grow up to be a gangster or a ball of fire for the Lord. Now we know which one." Then Cliff and Dad laughed together.

Beverly and Pauline listened quietly as tears slid down their faces. Mom and Dad had already told them about Andy's decision, but hearing the pastor describe Andy's choice to have forgiveness and follow the Lord made it more vivid to them.

Mom looked pale and numb while the pastor told her she should take great pride and comfort in what Andy had done. Then the pastor moved right to emphasizing May 9, this past Sunday. Andy had surprised everyone again, even the pastor.

On Mother's Day, we'd gone to Grandma Riposta's apartment after church. We visited Grandma every Sunday, not just Mother's Day. Grandma hugged and kissed us. Uncle Sal was already there and seated at the table. He said his kids had colds, so he'd come alone.

Grandma dished out platefuls of food for all of us and told us to "*Mangia, mangia.*" To Andy she often said, "*Che Dio vi benedica.*" He would just smile and eat the food she gave him, all of it. Andy often asked for more. That always made Grandma smile.

On any Sunday visit to Grandma's, we would try to leave by four thirty in the afternoon. If traffic didn't slow our driving, we might get an hour at home before we had to leave for the evening service at church. Sometimes Mom and I had a scheduled responsibility of watching the babies and toddlers in the nursery, but not this Mother's Day Sunday.

I didn't expect the day to end with an unusual event, but it did. The church always had lots of music and the typical altar call. Just like the previous Sunday and most other Sunday evenings, the pastor started with his invitation for people to come forward to the altar if they wanted forgiveness for their sins and for Jesus to be the Lord of their life. Andy got up, squeezed by Mom and Dad, and stepped into the aisle before we realized what he was doing.

Dad took a firm hold on Andy's arm to stop him.

Mom leaned over and said, "Andy, you went forward last Sunday. You only have to do that once. God has forgiven you. He loves you. You are his child. You don't have to go forward again."

"I want to be sure, Mom."

Dad let him go. We watched him walk to the front of the church again.

The pastor usually spoke quietly to each individual. A few people had gone forward this evening. Andy stood by the altar and waited his turn. The pastor talked to him briefly and laid his hand on Andy's head. A couple of deacons joined him to also pray with Andy.

In the car riding home, Dad asked, "What did the pastor say to you, Andy, when you went down front again?"

"He said what Mom said. One time is enough."

"And what did you say to him?"

"I told him I wanted to be sure."

That May 9, Mother's Day, our family stayed at the church until it was almost time to lock the doors. Mom and Dad talked quietly with the pastor. They had me take the boys to the car.

Now, in Lucille and Ed's living room, everyone heard the whole story of Andy asking a second time for forgiveness and for Jesus to come into his heart again this past Sunday, Mother's Day evening. They heard Andy said he wanted to be sure he was God's child. Everyone in the room shed tears except for the pastor and me. I wasn't invisible, but the pastor didn't look at me.

I wondered if it was because I was a child or because I was

the failed babysitter. I'd rescued his son, not Andy. He probably felt both grateful and bad when he looked at me. After the pastor prayed, he asked if they were able to talk about the funeral service. It would be on Saturday, May 15, at the church.

I was halfway up the stairs when Dad started coming down. I stepped to the side and pressed my back against the wall so that Dad could get by me easily. He didn't say anything to me as he passed.

What would he say or do when he got to the bottom of the stairs? He would see the pastor facing the four women, talking to them, with the Bible, paper, and a pen all on the coffee table between them. If I continued upstairs to be with Mark, I'd miss what happened when Dad heard they were planning the funeral.

Dad could be so strict about sharing and being generous in helping others, but he was often like a dictator with us. I had no idea what he would say to everyone planning the funeral. Being on medicine, he hadn't talked much.

I decided to stay downstairs. I followed Dad to the living room but kept my distance behind him. I sat again on the little straight chair that seemed to help me be invisible. I had no idea what would happen now. Was God really here with us in this mess?

To me, it seemed that God must measure how much we loved Him by how involved we were at church. My parents had us at church almost every time the doors opened. Sunday morning, Sunday evening, Wednesday evening Bible study, Thursday Royal Rangers and Missionettes, Friday night special services, and Saturday youth events. This didn't include times like weddings, funerals, missionary visits, or weeklong evangelistic meetings that would override regular schedules every night.

My father had risked rejection by his family at age nineteen by going to an Italian Pentecostal church instead of the Catholic church, but he saw the flaws in Protestant churches. He said Protestants were soft on teaching and memorizing. Because of this, he made up his own catechism practices for us.

We had family devotions time almost every day, with Bible reading and prayer. Besides readings, acting out Bible stories, and discussion of verses, we had assignments. Dad chose poems, verses, and chapters for us to memorize, and he gave us a deadline. If we didn't learn the assigned passage, we'd have no television until we could recite it.

Dad admired hard work and discipline, obedience, and persistence. I could tell by his tone of voice when he thought less of someone. Usually, they couldn't tell because he still sounded polite, but there was an underlying frosty sarcasm. I'd heard him use this tone with this pastor before, but the pastor didn't seem offended.

Dad sat down on the couch next to Mom. The pastor stood up, reached over, and shook hands with Dad. Everyone looked miserable. I wished Mom and Dad would hold hands or put their arms around each other, but they didn't. Aunt Bevy and Aunt Pauline didn't say anything, but they stayed in the living room. Aunt Marie had gone to the kitchen for coffee, but she came and stood in the doorway near me. Even though she didn't say anything to me, she put a hand on my shoulder.

In a gentle voice, the pastor started to review the funeral plans for Dad. After he went through it, Dad abruptly said, "I want you to give the Gospel. It should be as clear as it was to Andy, simple so anyone will understand the way they can have forgiveness of their sins and know they will go to heaven. There will be people at the funeral who have never heard the Gospel and may not be in a place where they'll hear it again."

I wondered if anyone in the room felt the surprise that I did at hearing Dad talk in full sentences. His voice wasn't regular. He sounded hoarse, but speaking in sentences should be a sign that he felt better.

How many people in the room knew he had not spoken in complete sentences since he asked me the question, "If you could get two out, why couldn't you get three out?"

The pastor seemed startled. He asked, "You mean you want a salvation message and altar call as part of the funeral?"

"Yes." Dad looked directly at the pastor.

I had heard Dad tell the story of how unhappy his family was when he left the Catholic church. Even though Grandpa rarely went to church more often than on Christmas and Easter, he argued with Dad over the one true church. Grandpa kicked Dad out and forbid anyone else in the family from letting Dad back in or even speaking with him as long as he did not return to the Catholic church.

Whether Grandpa knew it or not, the brothers and sisters did talk to Dad. Grandma did too but only through her daughters. They all hoped and prayed Dad would come back to the Catholic faith. The hope lasted until he met and fell in love with a Protestant girl when he visited a much larger Assembly of God church in Newark.

In Dad's family, the man made the rules for the household and had the lead role, but the wife provided the spiritual heart for the home. Grandma did that. She prayed daily for her family and friends and went to an early-morning mass almost every day. Grandma required the children to go to church with her on special days.

Grandpa and Grandma thought that if Dad married a Protestant girl, he would probably never return to the Catholic church. Grandpa tried threatening. If Frank went through with this idea of marrying a Protestant girl in a Protestant church, Grandpa said he would not attend the wedding. He did not forbid the rest of the family from attending, but he did not come into the church. He only showed up afterward for family photographs.

Anthony (Grandpa), Katherine, Frank, Angelina (Grandma),
July 21, 1951

NOT UNTIL DAD went off to Korea and Mom was pregnant did Dad's family relax and include her. Having a baby, especially while Dad was in Korea, caused them to care for Mom. That's what she told me. They looked after Mom and invited her to their homes. Dad's sisters did their best to teach her how to cook and keep house Italian style.

Grandpa forbid talking about religion in the home. Though he and everyone in the family could tell that faith meant more to Dad in practical and spiritual ways, Grandpa didn't want to speak about any of it. Prayers were allowed, but no discussions about faith or salvation or the Bible could occur because of the different views of God's relationship with people.

A wedding was typically the only time that some of my dad's family would go into a Protestant church. For funerals of Protestant or Jewish friends, they'd go to calling hours or the service if it was in a funeral home but usually not if it was in a church or synagogue.

I knew how much everyone loved Andy. The whole family, from Grandma to every cousin and family friend, as well as employees and coworkers of my uncles and aunts, would come to the funeral. Showing love for Andy and support for the family mattered to all of them.

Dad offered no opinions on songs for the funeral. Once he told the pastor what he wanted said during the service, he went back to sitting without focus or talking. He left the rest of the funeral planning to Mom and the pastor. She chose to include songs that would help her even if they made her cry. Dad stayed still and silent.

I slipped past Aunt Marie and went into the kitchen, where everyone was talking softly, sharing memories of Andy while they nibbled on food and drank coffee. The voices caught on some words, but sadness seemed second to enjoying the memories. Why couldn't Dad be like them?

When the pastor left, Dad returned upstairs to bed. He showed no interest in being with anyone. I watched his back and wondered if he still talked to God, and if he did, what he said. Or did he just cry, take more medicine, and sleep?

Everyone around me had shed tears, but I hadn't. I wondered what was wrong with me to have dry eyes when my heart ached. The grown-ups around me cried. I realized I had not prayed since begging God to rescue Andy. I'd thought about God. I'd thought about praying for Dad and Mom to be normal again, about finding a place to live, about getting through all the mess ahead, but I didn't.

Both Dad and our church taught that God knew our

thoughts. If God knew my thoughts, then couldn't my thoughts be prayers? Probably not. God wanted us to talk to him. God knew I was angry over Andy's death. I didn't want to talk to a God who had allowed Andy to die. I wanted to yell to God, "This whole miserable situation stinks!"

11

STINKERS

S tink? I've never heard or thought the words *stink*, *stinkers*, or *stinking* without remembering one time I rescued myself and my brothers from an awful smell. The summer before the fire, on the last Saturday we had in Maine, Grandpere had brought all the rocking chairs and Adirondack chairs to the side of the farmhouse that faced the fields, garden, and barn. Grandmere; her older sister, Winnie; younger sister, Caroline; Caroline's daughter, Janice; and Mom all settled into the chairs in beautiful sunshine. In their summer clothing, the women could have been a painting by Mom's favorite artist, Monet.

The men—Grandpere, Uncle Bob, and Dad—stood near the barn talking. Grandpere smoked a cigar. Grandmere never wanted him near the house when he did that.

Mark and Andy played catch near the men and were given tips on how to throw, stand, and catch. Then Dad called to me, "Take your brothers for a walk. They'll be in the car most of the day tomorrow."

Dad's suggestions were commands. Mark, Andy, and I

knew they were orders. Dad might require a sharing house, but most of all Dad expected quick obedience.

"We'll walk to the sandpit," I announced. Mark and Andy happily gave their mitts and the ball to Dad. The sandpit provided opportunities for climbing, rolling, digging, and building, and it was a thousand time bigger than any playground sandboxes we had in New Jersey.

I could feel the audience of family eyes following our progress down the driveway to Bremen Road. The boys could never cross the road alone, but if they had me or an adult with them, then they could. That had been a rule since they could walk.

We crossed the street and started up the overgrown dirt road that led to the sandpit. After one curve, no one back at the farm could see us. I often noticed how much the adults trusted me.

While I walked on the old road, the boys ran back and forth and in and out of the trees that grew thick not far from the street. I watched for poison ivy. We all knew to steer clear of those shiny trios on vines.

Suddenly they stopped. The one hill in front of them had a huge indentation revealing tan sand that looked amazing. I wondered who had been the first person to dig into it and realize that the entire hill was sand.

"Can we climb it now?" Mark asked.

"You can if you want to. You can even race up and down it if you want to." I figured Dad and Mom wanted them to get tired out so that they would sleep well.

Mark loped off to the right because someone had worn a path to the top of the hill in that visible side of sand, probably many someones. Andy ran up right behind him, but then Mark stopped abruptly. Andy crashed into him.

Mark pointed down at the thick tufts of grass that alternated with rocks at the base of the sandpit. "Something's moving."

I went close to the base of the sandpit that had a slope like Bob Hope's nose. Something was moving. The grass behind a couple of medium-size rocks swayed back and forth. Some little thing might be crawling through it. A small animal?

I had heard about rabies. One of the neighbors on Bremen Road had been bitten by a rabid cat, and the cat was caught and killed. The neighbor had to get many needle sticks over weeks of time.

Mark slid down off the path into the sand and toward the place where the grass moved. Andy came back down the narrow path and stood in front of the rocks and swaying grass. With some kind of instinct, they wanted to surround and trap whatever they found.

"Stay back, you two. Let me look first. It could be an animal with rabies."

"I want to see the babies."

"Rabies, Andy, not babies. Rabies is a terrible disease. You have to get lots of needles if you get rabies."

Both boys backed up and stopped moving. Neither of them liked needles. I grabbed a stick, part of a branch that was beside the road. Mark stayed where he was on the side of the sandpit. Andy moved alongside me.

"What do you see?" Mark asked.

"Nothing yet. Be quiet."

I moved closer and used the stick to part the grass. A hole appeared, a scooped-out hole as deep as a big salad bowl. In the hole filled with twigs, leaves, and grass, three little creatures moved. "Skunks! Baby skunks!" Andy said loudly.

"Shhhhh, quiet! If you scare them, they might spray us. You know how bad a skunk can stink. Plus, the mother could be nearby!"

"They're so little," Andy said as Mark slipped and slid down the hill to join us.

I leaned down and saw that their eyes weren't even open. I knew skunks sprayed by lifting their tails. If we picked them up and held the tails curved down and under them, they should be okay to carry.

"I want to touch one! I want to hold one!" Andy said. Mark just watched both of us. At least Andy was waiting for me to respond.

Right now, I agreed with Andy. I wanted to touch one of the wriggling little black-and-white babies with their tiny pink noses and closed eyes. Mark edged up close to me. "I want to hold one too."

"Okay, we can each pick one up. They're very little. We have to be careful and gentle. Fold their tails down under them while you hold them. If the tail is folded down under them, they can't spray, and maybe babies don't have much spray."

"What if the mother comes back?" Mark asked.

"They we'll put them right down. She'll want to go to them, and we'll run as fast as we can back to the farm. Okay?"

They nodded. I knelt down and reached for the one that looked the largest. He stumbled around with his eyes still partially closed, bumping into the other ones and my hands. He felt soft and warm and as light as a fuzzy slipper when I lifted him. I folded his tail under his body and held him close to my chest.

Mark went next. It wasn't often that Andy didn't try to go ahead of Mark; now he seemed glad to watch me and Mark go first. Mark lifted the baby skunk, keeping the tail curved under the body, and held it snug to his chest. Andy did the same.

We turned back toward the farm. I walked quickly. The baby skunk snuggled to my chest smelled to me like any furry baby animal—a kitten, puppy, rabbit, squirrel, gerbil, hamster, guinea pig. I'd been close to babies of all those.

Just as we got to Bremen Road, Mark said, "It tickles." Mark smiled at me and looked comfortable and happy holding the baby skunk.

What a strange parade we made as we walked up the driveway, our hands folded cuplike against our chests. Anyone passing by quickly might have thought we were praying. I knew the grown-ups could see us from where they sat or stood.

I could hear Mom and Janice laughing. Carolyn, Winnie, and Grandmere just watched us. Dad, Grandpere, and Bob stepped away from the barn.

"What is it? What do you have?" Dad called.

I wanted to answer but thought I shouldn't shout. The little skunk seemed to have fallen asleep against my chest. Dad took a few more steps toward us. Grandpere and Bob came with him. They stood on each side of him. Now all the women were looking at us too. Mom, Janice, and Aunt Winnie stood up, waiting for us to answer.

"Skunks!" Andy shouted. He laughed before he added, "We have baby skunks!"

The skunk must have felt the difference in his body when he shouted. It moved. Andy had to reposition his hands to try to keep it close to him with the tail held under.

Grandpere and Bob laughed, but they didn't come closer to us. Dad's mouth fell open about the time Mom and Janice shouted, "Get away! Get away!" All the women rushed into the house like rainbow confetti blown inside on a strong gust of wind.

I opened my hands just a little so that the men could see the size of the baby skunk. "Grandpere, remember when Grandmere and I met the lady with the pet skunk in Camden?"

"I do."

"These babies are so little; they could be fixed by a vet. They'd be good pets."

"'Fraid not. They're so little that they still need their mom."

"We could feed them with a little bottle, like people do with other baby animals."

"They can't eat cow milk or formula. Only the vet might know what they can drink to survive."

"Can we check? They aren't afraid of us. They're too little to be afraid of people. They won't spray us now."

"I have an old birdcage in the barn. I'll put some soft rags in the bottom; they smell like hay. I don't think they'll mind that. They can snuggle down together. We'll leave them by the old chicken coop while we go inside and talk about this."

Dad squelched that idea fast. "We are not having pet skunks." No room for a different opinion appeared when Dad spoke in that tone of voice.

And that was that. I knew we would never have pet skunks. Mom was allergic to cats, but she'd had them when she was young. They were her favorites, but when her allergies developed, she couldn't have cats around her anymore. Dad had allowed turtles, gerbils, hamsters, and rabbits. Sometimes we took care of friends' dogs when they went away on vacation.

Grandpere had gone into the barn and came out with the birdcage. There were rags in the bottom of it. We three carefully placed the baby skunks in the cage as gently as we had picked them up. They still seemed sleepy and unafraid.

"I'll take them back to their home in the sandpit and hope the mother isn't there," Grandpere told us.

"Right at the bottom there's a hole, about the size of a big bowl, and there's stuff in it like a nest," I said. Mark and Andy looked like they might cry.

"I can't believe you carried skunks over here," Dad said to

us. Then he smiled and rubbed Mark and Andy on their heads. They had crew cuts. Rubbing their heads felt like rubbing bristle brushes. Almost everyone in the family rubbed their heads when they had fresh new crew cuts.

Uncle Bob said, "Most crazy thing I've seen in a while—kids parading up this driveway with baby skunks."

We had to go to bed early that Saturday night because Dad wanted to leave for home by eight. He really wanted to leave earlier, but Grandmere wanted to make breakfast for us. It turned out we didn't get to leave until late Sunday afternoon.

Mark and Andy were dressed and outside just after sunrise. I didn't know it. No one knew it. They were allowed to go outside and play whenever they got up. They just had to stay on the property.

Andy wanted to see the baby skunks one more time. Mark followed his lead. They both went to the sandpit. That meant they crossed Bremen Road alone, which they were not allowed to do. There wasn't a sidewalk or even a decent shoulder of dirt or grass. Cars went superfast down the long straight section of road. The boys had never disobeyed this rule before, but early on a Sunday morning, no one was zooming over Bremen Road.

Because he loved to run, Andy ran far ahead of Mark once they crossed the road. The mother skunk had returned and was with the babies. Andy got sprayed, and he hollered and cried. Mark stopped far back down the dirt road because he could smell it. The scent might not have floated far on the still morning air, but it was powerful enough that Mark felt and smelled like some of the spray had hit him.

They were crying loudly all the way back up the driveway to the farm. Grandpere was outside and turned the hose on the boys. They were lucky that this late August morning was warm. They had to undress before they came in the house. Grandpere would burn all their clothes, even their gym shoes.

Grandmere sent Dad off to buy large cans of tomato juice. The boys would take a bath in that. Then Grandmere had some homemade mixture they could use after the tomato juice. I watched her mix it—hydrogen peroxide, baking soda, and dishwashing soap. They had to use it right after they finished rubbing the tomato juice all over their bodies.

They still smelled of skunk, so Grandmere called her oldest sister, Winnie, who always seemed to have some ideas for household items that could be used for different problems. She said to mix apple cider vinegar with water and have them sit in it for a while. Grandmere and Mom did that and especially rubbed it on the boys' crew cuts. They rinsed it after ten minutes. Winnie had said if they still smelled like skunk, mix a bottle of vanilla extract into a gallon of water and rub them down with that. Mom and Grandmere had to do this step too.

Dad didn't spank them or reprimand them. He said the smell and what they went through was enough of a punishment. I thought their stink was punishment for everyone who had to be around them. It made us all miserable.

The calling hours and funeral would make us miserable too. The whole situation could not be washed away. I knew it was probably sacrilegious to blame God for this stink, but I did.

12

CALLING HOURS AND SOMERSAULTS

C alling hours would happen over two days, Thursday and Friday. Only one person came to the Clauss home on Thursday after Ray and Ed had gone to school and Ed had gone to work. Uncle Sal came to take us to the funeral home. We knew he could help Dad to leave the house.

I heard Mom talking to Lucille. She wondered if Dad could even make it through the few hours. He had taken all the medicine the doctor allowed. I watched them each day and felt angry that she worried about him. Dad seemed to have no idea that she suffered too.

Uncle Sal had a son and a daughter. Would Uncle Sal fall apart so much if one of his children died? Uncle Sal went to church maybe once a year, so did being an active Christian who read the Bible and prayed every day not help a person any more than not having any kind of active Christian habits?

Dad often talked about wanting to be a good Christian witness to his family. Did he think about that at all while he was on the medicine that caused him to exist like a frowning zombie? Why had he fallen apart so much? God didn't seem to be answering anyone's prayers about Dad.

The funeral home had three areas for calling hours or funerals. On this Thursday, only our family had calling hours. The casket was closed. Dad did not want to sit in the room with it. Until people arrived, he stayed in one of the other empty rooms.

Mark and I sat at the back of the room in an alcove meant for two or three people to sit together. We had a clear view of Andy's casket. It was covered with a material that looked like white satin brocade with a pattern on it but no specific design. Lots of flowers and plants surrounded the closed casket, and the funeral home staff kept bringing more in to place around the small white casket.

"Are they going to open it?"

"What?" I looked at Mark. I had heard his question, but there was no way could I tell him what I knew about Andy's body.

"Are they going to open the casket?"

"No. They aren't. Mom wants people to remember Andy the way he was the last time they saw him."

I heard Mom talking to Aunt Beverly. She had not sounded so shaken since Tuesday morning when Dad had asked me the question, and she'd cried out, "Oh Frank!"

Beverly could see that Mom was upset. "What, Katherine? What is it? Something new about the funeral?"

"It has to be closed, Beverly. The casket has to stay closed. I didn't tell you, but I had to identify Andy at the hospital. They said the parents had to identify the child. Frank couldn't. He didn't even say he couldn't. He just sat on the bench outside the room where they kept bodies.

"So I went in the room alone to see Andy's body. What the fire chief said was true. Andy didn't die from the fire. He died in that top bunk while he was asleep from the smoke, but fire did get to him.

"His little body, it . . . it—" She stopped but then took a breath and went on. "His body looked like charcoal, a sculpture in charcoal—in the position he was always in when he was deeply asleep. Left arm across his body, right arm thrown back and above his head. Left leg straight, toe toward the ceiling, right leg bent so that his foot was flat down and his knee was toward the ceiling. He was frozen in that favorite sleep position but burned up." Mom sobbed and cried; Bevy did too.

I looked at that child-size casket and at the flowers and the wavy patterns in the white satin brocade. Some other family members arrived. When Sal brought them into the room, they stopped, almost gasping at the sight of the small white coffin. They hugged Mom. They cried on each other and with one another. Mark snuggled closer to me while we watched the adults.

Aunt Bevy had told me that the parents needed to sit or stand near the coffin to greet anyone who came for calling hours. Sal was going to bring Dad to stand near Mom. The funeral director gently guided them into the expected positions. I guessed no one learned where to sit or stand at a funeral except when they actually had to be the family at one.

"Mark, do you want to stand near Mom and Dad?"

"Do we have to?"

"No."

"Can we just stay here together?"

"Sure."

So we did, and after people greeted Mom and Dad, they usually came back to talk to us but only briefly. The grown-ups didn't seem to know what to say to us. Some gave hugs, some cried, and some gave us kisses. Only a few people actually sat down near us and told us some memory they had of Andy.

Most didn't say much. Maybe they'd never been to a child's calling hours before they came to Andy's.

For a minute, I thought, *Andy had never been to a funeral.* Then I recalled a time when he had. I wondered if Mark remembered.

"Hey, Mark."

"Yes?"

"Do you remember our spotted turtles' funeral?"

"We each had a turtle and we used to race them."

"Yes. Andy took his out the most to play with it."

"It died."

"Yes, so we had a funeral for it."

"Mom gave us a small gift box for a coffin."

"We lined it with tissues. Andy made sure the cover of the box fit tightly."

"And we buried it in the backyard."

"Andy put the box into the hole."

"Yes, and we all pushed the dirt around the hole on top of the box until the hole was filled. I patted it down."

"You did, and then we all recited Psalm 23."

Mark nodded and said, "Then we played with our G.I. Joes."

"Andy wanted to play."

"Nobody here wants to play anything." Mark looked pale. He sighed and leaned lightly against me. I thought about Andy and how easily he switched from burying his pet to playing with toys. Mark didn't transition from feelings so quickly.

Dozens of people came to the Thursday calling hours, maybe even a hundred. The foyer had a stand with a book on it that people could sign. We saw people we had not visited in years.

All of Dad's brothers and sisters and their children arrived. We saw them sign the guest book, and we saw them stay and talk for hours. Beverly and Pauline stayed the whole time. People from our church and friends of Mom and Dad who had children stayed for a just a little while.

Everyone who came had a story to tell about Andy. Their stories comforted Mom, but Dad grimaced. Sometimes he even stepped away from Mom to sit down away from everyone.

When people from church came to the calling hours, they prayed with Mom and Dad. As the friends prayed, Dad stood or sat very still. I wondered if he could pray now. I still hadn't prayed since begging God for Andy to be rescued, but sometimes it was automatic for me to ask God about something. I'd stop myself then.

Uncle Sal drove us all back to Lucille and Ed's. When he escorted Dad in, they stood on the porch and talked. We went in the house but could not hear what they said. Sal might be the baby of Dad's family, but he sure was acting like an older brother now.

I'd found out something else by listening to conversations during the calling hours. I didn't think Mark had understood it, but people talked about how wise it was to have two funerals. We would have the funeral here in New Jersey, since most of the family and longtime friends lived here. They complimented Mom on deciding to have another funeral service in Maine for all the relatives there who could not come down to New Jersey for the funeral.

We would have two funerals for Andy. I had never heard of someone having two funerals, but it must happen sometimes if our family had decided to do so. No one seemed shocked. One would be this Saturday, here in Elizabeth, New Jersey, but then the body would be taken to Maine.

We'd have a funeral service in the Assembly of God church in Thomaston. Then the funeral director would drive Andy's casket and ash body back to Waldoboro. Burial would be at the cemetery near the old German meetinghouse, a protestant church we could see from Grandmere and Grandpere's farm.

The traveling and driving the casket around was probably what made funerals more expensive. I knew Mom was worried about expenses. That was another conversation my sleeping Dad had missed, but I'd heard Mom talking with Aunt Beverly.

"Beverly, I don't know how we'll pay for all this. It's thousands, and we had a tight budget before we lost everything. We don't even know where we're going to live when we get back from Maine. Frank's family has done a lot, and Lucille and Ed have been wonderful, but we have to plan something else."

"You will. I'll help. Other family members will help."

"Bevy, no one knows when the insurance will come through. They want to say the house isn't a total loss. They haven't sent an adjuster yet, but they told us it's not a total loss. How do they know? Anyone can see that no one could live in it."

"They don't know. They probably say that to anyone who submits a big claim because they don't want to give out the money. Have you been to the house yet?"

"No. I haven't been to it yet, but . . ."

"Katherine, they're wrong. It is an entire loss. I'll talk to an insurance guy I know to get some suggestions for getting your full amount."

"I'm sorry to put all this on you. You know Frank—he's just stumbling through each day. I don't know if he'll be like this for a long time or just while he's on the tranquilizers."

"He'll get better. We're all praying for him." Then Aunt Bevy prayed with Mom. She did this every day before she left.

One summer Aunt Winnie had taken me to see where her family had cemetery sites in places on the coast of Maine, Owl's Head, Spruce Head, and Waldoboro. Near Grandmere and Grandpere's farm in Waldoboro, just a quarter mile away, stood the German Protestant church, called a meetinghouse, that was built in the 1600s. No one from Mom's family had been buried there until after America's Civil War.

Now Andy would be buried in that Waldoboro cemetery. The scary old part lined with dark gnarled trees and filled with four-hundred- and three-hundred-year-old graves was right next to the meetinghouse. I'd walked among them to read names and inscriptions. Andy would be buried a long way away from them on a high open hill.

And the funeral? I heard Beverly tell Pauline that the second funeral would be in a week at the little Assembly of God church where Grandmere played the piano each Sunday. Grandpere drove her there every week. He didn't go in for services except some special ones of music. I didn't even know what Grandpere believed about God and heaven, but he would go into the church for Andy's funeral.

And when we came back to New Jersey, what would happen then? No one had said much about where we would live or when we would go back to school. I had heard enough to know that we would come back to some other place besides Lucille and Ed's house. We couldn't live with them forever.

I reached out and put my arm around Mark. Soon after he rested fully against me, he fell asleep. I wondered if he slept well at night or if he woke up looking for smoke like I did.

WHEN I WOKE up in the night, I told myself I was silly to worry about a fire in the Clausses' house. When I lay awake, I thought about Andy. Even though he could make me really angry, I remembered lots of times when Andy had made me smile.

Mom and Dad often visited the elderly people from

church. They called them shut-ins, meaning the people couldn't go out for errands or to church or anything. Taking care of people with needs and old people was very important in our church.

I preferred visiting shut-ins with Mom. Her style of visiting seemed relaxed and aimed to have everyone feel happy. Dad took visitation as a responsibility to let the shut-in people know they were not forgotten. He aimed to give them encouragement from God's Word and by letting them see us to show there were good kids.

If Dad took us, he would have a conversation with the person, and we would have to sit still, hands folded, until he asked us to stand. Then we would recite Bible verses he had made us memorize or sing church hymns or choruses. We had been memorizing Scripture verses before we went to school and knew whole chapters of the Bible by heart, along with scattered verses and a dozen songs from the hymnbook.

When Dad told us to recite something or sing, Mark mumbled and sang softly. Andy spoke like he had a microphone in his mouth and sang loudly off-key. I spoke clearly but not as loudly as Andy. Andy had the loudest voice in our family.

If Mom took us to visit the elderly, it was not such a stand-up show. We had to be friendly, make conversation, tell some stories about school, tell a joke, answer questions, and above all be loud when we spoke. Mom explained that many of the people we visited could not afford good hearing aids. To make her point, she would turn down the volume on one of our favorite television shows, have us watch it for a few minutes, and ask how much we enjoyed it when we couldn't hear what the people said.

One day we went to Mrs. R's house. Her home always looked neat because she had someone who cleaned for her, but the whole place smelled like we'd fallen into a pile of baby powder. Once Andy said that out loud to Mrs. R. She just laughed and said it could smell like worse things.

Mom reminded Mark and Andy that she counted on their best behavior. As she guided them up the stairs to Mrs. R's front door she said, "Behave yourselves and speak up. Remember to speak loudly and clearly. Mrs. R is almost totally deaf."

Mom rang the doorbell. It clanged loudly enough to signal the end of the world. When Mom pushed the button the second time, we could feel it from our ears to our toes, even though we weren't standing close to the door. We heard Mrs. R struggle to turn the locks on her door. She had many extra locks. Then, working to balance while she leaned on her walker, she opened the door for us.

"Come in, come in! It's been too long since I've seen you. My! You children have grown so much, especially you boys!"

Mrs. R led us way into her living room. She sat in a large chair that I knew was called a wing chair. It was a rose color that matched the heavy rouge on her cheeks. Her white hair was arrangement in a high French twist. I wondered how she did that with arms as thick as highway cones and covered with sagging skin. She had wide wrists and swollen fingers.

Mom sat at the end of a sofa. Her simple navy blue and white dress stood out on the couch covered with floral fabric. Flowers were on almost everything in Mrs. R's house, even the lampshades. I sat next to Mom. Mark sat next to me. The couch was full, so Andy leaned against the end of it.

"I can do somersaults," Andy suddenly announced in a shouted sentence.

"Go ahead, Andy. I would love to see your somersaults." Mrs. R smiled at him.

Andy looked at Mom, and she nodded approval. He

retreated to the small entryway until only the front door was at his back. Clearly, he intended to somersault toward Mrs. R. With a smile and a spin forward, he began his row of somersaults toward Mrs. R.

In his first roll, just as his bottom faced the ceiling, he farted. A multiple rapid fire of farts emerged with every single roll. Mom gasped.

Mark and I looked from Andy to Mrs. R. She smiled calmly and stared at Andy. She was not laughing, not shocked. We realized she hadn't heard the kerfuffle of his gas pops.

Andy kept somersaulting and passing gas all the way across the room. Mark and I looked at Mom to see if we could laugh, but she shook her head no. I felt like I would explode, but somehow Mark and I kept polite smiles on our faces. Andy giggled at the noises he made but kept rolling until he stopped against Mrs. R's knees.

She reached forward and put her hands on his shoulders as he sat up. "That was wonderful, Andy."

For a few moments before I fell back to sleep, Andy had made me smile again.

∾

Later Lessons Learned: Needs of Children after Trauma

At age twelve, I felt curiosity about and concern for what Dad would do or say. It upset me that he had not acted at all like the father I had before the fire. I hoped for that dad to reappear.

I was years away from learning that, after trauma, children need parents and caregivers who will provide love, respect, and security. Without this support from these crucial adults, children internalize negative behaviors and feelings such as fearfulness, withdrawal, anxiety, apathy, and depression.

After traumatic events, it helps children to have familiar routines, but that did not happen for us, even though family and friends gave kind help. Talking about the traumatic event or one's feelings during and since the event also support a child's ability to work through their emotions. A caretaker relating as a stable support can reassure a child and help them to feel believed and valued. A caring discussion will also allow opportunities to think of ways together to cope with fears and emotions.

13

BIRTHDAY CLOCKS

Friday did not seem like a day that would have any smiles. Mom and Dad had received a notice that they could go to the Magie Avenue house and look for anything they could salvage. Dad did not want to go. He took his medicine and slept. Lucille said she'd watch Mark and me, but I said I wanted to go with Mom and help.

Mom let me accompany her. I knew she did not want to go to the burned-down house alone. She shouldn't have to. I didn't know why she wouldn't ask Aunt Bevy, Pauline, or someone else. The house would be a scary wreck.

Lucille gave Mom an old-fashioned wooden box and a large cloth tote bag, plus a couple of large garbage bags, and off we went in our car. Looking at the small number of containers, I knew that Lucille didn't expect we would find much of anything worth saving.

The hedges around the front porch were crushed and broken. Yellow and orange sawhorses with No Trespassing signs stood at the base of the front porch steps. Mom looked at those and said, "We'll go to the side door."

A sawhorse and sign stood by the side door steps too, but Mom went around it. She didn't have to unlock the door. The glass was gone from the windows, but when she turned the knob, it opened. Glancing to the left, we could see that there was still deep dark water in the basement.

Mom turned right and went up the steps into the kitchen. There was no ceiling over the nook where we had our kitchen table and chairs. I could look up at parts of the floor of the bathroom, pipes, and some pieces of floor from my room. Spaces, ragged holes, seemed scattered in the structures above our heads. Over our old eating area in the kitchen, blackened sections of back wall remained, but the windows had disappeared.

Mom turned to her right, toward the sink where we both had washed dishes. Once Mom had asked Dad about getting a dishwasher. I thought it would be super for us. Dad had laughed and said, "I gave you three dishwashers."

Now Mom looked up above the long rectangular window over the sink. I wondered if she remembered Dad's answer about a dishwasher. She didn't ask for things for the house hardly ever. What could she be thinking as she looked at this mess?

The window was gone, but the cat clock she had bought when we moved into the house still hung above the missing window. Mom loved cats. She'd always had a cat as a pet when she was child. She still loved cats, and the black cat pendulum wall clock in our kitchen clued people in on what she enjoyed.

The black cat looked sleek from the back of the head, neck, shoulders, seated body, and tail. People saw its back. The cat's head, slightly turned to the side, showed the profile, and one eye dared people to read the time. The cat's long black tail curled upward, and the end had a white tip. A white hour, minute, and second hand sat in the middle of the cat's black back. The numbers and small lines to mark the minutes also were white.

My friends thought the cat clock showed that my parents had cool personalities. I knew the only reason we had the clock was that Mom loved cats, and Dad loved Mom. He would never have chosen a cat clock on his own. He liked plain practical clocks.

None of the hands moved on the cat clock now. The clock showed the time when the electricity had gone off on Monday night. Mom stared at the clock. I thought she looked paler than she had when we came into the kitchen.

"That's the time the power went off?" she asked, looking at the clock.

"Yes."

"You said it went off all at once."

"Yes."

"When you were going upstairs?"

"Yes." Mom obviously listened to me and remembered everything I'd told the men from the fire department, even though she'd had some of the same medication as Dad.

"Climb up," she said and pointed at the counter beside the sink. I climbed onto the counter with a bit of a lift from her. I saw her reach to the left and unplug the clock.

"Take the clock down carefully."

"It probably won't work anymore."

"Just take it down carefully and hand it to me."

I lifted the clock from the hook and gave it to Mom. She took it, scrunched up the cord, and turned away, toward the room off the kitchen that should have been a dining room but that she and Dad had made into their bedroom. She hugged the clock. I followed her.

The room showed major damage from fire, the smoke, the firefighters' hatchets, and the water. Mom held the cat clock and pointed at her jewelry box on the long French Regency-style bureau. Mom liked styles from France. She did not have one piece of valuable jewelry, but I picked up the jewelry box.

She held the cat clock in her left hand and opened the jewelry box with her right hand. I noticed the jewelry box was white and gold. In some ways it reminded me of Andy's casket. His casket didn't have gold on it, but the white box reminded me well enough.

Mom opened the box. She took out the bracelet with the chunky and colorful stones that Andy had given her for Mother's Day. She hadn't worn it to the meeting on Monday night. Now she put it on. I wondered if she had thought about it since Monday. I wondered if she would ever take it off again.

"You can put the jewelry box in the tote bag." There were other rings and a couple of necklaces in it, plus a small envelope. I didn't know what was in that. Mom's voice sounded choked as she turned to look around the room. Against the opposite wall stood a tall chest of drawers in the same French Regency style. Centered on it was a clock that stood about one foot tall.

This fancy clock had three curved legs and looked like the clock that came alive in *Beauty and the Beast*. The French style mantel clock had a simple round white face surrounded by waves and curlicues of fake gold. The hours, minutes, numbers, and lines to show the minutes were slender and black. The thinnest hand marking the seconds lay as a thin needle of red.

Mom stared at the dresser and the clock. Photos in frames had been on either side of the clock, but they were gone, on the floor, in pieces. The large painting of lilacs that had hung centered on the bedroom wall between the windows was also on the floor. I walked around so that I could see the rips and breaks in it.

As Mom handed me the cat clock, she said, "Put this in the

box. Be very careful with it." Then she walked to the tall chest of drawers and picked up the fancy nonworking clock. She stared at its stopped face, then turned to look at me. I waited.

She seemed to want to say something, but she didn't. Maybe she couldn't. Something about the clock bothered her. She pulled the cord that went down behind the dresser to the outlet and picked up the clock. She hugged it to her.

Then we went to the open space where folding doors had stood. In the corner of the bedroom on the wall backed by the kitchen, she looked at the plastic hamper she kept there. That hamper had clothes in it that needed washing or repair. She did not sew often, but she did laundry twice a week. Now she reached into that hamper and stirred through all the clothes.

"Virginia, put these in the tote bag too." I took them from her. I saw that they were Andy's clothes: a sweater a woman from church had knit for him that had a hole in the cuff area, a pair of navy blue pants with a tear in the knee, a T-shirt with G.I. Joe on it, a blue and white checked shirt, and a pair of blue-, red-, and white-striped swimming trunks that needed a new elastic. I put them all in the bag. Mom had moved on and wasn't watching me.

I followed her into the living room. The sight of all the ruined furniture there made my head hurt. Every room smelled horrible, and I felt a tightening grip on my chest. I started to take a deep breath but changed my mind.

Mom and I looked at the broken television and tables, the ripped and soaked couch, the phonograph, and the chairs and carpet. There were two bookcases below the two broken windows at the front of the house. The bookcase closest to the corner had a clock on it.

Grandmere and Grandpere had given that old clock, an antique, to Mom and Dad. It was in a simple curved dark wooden case. The face, a circle of white, had three hands, the black hour and minute hands and one that looked like a thin line of brass for the second hand. Grandmere's parents used to wind that clock each day. Then Grandpere rewired it so that it ran on electricity.

In slow motion, Mom walked toward the bookcase. I could see she had focused her attention totally on the clock. Another stopped clock had grabbed her attention. Why did she stare so much at these ruined clocks?

She put her hand out to touch the top of the curved hill of wood that framed the clock. Then she turned and looked back at me. "They're all the same."

"What? The stopped clocks?"

"Yes. The clocks are all the same. Take this." She handed me the clock from her bedroom and turned her full attention to the old clock Grandpere had rewired.

I felt a surge of fear. Was Mom losing her mind? The clocks didn't have anything in common in their looks except that they were clocks. They had stopped, and they were ruined.

Even when they worked, they never had the same time. That used to make Dad grouchy. He wanted the clocks to show the same time and the right time. These three clocks never matched.

The kitchen clock usually ran ahead of the one in our parents' bedroom. Their fancy bedroom clock lost minutes each week. It had lost almost two minutes a day the last time we checked. Dad worried about being late for work if he depended on that clock. This living room clock always matched the television and radio time.

I knew about the clocks' quirky speeds and mismatched times. So did Mom. She looked at me and must have been able to see I did not understand her. She repeated, "Virginia, they all show the same time."

"They went off when the electricity went off. That's what the firemen said."

"Virginia, they all show the same time," she repeated. "Look at them."

I tipped the tote bag so that I could see the black cat pendulum clock: 10:18:57. I looked at the fancy French-style clock I held: 10:18:57. I looked at the old clock from Grandmere and Grandpere: 10:18:57. How could that happen? The clocks never matched. They would have had different times when the power went off.

"Virginia, I think it's a message from God."

"From God?"

"Yes. Andy was born on October 18, 1957."

She stopped and stared at me, waiting for me to realize how amazing these matching clocks were that showed the date of Andy's birthday and how they made her feel. I looked at all the clocks again and then at her. She seemed almost peaceful. She had a real smile on her face.

I glanced again at all the clocks stopped at 10:18:57, the exact date of Andy's birthday. Since someone else could see this set of clocks with matching times, Mom wasn't imagining this. It had to be a message. Mom probably felt relieved. She wasn't imagining this odd set of matched times on the clocks. They had all lost power at the same moment.

"Virginia, I think God is showing me that Andy died at this time, right when the power went off. I think God knew I needed to know He's in this. He doesn't want us to suffer, so He's reminding me that He was right here. He took Andy in an instant. Andy went to sleep in this house and woke up in heaven. He never felt any pain. The Lord will carry us through all of this. God did this with the clocks to comfort me, and it does. It does."

Mom smiled and burst into tears. I could see they weren't just sad tears. She unplugged that oldest clock and hugged it.

We didn't go upstairs. Mom didn't look in the front hall closet either. We took the three clocks, the jewelry box, the clothes from the plastic hamper, and Andy's bracelet back to Lucille and Ed's house.

What Mom said made sense to me. I could understand how the matching clocks gave her comfort. Getting a message from God—Andy's birthday three times over on stopped clocks that were all plugged into the house power but that had never matched in time—did seem pretty amazing.

Did it count as a miracle? Wouldn't some people say it was a coincidence? Who else would think these matching times truly showed a message from God?

Mom would tell everyone about the clocks. I'd wait and see who believed that God had given her a sign of His help and comfort through the clocks. If anyone believed that the matching time on the three different stopped clocks was some kind of miracle, maybe they would believe what Mark and I could tell them about the young man who helped us.

Mom laid out the clocks on the counter in Lucille's kitchen. Lucille was amazed and said, "Katherine, this can't be an accident, a coincidence. It must be meant as comfort for you. I think it is a miracle!" They hugged and cried together.

"Is Frank upstairs?" Mom asked, and Lucille nodded. "I'm going to ask him to come down and look at these."

Lucille didn't say anything. We both watched Mom leave the room and go upstairs with more energy than she had showed all week. If the clocks were a miracle, maybe the news of their matching times would make Dad come back to his senses.

After a half hour, Mom came downstairs; she was dressed differently. She wore the same outfit that she'd had on on

Thursday for calling hours. Mom didn't mention Dad. She had not lost the aura of peace that had come from the clocks, but she made no comment about Dad's reaction to the clocks all matching Andy's birthday.

I guessed Dad was still the silent stranger. If the clocks were a miracle, it hadn't affected him. Would anything?

14

MOTHER'S DAY BRACELET, NO GUARANTEE OF HOURS

Mom wore the bracelet from Andy to the Friday calling hours. I looked at that bracelet on her wrist while she stood in the line meeting people and found it hard to believe that just a few days ago we'd had such a happy Mother's Day. Dad helped us make her breakfast in bed.

After she ate the breakfast we had fixed, we gave her gifts. Dad gave her a beautiful soft sweater the color of lilacs, her favorite flower. The sweater was cashmere. I did not know what cashmere was, but I could see Dad's gift had made her smile, and she sent him a special look.

Mark and I gave her a spray bottle of her favorite scent, Arpège. Mark had saved three dollars toward the gift, and I paid the rest, since I had money from babysitting and from the treats my namesake, Aunt Virginia, had mailed to me.

Andy gave Mom a clunky rectangle bracelet of different-colored pieces of glass. I couldn't resist telling Mom how Andy had afforded that bracelet.

"You know that little junky store near the Acme?"

"Yes."

"We went in there last week. Mark and Andy had stopped to look in the window."

"Everything always looks jumbled together in that store's window."

"Yes. There were all kinds of things lumped together, stuffed squirrels, gloves, a cane, dishes, vases, ashtrays, and jewelry. Andy looked in there and said, 'I want that bracelet for Mom, for Mother's Day.'"

We had all peered at what caught his attention. The bracelet lay on a dark cloth. The chunky fake jewels glittered enough to catch the eye of a little boy or a crow. Nothing in the window had a price on it. I warned Andy.

"That probably costs a lot more than what you have, Andy."

"I have a dollar and eighty-three cents."

"I think it will be more than that."

"Can't we go in and ask?"

A bell jingled when we entered the store. Mom remembered that.

"Yes, I remember it was a bell, but it almost sounds like chimes."

"The old man in the back of the store, the one with the glasses that look like the bottom of jars, do you remember him? Do you think he's the owner?"

"Yes. I talked to him once, and his glasses do look very thick."

"He said, 'Hello, welcome. How can I help you?'"

"His voice sounded like a tuba," Mark added.

Andy said, "I want to buy the bracelet in the window for my mother."

"He wants to give it to her for Mother's Day," Mark explained.

"'The chunky one with the different colored stones?'" the man asked as he came out from behind the counter. He put a hand on each boy's shoulder and moved them toward the front of the store and the window display. The man used both his hands to pick up the bracelet, and when he turned toward the boys, he held it out like it was treasure. Dangling, it caught the afternoon sunlight and sparkled.

Andy blurted out, "I have a dollar and eighty-three cents."

"The man walked back toward where I was standing at the counter. He turned toward Andy and said, 'Really? A dollar and eighty-three cents?'"

"Yes. I told him yes." Andy smiled at Mom. He enjoyed telling of his search and purchase.

"You know what the man said?" I asked Mom.

She shook her head.

"He said, 'A dollar and eighty-three cents? That's amazing. That's the exact price of this bracelet.'"

Andy leaned in for a hug from Mom. Then we each got one. After that, it was time to get ready to go to Sunday school, then the worship service, then over to Grandma Riposta's for lunch.

All my happy memories from Mother's Day disappeared as Grandma came into the viewing room on Uncle Sammy's arm. He took her to stand in front of the small white casket. Grandma held tight to Uncle Sammy and cried. That was hard to watch, but it was not as shocking as the next person who came through the line and burst into tears.

Andy's teacher arrived. Mom and Dad had talked about her because Andy liked her so much. One time at supper he told us he was going to marry her when he grew up. I laughed. Mark looked confused. Mom shushed me.

Dad said, "You think that now, but you'll fall in love with someone your own age."

Most of the calling hour visitors looked like dark winter days. Out the funeral home windows, I could see May blossoms on trees and flowers in yards. Andy said his teacher was beautiful; he had been dazzled by her from his first day in second grade.

I had seen her when I sat with my parents to watch my brothers in the elementary school's music and drama presentations. Ms. M worked efficiently to have an organized classroom, but she had a playful attitude, and she usually looked like a model.

At the funeral she didn't look beautiful. Her dress was plain and as black as a crow's wings. Ms. M held a white lace-edged handkerchief in one hand that she crumpled and released. She walked toward where Mom and Dad stood as if toward a guillotine.

Her hair was pulled back in a low ponytail, and I don't think she had any makeup on or else she had cried it all off. Her face around the eyes and nose was swollen like people get when they have cried so long it hurts. She was sobbing softly in the line that had formed; people took their turn like an assembly line, walking forward to give their condolences to Aunt Beverly and my parents.

Andy's teacher was the first person other than family who had come through the line sobbing so hard she could hardly talk. My father stood like a Roman statue in a dark suit, white shirt, dark tie, and shiny black shoes. His brothers and sisters made sure he and Mom had good dark outfits for the funeral week.

Dad was the last person people spoke to in the family line. He wanted it that way. I had heard Mom tell Beverly that Dad hoped by the time visitors got to him, they would just leave the line or pat him on the arm or shake his hand without talking to him. I wondered how many people knew he had to take a lot of drugs just to stand there so calmly.

Beverly stood first in line because she was the oldest aunt and the one Mom leaned on most. Dad's brothers and sisters, along with their spouses and children, filled a section of chairs at each of the calling hours. Their friends all came and stayed for a while. They hugged, cried, and talked quietly.

Mom stood second in line, and I knew she took some medicine to calm herself before coming to the funeral home. A few tears appeared on Mom's cheeks as people spoke to her. She had a couple of handkerchiefs in the pockets on each hip of the dress she wore. Through the hours, she alternated which pocket she reached into for a handkerchief.

The dark-blue dress she wore showed her slim figure. The dress had a patent leather belt. Only that belt, her shoes, and the tears on her face were shiny. Mom didn't usually wear any jewelry or makeup, but she did have her good watch. She'd been wearing it the night of the fire. That glittered, as did the bracelet Andy gave her for Mother's Day. She hadn't taken that off since she took it from the jewelry box.

"Ms. M," my mom said, "thank you for coming. Andy loved you."

"Andy was . . . I never expected to have a student die. They are so much younger than I am, than anyone who works at the school." She began to cry in miserable ugly sobs. Her handkerchief quickly appeared, soaked, worthless. She talked through her tears.

"I wonder every day, did I waste any of the time Andy had? I wonder if I did my best with him. Did I give enough to him in the time he had in my class? I always thought my students had so much time ahead of them."

She stepped closer to my mother. Her choked voice was loud enough for everyone to hear. "I keep asking myself, did I do enough to make Andy's days good? All those hours I had him in class, were they good hours?" She sobbed so hard her body shook.

Mom hugged Ms. M, then held her out to look into her face. That pretty face that was now swollen from crying also had a runny nose. Mom looked at her and said, "Andy loved you. He loved coming to school. He loved every day with you."

Beverly patted Ms. M on the back, which caused her to move on to my father. She took his hand to shake it and seemed about to say something but started to cry again and could not speak. He took his hand from hers and looked over her head for something that wasn't there. Ms. M turned away and moved on slowly to stand in front of the small white casket.

She cried in front of Andy's casket for minutes. Then she turned and left the room in a rush. I couldn't guess if she would come to the funeral.

Mark came up alongside me. "Ms. M was really sad."

"Yes."

"She's sad about Andy."

"Yes. She feels bad."

"Because she misses him?"

"Yes." I kept agreeing with Mark's ideas. I couldn't explain that having a seven-year-old student die had made Ms. M wonder about her teaching, about using up hours of a person's life. I wondered how many teachers would go through their days differently if they looked at their students and thought that each day could be their last. Anyone could die before the end of the school year or the end of the month, week, day, or night.

Anyone's used-up hours could not be given back. How many teachers thought about that? Grandmere had been a teacher. I would ask her if she ever had thought about having one of her students die.

Having Mark or Andy die had not occurred to me either. They were little pests, my younger brothers, that's all. Did Andy have any good thoughts of me before he fell asleep? I had memories of yelling loudly at him on Monday night. *Be quiet. Go to sleep. Stop being a brat.* My words ran in a regular loop through my mind. The last he'd heard from me were words yelled in anger and aggravation.

Most people sat or stood talking to one another after they spoke to Mom and Dad. Everyone stayed for different amounts of time to look at the casket. Some people seemed to look carefully at the cards and ribbons that accompanied the flowers. I did that before anyone else arrived.

Mark had been sitting by Uncle Joe and Aunt Mary, Uncle Jerry and Aunt Nora. From where I sat, I could see everyone in the room—aunts, uncles, cousins, neighbors, people from church. Mark walked between and around them as he came toward me and sat down. We were almost in the same spot where we had spent Thursday evening.

Just like Thursday, he leaned against me. Even with so many more visitors this night, people talking in clusters all around us, Mark again fell asleep leaning against me. I wished I could fall asleep as easily as he did, and I wondered if Mom and Dad would ever be able to sleep without medicine.

15

COMFORT AND A FUNERAL

W e'd already received sympathy cards. Some even arrived by hand delivery on Tuesday, May 11. A card came from Mark and Andy's elementary school signed by all the staff and teachers. Then Lucille handed Mom a large letter-size envelope. The stationery had a letterhead, Township of Union Schools, Kawameeh Junior High School, Principal John R. Berrian, Administrative Assistant, John M. Leese. This big card came from my junior high school.

The note signed by the student council adviser, Nicholas Wellner, said on behalf of everyone at Kawameeh, he expressed deep sympathy to our family because of the tragedy. The students, faculty, administration, cafeteria workers, janitors, and office secretaries wanted us to have a check to help us through this time. Mom held the note in one hand and the check in the other—it was for over $2,000.

That was a lot of money for us, and the faces of the students, staff, and teachers whirled through my mind. I liked almost all of my teachers, even the seemingly unbalanced math teacher, Miss Murphy. She dyed her gray hair green on St. Patrick's Day and gave an A for the year to anyone who could sing an Irish song from start to finish. One student, Paul, sang "Oh Danny Boy." He had a good voice and sang all the verses. Miss Murphy cried, and Paul got an A for the year.

My French teacher had a foreign-sounding first name, Henrietta. She was the only teacher or staff member I disliked. She gave quizzes every Monday and took points off for wrong answers, but she seemed to do this differently depending on whether she liked a student. My best friend and I had shown her our quizzes with the same items wrong and two different grades. She said my friend tried harder and did not change either grade.

In Kawameeh, like other middle schools, fights happened even among girls. We had an older woman who was hired to sit on a folding chair in the girls' bathroom every day. She wore a uniform, and her job was to make sure no one fought or smoked or passed drugs there.

I thought about the school and how someone had organized a collection for my family. The card was signed by only one person, but it was on behalf of everyone. We would never know all the people who contributed. Maybe Henrietta had even given something to the collection for my family. I had not appreciated people enough in my time at Kawameeh. I'd need to do better when I finally returned to school.

Receiving such a gift reminded us that many people knew of our trouble and wanted to help. Everyone in my family would say it was care and comfort from God, but maybe some of the people who gave money didn't even believe in God. I had trouble falling asleep as doubt, guilt, anger, and fear filled my mind.

～

WHEN I WOKE up early on Saturday, May 15, I stayed for a while on the couch in Ed's study. We had only one more day at Lucille and Ed's house. Sunday morning, early, we would leave for Maine. The second funeral wouldn't happen until the next weekend.

Lucille and Ed's boys had been at school and other activities that week, but today our family misery would be theirs too. Lucille and Ed planned to take them to the funeral. I knew that many of my aunts and uncles would not bring their youngest children. They didn't know how to explain death to them and didn't want to talk about the death of a child. I'd heard them saying that to one another at the wake.

The funeral would take as long as a Sunday church service, a couple of hours. Where the Clauss family went to church, people walked in for a service and out in an hour or less. At our church people came early, sang for a long time before the reading of Scripture, sermon, prayer time, and lots more singing before parting after at least two and a half hours.

No service could be predictable in time or content at our church because no one could know what the Spirit might cause people to do, say, or sing. We also had unique Spirit-filled people like Sister Dickerson, a woman in her seventies. Sister Dickerson often felt the Spirit's leading to jump up and praise the Lord. She had loved Andy and had been one of the loudest shouters of *Amen* when Andy had walked to the altar.

I bet Lucille and Ed and their boys had never seen such a thing as people standing and shouting in church. Dad's family certainly never saw such doings in their Catholic churches. They'd be shocked and offended if Sister Dickerson or someone else broke into one of the surprising actions under the influence of the Holy Spirit.

When we got to Trinity Assembly of God in Elizabeth, there were no empty parking spaces in the church parking lot or on both sides of the street. Inside the church it was standing room only. Several of the front rows had been ribboned off for family, and most of our relatives were already seated. We were among the last to arrive.

As the funeral director led us inside, I didn't look directly at the faces of the people present. I held Mark's hand in mine as we advanced to the front row reserved for us. Mark kept a tight hold on my hand but didn't look at me.

There were lots of hymns sung that day, but I only remember four. The service started when the pastor asked everyone gathered to sing "God Leads Us Along."

Even though I knew Mom had chosen all the songs, the first verse made me cringe.

> *Some through the waters, some through the flood*
> *Some through the fire, but all through the blood*
> *Some through great sorrow, but God gives a song*
> *In the night season and all the day long.*

I looked to my right at Mom and Dad. Mom sang and let the tears run down her face. Her right hand was on Mark's back.

Dad did not sing. He stood and stared straight ahead, but he kept his left hand on Mark's back. Dad sat closest to the aisle. I wondered if he would leave at some point during the service.

Although I was looking at the pastor during the funeral, I didn't hear many of his words, but I paid attention to the songs. Evie Tornquist and her mother, Inga, sang "Jesus Loves the Little Children." The Tornquist family had been in the church as long as we had.

Evie, a beautiful representative of her Norwegian ancestry, was a rising star in the Christian singing circuit. From the time she was a toddler, she sang duets with her mother. Evie had known Andrew, had been in Sunday school activities and junior church with him. She was just ten years old and broke down a couple of times while singing the duet. Her mother took Evie's hand. They finished the gift of that song to us.

> *Jesus loves the little children*
> *All the children of the world*
> *Red, brown, yellow*
> *Black and white*
> *They are precious in His sight.*
> *Jesus loves the little children*
> *Of the world.*

When Evie and her mom sang their duet about Jesus loving little children, no one had dry eyes except Mark, me, and some of my cousins who were not teenagers yet.

Dad had offered no opinions on the songs. He'd wanted a salvation sermon, but he didn't look like he heard anything the pastor said or the songs that were sung.

I never saw any expression on his face except grim lines and scowls. Sometimes he frowned more deeply, like he did when the pastor led us in singing the words to "Ivory Palaces."

> *Out of the ivory palaces,*
> *Into a world of woe,*
> *Only His great eternal love*
> *Made my Savior go.*

When the sound of the pastor's voice changed to the tone and rhythm of a closing, I realized how long I had stopped listening. Maybe I had been sleeping while sitting up because I did not sleep soundly at night.

The pastor reviewed Andy's decision to believe in the way the Bible showed God's plan for forgiving sins and providing a way for people to know they could go to heaven. A glance at Dad showed no change in his scowling, and the pastor was doing just what Dad had requested.

"Andrew walked to the altar at the front of this church just last Sunday," the pastor said as he moved to the edge of the platform. "Why did Andrew come forward? Andrew came forward because he had listened to messages about God's love, about sin that all people have, about needing forgiveness, about needing a close personal relationship with Jesus.

"If there is anyone here who wants to let the Lord forgive all their sins and take control, who wants to live on this earth showing God's love to others and know they will go to heaven, I give that same invitation now. God gives that same invitation to anyone who hears how much He loves them. Come forward now. The deacons and I will pray with you."

The pastor paused. He looked out over the crowded sanctuary. The full weight of the choice before every person held down even the sound of a sniffle. No one moved.

The pastor continued, "I'm sure Andrew wants to see all of us in heaven one day. Just as you loved him, he loved you. The spark of his short life caught our attention and our hearts. He let his little light shine. That's what God wants all of us to do, and we can with the full bright light of God's love in us." Still no one moved.

With a much more subdued tone, the pastor said, "Please speak to me after we conclude if you too want to learn more about God's love and forgiveness and how you can know for sure you will go to heaven. No one knows how much time they have on this earth. We all need to be ready to face God and be welcomed into His presence. Andrew Frank Riposta was ready to face God. He has been welcomed and brought into the presence of the Lord."

I looked at my father. His grim stonelike shell cracked. He put his hand up over his face and tipped his head forward as tears glistened and fell from his cheeks. My mother leaned toward him and put her hand on his arm. Mark hugged Dad's arm.

Tears still did not fill my eyes. Whatever had happened the night of the fire seemed to have flipped a switch and set up some kind of wall against tears. I felt like I had a hard shell of protection around my heart. I looked at my family and thought I should cry, but the tears just did not come.

Everyone was asked to stand, and the pastor said, "We're going to sing another hymn to conclude the service, one of Andy's favorites. Andrew sang this song loud and strong, though he only knew the first verse word for word. Since he didn't know all the other verses, Andy would repeat the chorus with great enthusiasm. He knew he was part of God's family and could look forward to a big celebration in God's presence one day. Let's sing."

And people did sing. Almost everyone I could see tried to sing Andy's song. I remembered Andy singing this song whenever he was afraid, and that I had been the cause of some of his fears, starting with the moving bookcase. I sang along but my head and heart ached.

Our church's piano player had confidence, skill, and love for God. The music of "We Shall See the King" carried everyone along with the joyful enthusiasm Andy had when he sang.

> *There's a blessed time that's coming, coming soon,*
> *It may be evening, morning, or at noon,*
> *The wedding of the bride, united with the Groom,*

We shall see the King when He comes.
CHORUS: We shall see the King, we shall see the King,
We shall see the King when He comes;
He is coming in pow'r, we'll hail the blessed hour,
We shall see the King when he comes.

Andy sang this song with confidence that God would be right there taking care of him. Usually, Andy had smiled and shouted the chorus. He was better at shouting than at singing. That memory stuck in my mind.

Guilt over my mean actions, teasing, and harsh words to Andy plagued me. My father's question when he first saw me after the fire would never leave me. Something had happened while I sat and begged God to save Andy last Monday night. Something in me had clicked off.

I could think about emotions and see them in people around me, but I felt numb. Would I cry in Maine? Would anything seem more settled when that second funeral was finished?

The grown-ups were crying more over the death of a seven-year-old than I had seen them cry over some adults they'd known for many years. I'd been to other funerals but none with the church as full as it was now. I didn't understand why the death of a child upset grown-ups more than the death of someone their own age.

Mom and Dad were holding hands now. Mark was hugged between them. Would the second funeral make our family better or worse?

16

CURVED AND WHIRLED

Maine was a comfort. Whenever I arrived there, I felt like I had entered home. The farm in Waldoboro seemed like my most settled home. I felt safe with Grandmere, Grandpere, and our relatives from Maine, Massachusetts, New Hampshire, and Connecticut.

I had known Pastor Brown from Thomaston for years, and he gave me some comfort. He led the Maine funeral service and did not give a salvation sermon. Dad hadn't demanded it.

Our pastor from New Jersey read the Scripture in the church and at the graveside service. The songs for this funeral were the same except that Evie and her mom were not there to sing.

I still didn't cry. Now I thought that might be good because not crying made me feel like I had strength. People had cried around me for two weeks, and none of them seemed any better by shedding tears.

Riposta family at Andy's gravesite

MOM SEEMED relieved when Bevy said the stone they had chosen for Andy's grave would be in place. Mom had selected a white marble stone with a lamb resting on top of it. Even Dad spoke up about what he wanted engraved on it.

A lamb? I remembered how easily Andy had accepted our lamb, Troubles, as a meal. He'd not shown any special affection for Troubles or any disgust at being given Troubles's body as a meat dish for the family.

Andy had enjoyed Grandpere's dog, Snoopy. Even the idea of pet skunks gave Andy more happiness than a lamb. He had enjoyed his small pets too. I knew Bible stories and verses about lambs; that's why Mom had chosen it. Andy was one of God's little lambs.

It still seemed sad. That little lamb was the only stone creature in all the gravestones I could see. Andy could sense when people were sad. He gave hugs or did something to try to make the sad person laugh. Andrew Frank Riposta preferred laughter to seriousness.

Because he preferred laughter to anything sad, and because of the lamb on top of his gravestone, I thought of Andy's laughter over another animal. While we stood on the highest hill in the cemetery listening to Pastor Brown talk about Andy,

I remembered the animal that had surprised and delighted Andy, a carnival's baby elephant.

Andy was five and Mark was six when a carnival came to a field between Elizabeth and Union. Mom and Dad had time and enough money to bring us to see the show, take topsy-turvy rides, and play some of the games. Inside the biggest tent, we saw an act with clowns, horses, an elephant, and one tiger. The carnival seemed like a small circus.

As a family, we'd seen the big Ringling Brothers and Barnum and Bailey Circus in New York once. This little traveling carnival had so much less to its show and grounds, but we had fun. After the act in the tent, Dad let us play some of the skill games. I had picked up another stuffed animal to add to my collection. Dad always won at least one stuffed animal for me whenever we went to a carnival, boardwalk, or other place that had them as prizes.

The boys always wanted to eat, and at a carnival we could see and smell unusual snacks. We all enjoyed the individual bags of peanuts, freshly roasted. We could break the shells off them and eat them while we walked past weird sideshow signs and toward the parking lot. The carnival animals stood in cages or were attached to ropes near the parking area.

The elephant we'd seen in the show was large, definitely full grown. Out here we saw a baby elephant, so I guessed the one in the big tent was the mother. We walked slowly toward the little elephant. Mom said a baby elephant was called a calf.

No carnival person seemed to care when we walked close to it. Dad estimated it was three and a half feet tall and probably weighed more than he did. We all thought the calf was cute, and it didn't seem afraid of us.

Andy held out a couple of peanuts in his hand. He kept his palm up and his fingers flat out. We had learned to do that when feeding farm animals. The baby's little hose-like trunk had wide pink nostril openings.

Mark, Andy and the baby elephant

The baby elephant curled and whirled his trunk around Andy's face and chest. Then it picked up those two peanuts. Light in touch and fast, he smoothly took the two peanuts from Andy's palm.

Just watching that baby elephant put the peanuts in his mouth made us all smile. It seemed to enjoy crunching them. We kept smiling while we watched him chew. The baby elephant rocked from side to side with enjoyment. Then its trunk waved through the air again. It tapped Andy's chest. Andy laughed and patted the wrinkled and creased gray trunk.

Mark wanted to feed the baby elephant too. He put a couple of peanuts on his right hand. With his left hand he held the remaining peanuts in the bag close to his chest. Just as Andy had done, Mark offered two peanuts on his flat right palm to the gray baby.

The trunk curved and whirled again. Then, in one smooth move, the baby elephant's trunk reached out and snatched the bag Mark held in his left hand. The baby elephant put the whole white paper bag with the rest of Mark's peanuts in its mouth. We all watched with surprise as the baby elephant stuffed the bag of peanuts totally in its mouth and chewed everything.

Andy looked from Mark's shocked face and outstretched hand with the two peanuts to the paper bag of peanuts being chewed by the baby elephant. Andy laughed and laughed. For the rest of the day, Andy just laughed off and on picturing that baby elephant snatching the bag of peanuts from Mark instead of the two peanuts he'd offered. For the rest of his short life, Andy laughed whenever someone mentioned elephants or whenever he saw one.

STANDING THERE on the high open grassy hillside, I could almost hear Andy say, "Don't be sad." I wondered what people would have thought if there had been a baby elephant instead of a lamb on top of the gravestone. Andy would have liked it.

I stood still and stared at the white stone with the lamb and information about Andy. Dad had chosen what would appear on Andy's stone. Words were carved into each side of the stone. The little lamb on top had curly wool, a sweet face, and a tail as long as its ears. The lamb was lying down and looking in one direction, which formed the front of the stone.

Andy's grave marker

If someone looked at the front side of the white gravestone that showed the lamb's face, it read, Andrew Frank Riposta, Oct 18, 1957 to May 10, 1965. On the other side of the stone, where the back of the lamb rested so peacefully, people could read, Little Andy had memorized Psalm 1, 23, 27, 42, 91, I Corinthians 13, and many others.

Besides real flowers, Mom put a small container with artificial flowers that looked like red, white, and blue daisies on the grave. Memorial Day would soon arrive, but we would be driving back to New Jersey. Mom also put some toys on the grave at the base of the white stone. They had been some of Andy's favorites: plastic dinosaurs, little toy soldiers, and Tonka vehicles, a police car, a truck cab, and a delivery van.

We stayed at the cemetery after everyone left except for Grandmere, Grandpere, Beverly, and Pauline. After a while, Mom told Mark and me to go back to the farm with the remaining four adults because she and Dad would stay for a little while and then walk back together. In a direct line, it would be less than a half mile back to the family farm, but they wouldn't cut across the hills, so they might walk a mile.

Mom and Dad would walk all the way through the new section, the midsection, and the oldest section, down the hill, through the tall wrought iron gates that closed at sunset, and down to Bremen Road. In their walk through the cemetery, they would pass the graves of relatives from the past two centuries. When Mark and I left the cemetery with Aunt Beverly, Aunt Pauline, Grandmere, and Grandpere, I turned and saw Mom and Dad's backs as they stood looking at Andy's grave. Mom reached out and took Dad's hand.

Back in New Jersey, life veered temporarily into riches. We came back to a mansion. The friends from the Town Committee who owned a motel and restaurant said we should stay with them until the motel units connected to the efficiency apartment were available. The motel owners had five children and enough bedrooms and bathrooms in their house for everyone, plus a couple of extra for company. I knew them too because I had been a babysitter for their five children.

Their house also had an indoor swimming pool and orchids growing in large containers around the indoor patio. Their four oldest children could swim. When I had babysat for them on Valentine's Day, I asked them to lock the pool doors and pull the drapes across so that I could keep all the children in sight in the playroom.

In the mansion, Mom and Dad had their own room. Mark shared with one of their sons who was also eight. I had a small bedroom of my own. This arrangement had looked wonderful, but for me the comfort didn't last for even one night.

That first night in the kind friends' house, I woke up and opened the door to the hallway to go to the bathroom. The corridors in this house had a lot of space, high ceilings, broad width, and chandeliers. A tall multipaned window was at the far end of the upstairs hallway. Since they didn't want to depend on moonlight, they had a hallway night-light. It was low, placed in an outlet on the wall opposite my room. With the window, the moonlight, and the chandelier's many bits of glass, the light cast shimmers and wavy shadows.

It looked like smoke. I thought the whole hallway looked like it was filled with smoke. I couldn't smell any smoke, but it felt hard to breathe. My heart beat like it was on a ramped-up drug. My mouth was dry.

I did go to the bathroom, but I also sat up the rest of the night. Books that filled the one bookcase in the small bedroom occupied my attention for the rest of the night. When Mom came to check on me in the morning, I told her what I'd seen when I went into the hall. She tried to help me reason through what I'd felt. She wanted me to stay in this beautiful house so that our family would be together.

"Virginia, you know it wasn't smoke. The chandelier makes any light look different, even very dim light."

"Yes, but it looked like smoke."

"This is a lovely room they've given you to use. They said we should plan to be here for about four more days."

"I want to go back to Lucille and Ed's."

"You have your own room here. It's a lovely room, and you can swim, and—"

"I want to go back to Lucille and Ed's house."

"Are you sure?"

"Yes. I don't want to sleep here. I can't sleep here."

"We could ask them to just take the night-light out."

"No. They have it for their kids. I don't want them to change for me."

"When I tell them why you want to go back to Lucille and Ed's, they'll want to take out the night-light."

"You don't have to tell them anything except that I want to go back to Lucille and Ed's."

"I suppose . . ."

"I really want to stay at Lucille and Ed's house, Mom. Do you need to ask Dad?"

"No. No, it will be fine with him. I'll call Lucille. You can probably go over later today. Did you unpack anything?"

"Just a little bit. I'll be ready anytime today."

After a few days, my family moved into the motel but without me. I stayed at the Clauss home until Uncle Louis found a two-bedroom apartment Mom and Dad could afford. He took care of the deposit and first month's rent. Mark had a bedroom. I had a bedroom, and Mom and Dad slept on a fold-out couch in the living room. All the furniture we had in that apartment came from family and friends' extra rooms, basements, and storage.

We stayed in the apartment until September when the insurance company gave us the money we needed to buy a new house, but I wasn't in that apartment as long as everyone else. I went to Waldoboro again as soon as school ended in June. The relief I felt at leaving my family to go back to Maine gave me more guilt.

Grandpere had his matter-of-fact, let's-move-on attitude, but he always looked for little ways to give me treats, whether they were strawberries, a day trip, or a visit to the largest horse boarding and riding stable in Knox County. Grandmere gave comfort in everything she did. She felt like a mother. My mom had turned into a person who needed protection and help. She talked to me like a friend instead of a parent.

My parents did not make the trip up to Maine with Mark for the last week of summer. They had too much to do moving into the new house. Beverly came to Maine for a few days at the end of the summer, and we took the train back to New Jersey.

When I returned to Union, we had a new house on a quiet street instead of on a busy main avenue. Our new home was in an area where Mark and I could attend the same schools that we had before the fire. Family and friends continued to support us with many kindnesses and prayers.

Sympathy cards arrived all summer, and Mom kept all of them. She wanted to show each of them to me when I got home. She kept them in a black suitcase, and she had me sit next to her to as she read through them. She would put the cards tenderly into the stack in that ugly little case. She squeezed them in beside Andy's clothes that had been in the laundry hamper that we opened on May 14.

Andy's clothes were rolled and folded. A pair of his sneakers were in there too. I didn't know when she had found those. She shut the cover slowly. "You can latch it, Virginia, and put it back in the closet."

Mom also wanted to talk about Andy all the time. Dad would leave if she or someone mentioned him. He would go into another room and stay silent. He often went into the basement where he would groan or pray out loud at the same time. Sometimes he shouted at God. I felt like shouting at God too, but I didn't ever do it.

Mom emphasized thankfulness for all the pictures of Andy that people gave us. Dad wouldn't look at them. With these pictures that we received from others, Mom filled new albums with photos of Andy by himself or with us or other family and friends. She tucked these albums into her closet too. Small albums she fit into the little black suitcase. Large albums she stored on a shelf under folded clothing. I knew she must look at them whenever she was alone in their bedroom.

One afternoon before Dad got home, when we were alone, Mom asked me to get the black suitcase and bring it to her in the living room. She had a new little picture album Pauline had made. It would fit in the black suitcase with everything else she kept for memories and comfort.

She opened the case on a hassock. "Thank you."

Mom opened a folder that was filled with papers featuring the wide lines of the early elementary grades. "Andy's teacher gave me all his papers." Mom put those in the suitcase next to the pile of sympathy cards and a book the funeral home had given to us.

"Would you put the suitcase back now? I'm going to start supper. You know, if you ever want to look at any of this, you can." She smiled like she was giving me a gift.

I did like remembering Andy and talking about him, so I wasn't like Dad. But I didn't want to hold Andy's clothes, papers, and photos or the sympathy cards, so I wasn't like Mom.

Mark continued to go through the days playing as he typically played, except now he was usually alone. Dad did give Mark more attention that fall. They played catch, made a pinewood derby car, and did activities related to Royal Rangers, a version of Boy Scouts for Christians. So I wasn't like Mark either.

Mark had started fourth grade, and I was in eighth grade that fall after the fire. We both noticed that teachers tended to treat us differently from other kids, and we guessed it was because everyone in town knew about the fire and Andy. But nothing any teacher said or did was worse than what happened at the first slumber party I went to that fall.

About eight girls were gathered for a birthday slumber party. After a supper of messy fun fondue and melt-on-the-tongue birthday cake, we got our sleeping bags and pillows together to watch a movie that the birthday girl had chosen, *Mighty Joe Young*.

Even though it was in black and white and really old, we liked the story of the girl who bought a pet gorilla when her family lived in Africa. Years later when they were back in the United States, Joe, an oversize gorilla, got into trouble because he just wasn't made for living in American suburbs. A judge was going to make a decision about Joe's fate, life or death.

Joe escaped from where he was being held. The police chased him, but as he was running away, he saw an orphanage on fire. With flames threatening him and the children, he rushed to save the orphans from the fire.

We were intent on the movie. I was into the story as much as any other girl who had never seen *Mighty Joe Young*. The birthday girl's mother had been sitting in an adjoining room. Suddenly she rushed into the room, and at the height of Joe rescuing the children from the fire, she turned off the television.

"You girls have had enough TV. Go play board games before it's time for bed."

I hadn't realized how many people would be sensitive about fire when I was with them. The girls glanced from the hostess to me. They got up at once and went to the room where we would play board games. Just like I had suddenly remembered the fire, they had too, but we didn't talk about it. No one ever spoke about it with Mark or me.

Maybe if people had talked with us, we would have shared the information about the guy we thought of as our angel. The story that Mark and I had not told anyone came out on October 18, Andy's birthday. Mom was teary all day. Beverly and Pauline came over to the house to have dinner with us.

Dad was glum. He did not eat much. Then he went to the basement right after supper. When other people were in the house, Dad did not do his usual loud grieving. We didn't know what he did.

Dad did not come upstairs before Beverly and Polly left. They had gotten used to his rude behavior. If Mark or I had acted like that, we would have been punished.

Mark and I stayed in the living room. Even with the television volume on very low, we could hear the three women talking about Andy. Mom said how much comfort the clocks gave her. Then she sighed and was silent.

I spoke up then and said, "Mark and I didn't tell you everything about the guy who showed up on the front porch and tried to help us. You know, the guy the fire department tried to find but didn't. Mark and I think he was an angel."

All three women stared at us and stayed as still as manikins.

I said to Mark, "Tell them about the guy upstairs before he was on the porch."

Mark did. He told them just what he had told me. His descriptions were simple, little kid observations. He told them how the guy had bright-white clothes upstairs but how they were just regular clothes when we were on the porch.

Then I took over. I retold how the man had gone with me upstairs, watched me, and stayed close but that he had nothing over his face. He didn't seem bothered by the smoke. I could hear him clearly when he insisted on leaving. I told how he had taken me down the stairs, protected me from burning my hand on the melting phone, and taken me outside. Then he told us to leave the porch. In the instant that I turned to move the boys and then looked back, he was gone.

Mom, Beverly, and Pauline stared at us silently for a few moments. Then they exclaimed and asked questions. We could only repeat what we had told them. Mark and I had nothing more to tell.

They cried again but with smiles too. I could tell they believed us. Looking at their smiles as the tears streamed down their faces caused some of the painful tight feeling inside my chest to ease. The tenseness didn't return until Dad came back upstairs after Pauline and Beverly had gone.

17

MR. GRIM AND RING DINGS

The fire took my younger brother, our house, and almost all the possessions from the early years of our family life. The fire also took Dad's unmedicated sanity and natural smile for more than two decades. He kept taking the medicine for years and refused to go to counseling. Mom asked if they could talk to the pastor. Dad refused. He said if Mom went to the pastor by herself, he would stop going to the church.

Every day, Dad's mood swings went from silent to angry, depressed to tearful. I had squashed down thoughts and fears from the fire, but I couldn't squash the anger I felt toward my father. I resented the quick changes in his moods that made us learn ways to tiptoe around anything that could cause an angry reaction. He could yell, but it was when he talked in a low voice that we knew he was really angry, and he threw things. If he wasn't close enough to grab one of us, he just threw something at us when he didn't like our noise or actions.

I felt such a growing depth of anger that it affected my view of God. I couldn't hear the word *father* without thinking of mine. Although I still prayed, I stopped saying the first two words of the Lord's Prayer. It seemed better to just concentrate on Jesus.

During the rare times when I was alone in the house with Mom, I asked her to consider leaving Dad. We could live with Beverly while we looked for something. We could live in Maine with Grandmere and Grandpere. Sometimes Mom's eyes filled with tears, but usually she just turned away. She said, "I'm not leaving your father. He needs me to stay. Marriage is for better or for worse."

I wondered how much worse. Was there anything Dad could say or do that would get Mom to leave? I couldn't tell if she really meant what she said or if she was just afraid to leave.

Mom got a job outside our new home. The insurance had given us enough for the down payment but not much more than that. We needed two incomes to cover the bills. Now she and Dad arrived home at the same time.

Mark and I came home on the school buses two hours earlier than our parents. We did homework. Mom left instructions for what I needed to fix for supper, and Dad left a list of chores for Mark to do. The rhythm, responsibilities, and relationships in our family's daily life changed for all of us. We went through the motions of living together as a family.

Mark and I did what we could to be good kids. We were alive but Andy was not. It seemed like the least we could do was try to be obedient and helpful to a mother who at least noticed how we acted.

Our obedience had its limits. For instance, Dad said no television after school, and the first thing he did when he arrived home at five thirty was go to the television and put his hand on the top and back of it. I guessed that if I put a wet washcloth in the freezer when we got home from school and then put that frozen washcloth on the top and down the back of the television when we turned it off at five, the TV would be cold and pass Dad's test.

Mark and I waited nervously the first day we tried this trick. Dad came in at five thirty as usual and with a frown went right to the television. He put his hand on the top and the portion of the back that we knew also got hot after the television was on for a while. Since it wasn't hot, he turned to us and said, "Did you get all your homework finished?"

The only thing Dad did that seemed like fun was learning some simple magic tricks. He would use them when teaching a lesson to children's church, a Sunday school class, the Boy Scouts, or a senior citizens group. He also made sure not to miss any of his family gatherings and practiced some of his magic tricks with them. They seemed relieved that he had a hobby that kept him social.

Most days seemed different for Mark. He had grown, and by playing sports he seemed stronger and more confident, plus he got a lot more attention from Dad. Even though Dad continued to stay moody and demanding, his pride in his son was obvious. When we were with Dad's family, he bragged about Mark in sports, Mark in Scouts, Mark in church activities. Mark wasn't a middle child anymore.

I told myself I was fine without a relationship with my father because he wasn't the father I once had. I just had to get through high school. Then I would go far away to college. If Dad was affected by the coldness between us, I didn't know. He looked grim most days at home, though he did smile when he was with his brothers, sisters, and mother.

Dad rarely smiled in church. Sometimes he frowned all the way through a service, but he went just the same. He resigned from responsibilities in the church, but he took on more community activities that he could do with Mark, like Boy Scouts and Little League. I'd overheard him talking to Mom about looking for another church, but they didn't make any moves to visit others.

Dad and I hardly talked, but unexpectedly he'd make some kind of observation. One day he came into the kitchen when I was taking a Drake's chocolate-covered Ring Ding out of a box of eight in the refrigerator. "You shouldn't eat that," he said. He wasn't saying I couldn't eat it.

I stood there with the box in my right hand and the individually wrapped one in my left hand and just looked at him. He stared me down with a laser look and made a vicious pronouncement: "If you eat those, you'll get fat and no one will want you." Then he left the kitchen to go down to the basement for his evening moody battle with himself or with God or both.

I took the box of Ring Dings into the empty dining room, peeled the cellophane off the one I had selected, and ate it slowly Then I opened the other seven and ate all of them. I left the empty box on the kitchen counter. Dad always got a glass of water before he went to bed, so I knew he'd see it.

18

THE LAST SPANKING, AN ESCAPE, AND A MOVE

Two years after the fire, Dad stopped giving his assignments to me and Mark about memorizing Bible passages. He never said why. Dad rarely explained anything he chose to do or say. Mark and I could still remember a time when Dad talked easily and could make us laugh.

He also stopped spanking us—but only after I almost broke his hand. One day, just after I started ninth grade, Dad thought I had a disrespectful tone, so he told me to meet him in the living room for a spanking. I could not believe he thought he should still spank us no matter what the Bible said about sparing the rod and spoiling the child.

In anger and thinking I had to do something, I rushed into my room and picked the thinnest hardback book I had. I lifted the woolen skirt I'd worn to school and slid the book into the back of my underpants.

Dad sat in a straight chair in the living room waiting for me. I would have to lean over his lap, and he would spank me with his hand. I knew it made him mad when I didn't cry when he hit me. His face conveyed his stern about-to-give-discipline expression, and he didn't notice the outline of the book through the fullness of my skirt. He lifted his hand back high and brought it down hard. I heard it whack the book, and I thought, *I'm either going to be in the worst trouble ever, or he's going to laugh and punish me some other way.*

He hit the book so hard it must have left his hand red and reverberating. There was silence for a moment. Then he laughed a coarse bark of surprise. He pushed me off his lap.

"You're too old for spankings. Go to your room." He stared at me as if he hadn't seen me in a long time.

So punishments moved beyond hitting for Mark and for me. Mom seemed glad. She had never agreed with Dad about spanking, but like with so many things, she didn't argue with him. She told me she prayed for God to change him. I waited to see some changes but didn't, so I continued to tell God he could read my thoughts as prayers.

Dad remained the ruler of the household. I thought he saw me more, and he still had a powerful protective energy. One humid hot summer night in our Conant Avenue house, a guy tried to break in. My room was the only one above the garage. My window was half-open, and a man pulled himself through it.

I hadn't fallen asleep yet, so I sat up in bed, and hollered as loudly as I could, "Dad!"

He and Mom were on the next floor. Before the startled guy took two steps inside, Dad was in the doorway of my room with a baseball bat in his hands. The guy turned and leaped out the window. Dad went after him but didn't catch him. I figured that was a good thing, since Dad would have used the bat as a weapon.

Dad entered the house through the back door. We all knew where the key to that door was hidden. He came up the stairs and stopped by my room. "Can you go back to sleep?" he asked.

I told him I could. I don't remember if I did, but I always had books to help me through sleepless nights.

Dad continued to learn more magic tricks. He even did some with live doves. Those poor creatures were kept in a cage in the basement, so rarely anyone was with them but Dad. He would use the magic when teaching a lesson to children's church, a Sunday school class, the Boy Scouts, or when visiting individual shut-ins or a senior citizens group.

He was doing more in the community and less in the church. Since he did not talk about personal struggles, we did not know what or why something had changed for him with our Assembly of God church. We still went to most meetings but not all of them.

Two years after the fire, we started visiting other churches. After just a few months, my parents sat us down and said we would be going to a Christian and Missionary Alliance church instead. We had visited the church and liked a lot about it. The youth groups, one for my age and one for Mark's age, had many friendly teens. The pastor's sermons didn't include yelling and jumping, but they had several interesting stories. The music had more traditional tempos than the lively music we were used to, but it was fine.

Mark and I adjusted to the move, even though we had no part in the decision. We didn't even know that Christian and Missionary Alliance was a denomination for years. We thought it meant that Christians from all other denominations allied together.

I had hoped the new church and the easygoing pastor with the good sense of humor would help Dad calm down. His mood swings at home seemed worse than ever, but still he never showed his wretched behavior in public.

Mark and I continued to want to protect Mom from the remote and sullen man Dad had become. We did whatever we could to help her around the house or with any projects she took on at church. She really hadn't seemed like a mom since the fire, just someone we loved who needed kindness.

Lucille, Aunt Beverly, Aunt Virginia, and Grandmere did a lot of mothering for us. I was thankful that summers in Maine continued until I was seventeen. Time in our house felt like emotional torture. I just didn't know how Mom could endure it. Could she for the rest of her life?

I couldn't or wouldn't, but college was a year away. What could I do to escape the house that Dad and Mom would both approve of? I did not want to be there at all.

An idea came to me that my parents would likely agree to, but I needed the pastor's help. I told the pastor it was my last summer to do something that could help me choose a path in college. I was thinking about being a teacher, a nurse, or a missionary or maybe a combination of those things. Experience with people in missions could give me direction before my senior year and before I applied to colleges. Was there a way I could work with missionaries for the summer? Our church supported many missionaries around the country and the world.

"Do you know another language?" he asked.

"I've had two years of Spanish."

"I think I may have something for you, but it will take me a few days to check on the details. You would be in more than one location over the summer."

"Near here?"

"No. I'm thinking of some missionaries we support in the Rio Grande Valley of Texas and some in northern Mexico."

Relief flooded my mind when the pastor arranged for me to spend the summer two weeks at a time with four different missionary families. My parents accepted this far more easily than I would have guessed. Mom worried about me being so far away but said they both were thrilled that I might actually choose to become a missionary after experiencing the work for a summer.

As soon as school got out in June, I left for Harlingen, Texas. I didn't come back to New Jersey until after Labor Day. The family in Harlingen mainly helped with migrant workers. They also worked side by side with them picking what was in season. I happened to be there when grapefruit was the crop to pick, so I did that too.

Grapefruit picking in Rio Grande Valley

IN THE EVENING, the missionary family alternated between tutoring in English and leading Bible studies. The whole Anglo family spoke Spanish fluently. On Sunday they had a morning worship service, Sunday school, a meal for anyone who showed up, and an evening worship service that mainly was singing with another meal.

The heat and humidity made Maine and New Jersey seem a planet away. My basic Spanish became conversationally fluent. My first location was in a small house in Harlingen, Texas, with a family of five. My second location was in a wooden shack in a rural municipality near Monterrey with two single women. My third location was a mud brick hut west of Saltillo where I had to look for tarantulas and scorpions before I put my feet on the floor each morning. The fourth location was in an outlier suburb of Monterrey.

With a full view of life in these locations, I saw I had much to be thankful for in spite of the fire and my father's problems. The efforts and attitudes of people struggling for the basics of life showed me all I took for granted. I had imagined this summer would be an escape, but it was a daily education that affected me spiritually. The frozen distant feeling from God began to melt. I started to pray again.

I began reading my Bible with my hosts and on my own. The focus of my efforts was aimed at doing the best I could with any tasks assigned to me. My goal was to make people feel valued in each interaction.

The excitement and freedom of the summer gave me time to think and plan how to do better at home during my senior year. The year itself would not be tough. I had planned and chosen courses that I would enjoy in my last year in Union High School. I felt sure the revival of my spirit would last and prayed that it would have a positive effect on the problems in my family.

My flight home landed in Newark. Looking out the window as the plane approached the airport, I felt this also was a foreign country. Our quiet street in Union, right near the Kennedy Reservation and a mile from Kean State University, had been a good home for us since the insurance gave us enough money to buy a house. If I could tune out Dad's moods, I would sail through this year at home. When I exited from arrivals into the main area, Mom met me with a smile and a huge hug.

We didn't talk much getting to the car or as we left the airport. I knew Mom needed to concentrate as she exited the terminal. When she got onto a familiar highway, she sighed with relief.

I looked around and said, "Mom, this isn't the way home."

"We moved."

"What?"

"We moved last month, to Morristown."

"Are you joking?"

"No, of course not."

"I'm going to have my senior year in a new high school?"

"Yes, and you'll do fine."

"Mom, if you'd been in an accident getting to the airport, I would only have had the old address and the old phone number!"

"That didn't happen, did it? You'll like the new house. It's a lot easier for your Dad's commute, and we're right across from the big park of Morristown. No houses will ever be built across the street from us. Union is expanding all the time. Who knows if they will even keep the Kennedy Reservation. The new house really suits our needs, and we did a lot of work on it. Your father painted the whole outside. Mark helped, even though it was a hot summer for that work. While you were away having fun in Mexico, we scraped, painted, wallpapered, and landscaped."

"Mark helped with all of that?"

"Some. He's in a new school too, eighth grade in the middle

school near the new house. He made the football team. They've been practicing for over a month."

She sounded proud of the work they had done and was hopeful that I would go along easily with this change. In the half hour it took to drive from the airport to our new home, Mom didn't ask any questions about my summer or the flight home. I heard details about the move and about the redecorating. She even sounded excited that she'd found toilet paper with little pink flowers on it that went so well with the wallpaper she'd chosen for the hallway bathroom.

Toilet paper with pink flowers? I wondered when I would tell her that in one of my locations there was community outhouse, not even individual outhouses for each family. Toilet paper, plain white, cheap, and thin, came when supplies arrived by jeep every two weeks.

Showers? Baths? We swam in a narrow river nearby. We had to wear clothes when we felt so sweaty or powdered with the dirt of the barren landscape. People in the community did not want the near nakedness of bathing suits.

I did not know what Mom imagined I'd been doing all summer. Probably she thought of it as being a tourist in Mexico. And learning more about my summer obviously was not a priority in her otherwise busy mind. I wondered if Mark or Dad would want to know about my time away.

LATER LESSONS LEARNED: **Inner Comfort Zone**

Unhappy childhoods with undependable caretakers and constant criticism can cause unhealthy self-consciousness, but I didn't have that. I knew who I was even when I was little. My parents had been supportive, as had other family members and friends. I'd done well in school and liked the positive attention that brought, especially since Mark didn't seem interested in school. He did only what he had to do. Most of his interest and energy was spent on sports and girls. We both learned how to adapt and make friends.

Neither Mark nor Dad asked questions about my summer working in the Rio Grande Valley or in Mexico. The pastor interviewed me in an evening service about the work I'd done. My parents and Mark heard that. That seemed enough for them.

Life would not be about me or for me. But no matter how isolated I felt from my nuclear family, God would always be with me. God's timing and perspective differs from ours. I had decided to trust that my view was like looking at the back of a piece of embroidery. God's view saw the finished product, the side I could not fully see.

A quiet tension pervaded our Morristown house. Other than trying to help Mom when we were home, Mark and I worked hard not to bother Dad. On my own, I still prayed more than I had before the summer, but the feeling of connection wavered. Trying to hold on to God as an inner comfort zone was like trying to see my way clearly in a roomful of smoke.

19

GROWING IN SPITE OF DOWNPOURS

Just up the road from our Morristown house, a major health care center hired me as a nurse's aide. Their pay was higher than what most teenagers could earn. I worked the three to eleven shift. This meant I had to do homework at school because when I got home, there was only time to change into my uniform and get to work. I turned into a night owl too because after work I was so keyed up that it took a while to wind down. Homework was often finished between 11:15 p.m. and 1:00 a.m.

Another world, an inside view of caring for elderly, sick, and crippled people, opened up for me from my first day on the job. Feeling upbeat and determined to do a good job, I greeted the first smiling sweet old lady. Her smile turned to a frown, then she leaned forward from her wheelchair and threw up all over my brand-new white working shoes.

I worked alternately in three different units, one geriatric, one for young people with crippling diseases, and one a mental health facility. No day was the same, and the education about the body and mind was not matched by any course

I ever took. In the year I spent working in the units, it became sadly clear how many people rarely had visitors. Trying to treat each person as if they were my family members helped me to stay positive and to work conscientiously.

School and work meant I didn't have to spend much time with my family except for the four days between shifts. I worked ten days in one building, had four days off, then went to work in another building or section. That was the pattern for my whole senior year. The four days at home varied in difficulty depending on whether they included a weekend. Having a weekend at home meant spending more time with my family.

By the time I'd been in this new home for a month, I realized that even though the commute was easier for Dad, he still acted remote and surly. Mark had adapted my strategy of staying busy with something that my parents would approve. They accepted him being away at practices or with friends. In eighth grade he looked like an older guy and actually had girls old enough to drive ask him out.

Mom did not like this, but Dad strutted like a rooster every time some girl drove up to pick Mark up for a date. "That's my son," he'd say out loud, even if only Mom and I heard him.

We all stayed busy with work and activities that kept us out or in our own rooms. Sports and dating caused Mark to get behind in his schoolwork, so when he had time at home he worked to catch up on assignments. Dad did yardwork, read, watched television, or slept when he was at home. Mom would often disappear into the bedroom to read or work on projects that I didn't know about until one day when a fat envelope arrived from Aunt Beverly.

The envelope was filled with photos Beverly had found from holidays when Mark and Andy and I were very little. "These are wonderful," Mom said with one of her teary smiles.

"Come with me." She led me to the bedroom that she and Dad shared.

There she opened the sliding doors of their large closet and pushed back the clothes at one end. When she emerged, she was holding the small ugly black suitcase. It was like a punch in the stomach. The last time I had seen it was when we'd gathered all the belongings we'd stored at the Clausses before moving to our new house.

This little black case was made of heavy-duty cardboard that had lumps to make it look like imitation leather. One center latch of silver held it shut. All the corners looked like they'd been battered. I hated the sight of it.

With a smile, Mom brought the case to the bed, flipped the latch, and exposed the interior that was filled with papers, envelopes, and cards on one side and clothes on the other. I had pulled those clothes out of the laundry basket on the Friday we went to the Magie Avenue house. They were all Andy's.

Under some of the papers, Mom retrieved a photo album. "I've been filling an album with pictures people give me of Andy and you and Mark. I keep all these things in this case because it's small enough to be out of the way and because your father doesn't want to see any of it."

She looked at me like I would understand. I did, but it made me furious. She wanted to see these things, and it had been five years since Andy died. I understood wanting to see pictures, but why keep his clothes? Why keep all the sympathy cards, the guest book from the calling hours, the pressed flowers from bouquets given by family, and that little white envelope that had been in the jewelry box? Why keep and fondle stuff that had outlasted Andy?

I didn't want to look at it or think about the fire. I had locked it all outside the armor around my heart. I left the bedroom.

ALTHOUGH IT WAS my senior year, Mark and I had heard my parents talking about another move. I hoped I would get to graduate before they moved us somewhere else. Morristown High School was bigger than the one I would have attended in Union. We had 898 students in our graduating class, and we were the smallest class in the high school.

A drug raid during drama class had police dragging two students out, and our year featured student protests over Kent State, Zionism, and Vietnam. Days in crowded classes, feeling like a cattle herd shuffling through hallways, and fights were the negatives of the school. Teachers who found ways to make requirements interesting made the days better. I didn't like regular gym classes, and Morristown had a variety of gym options from fencing to archery to bowling. The school also had a sex ed class that made the newspaper because of the content suitable for medical school and because it scared army recruits about sexually transmitted diseases. The course made the Morristown curriculum controversial and unique.

As a senior, I was automatically enrolled in the new controversial health class. People said it was too explicit for a sex education class. Parents who did not want their kids to attend could sign a waiver, and they could go to the library instead. Although my parents were much more conservative than those of other students, they said I could be in the class. In their estimation, I was old enough to learn how the world saw and thought about sex compared to how God intended us to have sexual relationships.

That health class and my Honors English class that included paperbacks considered controversial, such as *Last Exit to Brooklyn, Lord of the Flies, Catcher in the Rye,* and *The Sun Also Rises,* expanded not only my knowledge of different views but also my ability to listen, argue, and discuss. The paperbacks were alternated with the huge hardback English literature text. We spent three weeks on the *Canterbury Tales* in that text.

Our English teacher, Mrs. Grow, lived up to her name. She pushed us in reading, writing, and discussions. If anyone expressed a distinct view or belief, she honed in on that person and frequently questioned them. Because I spoke out for some positives of Christianity, especially when Chaucer made the whole faith look like a wreck, Mrs. Grow called on me anytime a story or an article connected to the Christian faith.

We didn't have devotional times as a family anymore, but we still prayed together before we all left for the day. Really just Dad prayed, but we could give prayer requests. I mentioned we should pray for Mrs. Grow to stop picking on me about Christian ideas.

Dad said, "No. We need to pray that God will give you the words to express your ideas. Your teacher is doing you a favor by picking on you. The world will challenge you every day." After his gruff response, he prayed, and we left the house for our day.

I knew there were other Christians in my English class. A couple of them went to the church my family attended, but they didn't speak up to Mrs. Grow. My one friend of deep faith, Brenda, became a best friend in my year in Morristown High School. She was petite, far smarter than me, and shy. As we were leaving English class after I'd had a long back-and-forth session with Mrs. Grow, Brenda tapped me on the arm and said, "I pray for you every time Mrs. Grow calls on you."

Ungraciously, I responded, "Why don't you say something too?"

On senior graduation day, after everyone was seated on folding chairs in the field, it started to rain—first lightly, then a downpour. Attempting to avoid electrocution from the storm, the announcer said, "Come by the school during the week to pick up your diploma."

The school colors were maroon and white. The color from the maroon gowns and caps ran. Graduates had maroon stains on their special outfits under the graduation gowns. I should have seen that graduation day as foreboding a tough summer. If my graduation got rained out, what would follow?

Topping off the rain-drenched run from the graduation was an argument at home, the worst one I'd witnessed between my parents. A person could stand at the sink in the kitchen and look out at the backyard or, upon turning, look directly into the living room and see the large picture window at the front of the house.

After we got home from the graduation fiasco, Mark went to his room to change. I paused in the kitchen to look out at the sheets of rain still pouring down. Then I heard my parents arguing. It wasn't loud, but it was angry.

I didn't want to turn around and see them, but I did. I looked just in time to see Dad give my mom an open-handed slap across the face. Mom's back was to me. She backed up a step. I saw her hand go up to her face, and she rushed out of the living room toward their bedroom.

That left Dad in my direct view and me in his. He fell to despicable in my thoughts. My face showed my feelings. I knew he was waiting for me to say something. What could I say? I had never guessed he would hit Mom. I wondered if he had done it before or if this was the first time.

I turned around and put one hand on the counter and one on the handle of a drawer. I slowly pulled the drawer partially open. It was filled with sharp knives arranged from cleaver, boning, and bread to small paring knives. I stared at the knives and thought, *This is how murders happen in families.* Backing up a step, I turned and looked at Dad with what I hoped was visible disgust. Then I went to my room. I suppose he shut the knife drawer because no one else went into the kitchen for the rest of the evening.

WE MOVED a week after the rained-out graduation. I had a chance to talk with Mark and tell him what I'd seen. I asked him if he'd ever witnessed Dad hit Mom. He said he had not. I asked him to tell me if he saw it happen again. If Mom wouldn't leave Dad when he slapped her, we would have to push harder for her to leave him. We could demand she choose him or us.

The Morristown house now had a different and worse feeling. Being so miserable there made me open to another move. Mark felt the same way. Moves always required lots of work, not just packing up. We worked as a family to fix up the new house, repairing, painting, wallpapering, and decorating.

Because my parents always fixed up any house they bought, they made a profit on it. The profit they'd make on the Morristown house would give them enough money to buy a business that interested them, a guesthouse at the Jersey Shore.

They bought a house built in the early 1900s, located one block from the ocean in Bayhead, New Jersey. It had sixteen bedrooms, eight bathrooms, three floors, a basement, and a main floor with the gracious old-time large entry hall, living room, dining room, bathroom, walk-in pantry, and large kitchen. The porch wrapped around the front and one side. Tall thick hedges made a green fence around the side and back-yards. The front yard had grass and shrubs, plus it faced the busy main route along the shore.

Because Bay Head had no motels or hotels, the few guest-houses had full rooms all summer. As soon as they owned the house, Mom had the sign out front changed to Andrew's by the Sea. We would live in the house, and there would still be sixteen bedrooms for guests, some en suite.

The rooms had been booked for the summer by the old woman who had sold it to my parents. This guesthouse had many repeat visitors who rented the same rooms for the same weeks every summer. They loved this quiet area of the shore, with no motels or amusement parks and only one other guest-house. Huge old houses lined the beach on the two blocks closest to the dunes and sand. A small grocery store was on the corner near the large white clapboard house that my mother named Andrew's by the Sea.

My father didn't say the name of our guesthouse and winced sometimes when he saw the large sign in front of the house. We knew Mom had chosen the name. Did he let her because he knew he had been so wretched to her?

A movie theater was also within walking distance. *Jaws* came out that summer, and the people who spent their days on the beach created long lines waiting to see that movie every day it played. I saw it two times on evenings I didn't have to work, but I missed having a friend to go with me.

In this new place with so many hours working each week, I had to accept doing activities on my own whenever I had a chance. Mark had once again made friends quickly, as he had qualified for the Point Pleasant Beach High School football team. In less than a couple of weeks in the new location, he had dates.

When we lived there, Bay Head had thousands of tourists in the summer and fewer than six hundred year-round residents. I got to be the guesthouse maid, and Mom was the hostess. Dad was a handyman, and Mark did the yardwork. I worked a shift almost every day as a waitress at the Ocean Bay Diner.

Living at the shore was idealized by many people, but for my family it included a constant variety of work. I also experienced more surprising life lessons, such as realizing that people drank vodka at breakfast. One day when cleaning, I asked Mom to bring me a glass of water. When I finished vacuuming the living room, I saw a tall glass of what I thought was water on the credenza in the front hall.

I rushed to gulp it down, and my mouth and throat burned with the power of the vodka in that glass. My mom hadn't put it there. A guest, a woman who worked in advertising in New York City, had left the glass there while she went to find her bathing suit.

The best benefit of this new move and life experience was that Dad decided it was too long a commute to work. He rented a room right near his office and stayed there Sunday through Thursday nights. It was a long drive to our church, but we continued to go there on Sundays in two cars. Mark rode up with Dad, but we both came back with Mom late on Sundays.

When Dad was with us from Friday evening through Sunday morning, the days were tense. I felt that he didn't like the independence he could see growing in Mark and Mom and me. Much of the tension remained due to finances. Mom seemed more comfortable with running a business than Dad did.

Halfway through the summer, Mom and Dad called me into the kitchen and told me they needed new carpet for the halls and stairs of the guesthouse and other repairs and updates. They wouldn't be able to give me anything for college. I'd been counting on $1,500 from them, but the carpet and repairs would be more than that amount.

As if to comfort me, Dad said, "If you don't get to go to

college, that's all right. Women get married and have kids. You don't need college. And lots of people go to college later in life."

With what I had saved from working, a small scholarship, and what I'd counted on from my parents' original intent, I would have been able to pay for college. Now what?

20

GORDON'S GIN

I wanted to go to Gordon College in Wenham, Massachusetts. Gordon was the antithesis of Morristown High School. It was small, situated on beautiful property, and had high academic standards, majors that interested me, a Christian outlook, and professors who had that faith. Plus, it was a short distance outside Boston. Even without a car, students could walk to the Beverly Farms train station and go into the city.

I had received early acceptance and decided to go for the first semester. I had the money for that, and I could talk to the guidance and financial aid offices about options. At the end of the summer, I went to Maine for the long Labor Day weekend. Years never felt complete when I didn't have time with Grandmere and Grandpere in Maine. I didn't talk to them about the money I needed because I knew they just got by with their retirement income.

They had always done a lot for me. Now they would bring me to the college in Massachusetts. It was less than a three-hour drive from Waldoboro to Gordon. They were excited to be the ones to drop me at college. They both felt confident I would do well, and Grandmere told me she prayed about my time at college every day. She was not a person who just said she would pray. She prayed every day for many people. I'd seen her prayer list in her Bible.

The day we were due to leave, I walked down to the mailbox. The sky was the blue of a Dutch painting, with scarcely any clouds in sight. I turned and looked up the hill at the farm that felt more like home than any place I'd lived in New Jersey. Then I pulled the mail from the box and started to walk back up the driveway. Shuffling through the mail, I saw one long envelope that had been forwarded to me from the Bay Head address.

Inside was a scholarship check from a foundation. Unbeknownst to me, a woman from church who was old enough to have been my parents' Sunday school teacher had put my name in for a little-known scholarship. I knew nothing about it, but it was the exact amount I needed to pay for the full year at Gordon. I shouted and ran to the house. I was shocked and amazed. I could hardly tell Grandmere and Grandpere what I held as I waved the check and tried to talk.

As usual, Grandpere was his reserved New England self; he smiled and expressed happiness that I had gotten such a scholarship. Grandmere gave me a hug and whispered in my ear. "I've been praying for the Lord to supply your needs if Gordon is really the place where you're supposed to be."

The scholarship seemed like a miracle. Who got a scholarship they hadn't applied for? With that scholarship help and my two part-time jobs while at the college, the bills got paid for the year. My namesake, Aunt Virginia, wrote to me at least two times a month, and there was always money in her cards, which seemed to arrive when I was down to pennies.

Finding out just weeks before I left for Maine that my

parents would not give me the amount for college that they had promised formed a sour memory. I held on to unforgiveness of my father for what I saw as a betrayal of parenting and husbanding. I knew Dad made the final decisions on finances. He might have let Mom name the guesthouse, but he decided anything that had to do with repairs, education, and big bills. He really didn't believe girls needed a college education.

My college roommate, Beccy, had a vibrant and practical Christian faith. As we got better acquainted, we had conversations about our early lives. Beccy missed her parents and siblings from the time they dropped her off at school. I was surprised to see that she even had tears in her eyes when they left.

When she heard me talk about being happy to be away from home, she asked about my family. I told her some of why living at college was a relief to me. I tried to help her see that life in my house was like tiptoeing over a tightrope while keeping an eye on other people who needed help walking on nearby tightropes. I told Beccy that all through high school, I had asked my mother to divorce my father.

He seemed like he would never come out of the depression he had fallen into. I thought Mom had ridiculous ideas about him changing. His mood swings could make anyone around him miserable, though he continued to only show these at home. It seemed ridiculous and wrong that he would think he was entitled to live with such moods as an adult. I did not think he wanted to be a hypocrite, but he seemed just like Jekyll and Hyde.

My first year of college, it was frightening that every day seemed like the best I could imagine. Dad had taught us that anything that seemed good had flaws. When things went smoothly, we should expect problems.

The fall colors on the trees around Coy Pond made every walk on campus feel like a gift. Frost Hall, like a piece of a medieval castle, was the oldest building at the college and seemed magical; I had a couple of classes there. The business office people were helpful and encouraging. The hard shield over my heart and emotions became as flexible as leather.

My college days and the school's atmosphere served as a new life and a fresh start with new friends, professors who cared about students, and interesting courses. These happy changes made it easier to keep everything disturbing locked away. The classes, the cleaning jobs on and off campus, making new friends, joining the drama group, campus special events, and trips into Boston for concerts and sports events filled each week with positive experiences.

I even had a new name. Although I had always been Virginia to family and friends, I thought since I was at Gordon, I would be Gordon's Gin. Uncle Sammy had given me a huge window display from his bar for Gordon's Distilled London Dry Gin. It featured a British guy walking under an umbrella on a London street and the words *Gordon's. It how the English keep their gin up.* By the day after I filled my dorm window with the display, I was Gordon's Gin, but most people just called me Ginny.

After a week, the president of the college, Dr. Okenga, walked across the campus and happened to look at my dorm, Sheppard Hall. Facing the open green and paths was my second-floor window with the Gordon's Gin display. As soon as the president got to his office, he called our dorm director, Eleanor Vandervort. "The display about gin needs to come down." Even so, I remained Ginny to most students and Gordon's Gin to some.

In spite of Dr. Okenga's concern, the Gordon atmosphere did not hold the tension or sadness that pervaded each day at home. Sometimes I felt badly that Mark was still stuck there, and I worried about Mom. Mark said he would call me if Dad became worse, but I thought Dad might act better without me there resenting and despising him. After he hit Mom, he could probably even see hate in my eyes.

Living with other women in our all-female dorm included plenty of time for conversation. I realized we had some dramatically different reasons for coming to Gordon. Some girls said they came to a Christian college to meet a Christian man to marry. Some said their families would pay for college only if they went to a Christian school. Some chose Gordon for reasons similar to mine—a desire for a learning experience very different from their high school and independence from their families.

Beccy and I and our closest neighbors, Lynne, Mary, and Judy, had long conversations about our hopes for the future. Since Beccy was my roommate, we had the most personal conversations that first year. Beccy was a good listener and a brave and an honest friend. While she extended sympathy, she also had enough courage to tell me she thought I needed to work on forgiveness for myself and my parents.

I told Beccy and our other close friends what my mother put up with in her marriage and that I'd rather never get married than live with someone who made me and my children miserable. My friends came from happier homes than I'd had since the fire. They hoped for marriages like their parents'.

No matter what they said, marriage did not seem attractive to me.

Men tried to dominate. Life choices would narrow if I married, and I definitely didn't long to have children. Some of my friends couldn't wait to get married and start a family. I didn't tell them that having children was where the real hurt could come.

With my roommate, Beccy, my next-door neighbor, Lynne, and my RA, Robin, I had many discussions about love, relationships, and choices. They were all young women with strong faith who tried each day to learn not only course material but also life attitudes suited to trusting God.

Our dorm director, Eleanor Vandervort, was friends with Elisabeth Elliot, author of *Through Gates of Splendor*, the story of her husband's murder and her forgiveness of the people who killed him.[1] Elisabeth Elliot came to our dorm a couple of times each semester for an evening of discussion about living out God's love and forgiveness in the world.

I felt sure I could live best by staying single. No matter the career I chose, I wouldn't have to answer to a man. Maybe someday, after I was thirty, I'd feel differently. I had seen Christians and non-Christians unhappy in marriage, so marriage had no guarantees of happiness even if someone was a Christian. I had my plans, and marriage was not a part of my foreseeable future.

21

NOT WHAT I EXPECTED

I met the man I would marry in the spring of my first year at Gordon. He lived in a house with four other young men who attended Gordon-Conwell Theological Seminary. Robin was dating one of the five, Jack, and had promised to bake cookies at the house. She felt shy about going alone and asked if anyone wanted to go with her.

Everyone had something to do or papers to write, so I told her I'd go along. I liked baking cookies, and it would be interesting to meet a bunch of guys who were training to be pastors. Only Robin's Jack and a young man from Maine, Fred, looked clean-cut enough to be seminary students. The other three guys had hair to their shoulders. One also had a beard. Two of the long-haired young men wore dashikis, jeans, and sandals.

I'd met plenty of pastors, missionaries, and evangelists in my lifetime but none who looked like these guys. They said brief hellos while Robin and I got ready to bake, and they did not appear again until the scent of the freshly baked cookies filled the house. Robin talked more with Jack and the others than I did, although Fred and I enjoyed speaking about special places we enjoyed in Maine.

That evening, back in the dorm, I got a call from Jerry, one of the guys I'd met at the cookie baking in Beverly Farms. He asked me out on a date for the following Friday, and I accepted. Beccy was surprised when I told her I'd been asked out by one of the guys I'd talked with so briefly.

"You don't ever act like you're interested in dating."

"I'm not desperate."

"But you think you'll enjoy going out with this guy?"

"I think he's interesting. He's older than college age, and I don't know anyone from Chicago."

"So that's why you agreed to go out with him?"

"Truth?"

"Yes."

"I agreed to go out with him because his long hair and looks would upset my dad."

"You're going to tell your dad about him?"

"No. I don't need to do that. Just being out for an evening with a guy who is so different from my father will make me happy."

Beccy was not pleased with that answer. She showed it in her expression and posture. Because I had a full course load and participated in many activities, plus the campus drama group, the spring passed quickly. The dates I had with Jerry were casual and varied from movies to picnics to bowling to bike riding. Conversation stayed in the get-acquainted category, with some theology and politics thrown into the mix.

One Saturday, Jerry asked where I was going to church. I wasn't and felt defensive. I told him I would bet I had been in church more than he had because my family tried to be at every service and event in all my years before coming to college. Then I admitted I wasn't attending church. Since coming to college, I enjoyed sleeping in and having a leisurely Sunday without church services. He told me about a church he went to and spoke so enthusiastically about it that I agreed to visit it with him.

I went a few times before the spring semester ended. That experience let me hear Pastor Howard Keeley, who also taught a practical course on ministry at the Gordon-Conwell Theological Seminary. His sermons never bored me, and I knew Jerry and others liked Howard's classes.

Howard's wife, Hazel, seemed more outgoing than other pastors' wives I had met. She managed their household, worked with Howard to raise their two children, and had a job outside the home for a real estate agency. Howard and Hazel hosted studies in their home and frequently had visitors. They seemed much more active and fun than any pastor families I had known.

Just before I left the college for another summer as a maid and waitress, Jerry came to visit and told me he would be working as a youth pastor with a church in Kensington, a part of Philadelphia. He asked if he could come visit me at the Jersey Shore, and I agreed. It was less than a ninety-minute drive unless a person came on a Friday or returned on a Sunday. Jerry said he could only come on a weekday. I didn't tell him that worked well because my father would not be at the house on a weekday.

Even though I warned Mom that Jerry, a guy in seminary, would not look like any pastors she knew, Mom was shocked, and Mark didn't help. He was on the side porch when Jerry parked his Vega in the guesthouse lot. Because he had driven over with the window open, he wore a headband to keep his hair from blowing into his face. As he got out of the car in the same dashiki, jeans, and sandal outfit I'd first seen him wear, Mark asked me, "Is this the guy?"

I said yes, and Mark leaned off the porch, making a wooo wooo wooo sound while tapping his mouth with his open hand, his version of a tribal war cry. Then he laughed and went in the house to tell Mom she was in for a surprise.

"Good thing Dad isn't here," Mark said with a laugh as he left me to greet Jerry.

Mom was polite, but when I had to get ready to go work, she took Jerry out on the porch and asked him how he could be studying to be a pastor and have such long hair. Didn't he know the Bible said, in I Corinthians 11:14, that it's a shame for a man to have long hair?

Even though I had warned Jerry about how conservative my parents were, he was surprised. Fortunately, when Mom paused after her question and mini sermon, Jerry didn't try to argue with her or point out that people like Sampson, John the Baptist, and the Nazarites were told never to cut their hair.

Jerry answered, "Mrs. Riposta, I'm just dating your daughter. If we ever become serious, I will be glad to cut my hair to help you feel more comfortable. Right now, in my work with young people, many of the teens and young adults have long hair."

She let the topic fade but told me later to make sure Jerry came to visit only when Dad was not with us in Bay Head. For most of the summer, Jerry drove over midweek when I had a day off from the diner. When he arrived at the end of July, I noticed that his hair no longer touched his shoulders. Now it was just a couple of inches below his ears.

Jerry and Ginny at the beach house

I DID NOT SEE the shorter hair as an attempt to be more pleasing in appearance to Mom. It wouldn't have worked anyway. She only liked traditional haircuts on men.

In August, Jerry asked if he could come over on a Saturday. He would leave the city early in the morning and go back when I had to leave for my waitress job.

"Jerry, my dad will be here then."

"I thought I'd like to meet him."

"He will not like your long hair."

"It's shorter than it was."

"All right, but be prepared to be told to go away. Dad can be harsh and rude when he's upset, and your appearance, hair, and clothes do not go along with his idea of how a pastor should look."

Mark and I were waiting for Jerry to arrive. Mom had fixed a big breakfast as usual for the guests, but we had a family table in one part of the kitchen where we could have our own breakfast. She thought we'd all eat together.

Mark spotted Jerry's car first. He called Dad and watched

as Dad stepped out onto the porch and caught sight of Jerry getting out of the Vega. Jerry's hair was still at his chin line, but he wore a cotton plaid shirt with his jeans and gym shoes. I was just exiting the porch when Dad pushed by me with a frown and went back into the house.

Jerry never saw Dad that day. Absolutely furious about Jerry's looks, Dad went into the basement and refused to come upstairs until "the guy" left the premises. Mom took breakfast and lunch down to the basement for Dad. There was a full apartment and a game room there. A lifeguard had rented the apartment for the summer, but Dad could stay comfortably in the game room, which also had a television, a couch, an armchair, a table, and lights.

Jerry came back one other time when Dad was present. It was in September. Jerry was going to drive back to Massachusetts for his seminary classes and had offered to drive me to Gordon College. I agreed, as I much preferred riding for hours with Jerry.

Dad again stood by the windows the day Jerry was due to arrive. Mark sat outside on the porch and promised not to do his war cry whooping. Jerry got out of the car without a headband. He didn't need one. He had a traditional haircut and wore a light-blue short-sleeved shirt with his jeans and gym shoes. When I opened the door to go out to greet Jerry, Dad called out to me, "It doesn't matter that he got a haircut. I'll never forget how he looked the first time I saw him."

We had a tolerably polite short time of visiting before Jerry and I left for Massachusetts. Mom seemed relieved but not relaxed. Dad's tension and lack of friendly conversation made for many awkward moments.

I did not have my usual sparkle either. I thought back to Jerry's first visit and Mom's lecture to him on the porch about the shame of long hair on a man and wondered if Jerry really was signaling that he wanted a serious relationship. I distinctly remembered Jerry's reply: "Mrs. Riposta, I'm just dating your daughter. If we ever become serious, I will be glad to cut my hair to help you feel more comfortable."

BECCY ALWAYS SEEMED concerned about my negative attitude toward family and marriage. "You're seeing Jerry again this weekend? First time since he drove you back?"

"Yes, but I've decided to tell him I don't think we should date anymore."

"What?" Beccy stopped folding her laundry and turned to look at me.

"I like him, but he's ready to be serious. I'm not looking for serious or for marriage."

"So you're going to stop seeing him?"

"Yes. It'll be better for both of us. The more time couples spend together, the more they have a chance of falling in love or whatever it is that blinds a person to all the problems of marrying."

"Have you prayed about this?"

"God gave me a brain to figure things out. I don't have to pray about everything."

"If you want what's best for your life, you should."

"Says a person who came to college open to the possibility of meeting a good Christian guy to marry."

"God's plans can often differ from our own, but God sees the whole picture in ways we won't until we're old."

"If we live to be old."

"All right, I'm not going to say anything else, but I'm not sure you're doing the right thing. Does Jerry have any idea how you feel about marriage?"

"We haven't talked about it."

JERRY ARRIVED without set plans for our evening. That seemed fine. I suggested we could find a quiet spot on campus to talk on this warm September day. He gave me the perfect lead-in. "You seem heavyhearted, not a mood for such a nice day."

I took the opportunity to say I thought we should stop seeing each other. I was not looking for a serious relationship, and I felt he was.

BECCY LEAPED up from where she sat cross-legged on her bed when I came back to the room after leaving less than an hour earlier.

"You told him?"

"Yes. I said he was a great guy but that I wasn't ready to be serious. I thought we should take a break from seeing each other."

"And?"

"And what?"

"How did he take it?"

"He was surprised but didn't ask a lot of questions."

"Where did you tell him?"

"We walked out by the stone benches near the path that goes around the pond."

"How do you feel?"

"Relieved and sad. But I know it's better to stop developing a relationship. Anyway, being married to a pastor would be even tougher than being married to someone in a normal career. Pastors get called out at all hours for good and bad reasons. Pastors' families are under a microscope, and their kids are angels or devils. I've babysat for pastors and missionaries, and their kids were either goody-goodies or terrors."

"Hmph. From a person who didn't want to consider marriage, it seems like you've thought beyond it to pastors' careers and a family."

~

Robin and Jack were getting serious. Because she was still our resident assistant, girls asked her about Jack. Robin answered the way a big sister might, informing but not blabbing about everything. I waited for Robin to say something about Jerry or to ask me what was going on, but she never did.

Jerry called one Saturday in early October. He said he just wondered how the semester was going and that he thought about me and prayed for me. I thanked him and said I thought about him too but wasn't ready to start dating again.

After hearing his voice, I returned to my desk and started making a list. Pros on one side, cons on the other.

"What are you doing?" Beccy asked when she set down all the books she'd gotten from the library.

"Making a list of pros and cons of continuing to see Jerry."

"You're thinking about seeing him again?"

"He called. I think he really could be serious about me, and I can't figure out if I could be about him. It wouldn't be fair to spend more months and then stop seeing him."

"If you're really making a list of pros and cons, you probably aren't in love."

"Why not?"

"I don't think people are that rational when they're in love."

"They should be. Look, the pros are easy. There's a lot I really like about the time I spend with him."

"And he is handsome."

"Yes. If you like the Northern European look, which I prefer to the Italians I grew up with. You know, the way I could always really annoy my father was to announce I would never marry an Italian, but that wasn't because of looks."

"You're Italian."

"Half, and it is different for the person who marries an Italian woman. We learn to serve and keep things running as smoothly as possible so that the head of the household is happy. Getting an Italian guy for a husband, especially one from Italy, is entirely different. At least, that's what I've seen. And it doesn't matter if they're Christian or not. Their role is to dominate."

"You think men from other ethnicities are different?"

"Maybe, if they come from a society where household responsibilities are shared and the parents have mutual respect."

"Even if the person isn't a Christian?"

"Even if. I have thought about it. I would only want to marry someone who had a strong relationship with the Lord, someone who would inspire me to grow in faith."

"Is that on the pro side of your list about Jerry?"

"Yes."

"What are you putting on the con side?"

"A few things, habits mostly. They should all be things I could live with if we did get serious."

"People change."

"But that's the problem. People get married thinking they'll change the things they don't like about their spouse. I think we need to look at what a person says and does, their moods, and try to imagine living with them without trying to change them."

"Good luck with that," Beccy said as she sat down on her bed amid her books and notebooks. "I have a research paper due at the end of the week, so you just go on making your list. I won't bother you, but I will say it seems a cold way of evaluating a relationship. You still haven't prayed about it?"

"I'm using the brain God gave me, and anyway, Jerry said he's praying for me and about us."

JERRY CALLED the next week and said he wouldn't keep bothering me, but he wondered if maybe by spending some time with me and another group of my family, that it might help me sort out my feelings.

"Another group of my family?"

"Your grandparents, in Maine. I know how much you love them and going to their house. I thought I could drive us up there for a weekend. You could invite Beccy or a couple of friends to come along with us so that you wouldn't feel like it was too much of being just the two of us."

22

CAN'T JUST SAY IT

Lynne couldn't go away for the weekend, but Beccy could. Jerry seemed fine with our trip being for the three of us. Even though Beccy sat alone in the back seat of the Vega, conversation flowed freely. They asked questions about my grandparents, my years of summers and even winter vacations in Maine, and what I did in all the time I spent there. By the time we pulled into the driveway, they were anxious to see the places I'd told them about.

Grandmere and Grandpere always welcomed visitors, even if it wasn't with the affectionate enthusiasm of lots of kisses and hugs. It felt good to see Jerry welcomed by the two people I trusted most in the world. We had time for a good walk before dinner, since Grandmere said she didn't need any help.

They wanted to see the German meetinghouse, as neither of them had been in a church from the seventeenth century. Once they went through the tall iron gates and up the hill to the building, they could see beyond it to the acres of the old cemetery. Only Beccy knew a little about the fire and the death of my youngest brother. I'd told Jerry an even more abbreviated version when he asked why the guesthouse was named Andrew's by the Sea. Neither of them knew about the funeral or that my brother was buried in the new section of this cemetery.

There was silence when I said, "We can walk through the old section of the cemetery and beyond it, past all the gnarled trees. Then there are open hillsides that have views of farms and the town. Grandmere has brothers and sisters buried right between the old part and the new part, and my brother Andrew is buried at the highest section of the new part."

We walked through the old part, stopping sometimes to read unusual names and verses on gravestones. We paused near the section where the cemetery transitioned to more open fields. My heart and mind paused there as I looked at the hillsides of the new section. Everything was mowed to grass height due to perpetual care.

We stopped. I didn't want to tell them this was the first time I had come to the cemetery on my own since Andy's burial. I stepped forward. I had no idea what my face or body language showed, but before I'd gone much farther, I felt Jerry's hand take mine. He and Beccy and I were silent until we approached the stone with the white lamb on top.

Jerry read the inscription on both sides of it, and we talked about how in the world a little child could memorize so much. We spoke about brothers and sisters, as we each had siblings. Then we walked back to the farm for a typical New England supper of baked beans and brown bread, homemade and delicious.

Saturday I guided the drive from Waldoboro down Bremen Road. Locals called it the Jersey Pike because of all the people from New Jersey who had bought property on the portions of the road with the best views of the water. Since neither Jerry nor Beccy had been in this part of Maine, we stayed out the full day driving along Muscongus Bay, Round Pond, Pemaquid, Chamberlain, and New Harbor and then looping back to Route 130, which took us into Damariscotta, and a right turn that took us to Route 1 and back to Waldoboro. Fantastic scenery, fresh lobster rolls and steamed and fried clams, water views, charming villages, and autumn colors made it a day better than I'd imagined.

Sunday, after visiting the church in Thomaston with Grandmere and Grandpere, we stopped at Moody's Diner. Moody's had the best home cooking in the area and a growing reputation since the family started it in 1927. I told them Moody's Diner had been in *Yankee* magazine and in most tourist information about Waldo County. Grandmere and Grandpere had been taking me there since the first summer I started staying with them.

When the time came to leave, I embraced Grandmere and Grandpere tightly. Every time I hugged them goodbye, I wondered how many more years I'd have them. They were in their late seventies and still active, but no one could know how long they'd have. I'd learned that lesson, but I didn't remember it as much as I should.

In the car driving back to Gordon, I let Beccy carry the conversation with Jerry. I thought about how much I took their friendship for granted and resolved to be more appreciative. I realized I'd told them more about myself this weekend than any of my other friends knew.

As for Jerry, he hadn't kissed me, but he had held my hand at scattered times throughout the weekend, and he really seemed to enjoy the time together. Grandmere had told me she thought Jerry was a fine young man. I had more pros to add to my list when I got back to the dorm.

∾

I saw Jerry a few more times before the end of October. We had supper with a married couple he had known since college. Gordon and Caryl had been married a few years and had a baby. I wondered if it was Jerry's strategy to show me more of his life and also to have me see a young Christian couple who had a healthy relationship.

There was almost a full moon at the end of October. On this Halloween night, it looked close to full, even though that wouldn't be true until the second day of November. On our way back to the college from a movie, Jerry pulled off the road by a picturesque field edged by a sturdy wooden post and rail fence. He came around and opened my door, then held out his hand. I took it and we walked together to the wooden fence. Standing there with a perfect view of the moon over the field seemed too romantic to be real.

Oh Lord, I thought, *don't let him propose! I'm just barely settled into accepting serious dating.* Jerry lifted our joined hands so that they rested together on the top rail.

"You know, Ginny, I love you."

I wondered if he could sense the tension in my hand, if it felt colder because of how terrified I was at the prospect of saying the wrong thing. I believed him, but I couldn't just say I love you back. Those words could not come out of my mouth just because he had said them to me.

I turned toward him. He met my eyes with his as steadily as he ever did. Jerry had no guile. I admired his honesty, but on the con side, it also meant he struggled with tactfully avoiding blunt observations. Still, my list had grown to more pros than cons.

"I believe you, Jerry, and I feel good spending time with you now, but I can't say I love you just because you said it to me. I can't say that until I'm sure. I haven't said those words easily since I was a child."

He squeezed my hand. "So I have a chance of having you say it to me?"

"Yes."

"Good." He hugged me, then let me go. "I was glad when you said your family invited me to come to your house for Christmas. I think it will help if you meet my family. I've had several visits with yours, but you haven't met anyone in mine. Would you like to be with my family in Illinois for Thanksgiving?"

JERRY and I had spent time with each other for eight months, even including the few weeks when we had stopped dating. Jerry knew my family felt conflicted about him. They admired his desire to be in Christian ministry but wondered about fully trusting him since they judged him as a liberal.

The second time he had come to the shore on a weekend when my father was present, I'd been vacuuming the front hall with a large industrial machine. I started to pull it toward the stairs. Jerry jumped forward and said, "Let me carry that for you."

My father was reading in the living room. "Leave her alone," he said. "She's strong enough."

Jerry carried the vacuum to the first landing and without words asked, *What now?*

I gave a nod toward the living room as if to say, *See if you can talk to him.*

Jerry smiled and went into the lion's den of our living room.

To go to Jerry's home for Thanksgiving, we drove seventeen hours from Wenham, Massachusetts, to Wheaton, Illinois. It was late evening when we arrived. We entered the house through the kitchen and walked through the dining room. From there we could see Jerry's parents in the living room sitting on the couch.

They each had a book but looked up and said, "Oh, you're here." They put their books down, smiled, and stood up.

Jerry's mom asked, "Can we get you something to eat or drink?"

The difference in their greeting was a sharp contrast to my parents. It was like one extreme or the other. Though my father would have lagged behind my mother in greeting any guy interested in marrying me, Mom's hugs, kisses, and enthusiastic welcome would have made up for Dad's reluctance. I wondered if Jerry and I could create a happy medium between the two different family attitudes and styles.

Beccy and Lynne never seemed nosy to me. They were like concerned sisters. When I arrived back at school after Thanksgiving break, we had a trio discussion almost immediately.

"Tell us about meeting Jerry's family!"

"Tell us everything!"

"I don't have time to tell you everything, but I will tell you that the only thing they have in common with my parents is that they're active in their church and devoted Christians."

"Were they welcoming?"

"Not with enthusiastic words and affection, but yes. Jerry's mom made a big rectangular pan of pizza for our first supper. I guess she did that to make her Italian visitor feel comfortable."

"Was it good?"

"Yes, not like my Aunt Vee's thick-crust pizza, but it was good. And Jerry's dad asked me what kind of neighborhood I lived in. I told him it was a suburban neighborhood. He said when he grew up in Chicago, people lived in neighborhoods of their ethnicities and when he went home from school, he usually had to fight some Italians."

"Was he serious?"

"Yes. He said it wasn't every day, but people wanted everyone to stay in their own neighborhoods. He's one hundred percent Dutch, but Jerry's mom is Croatian and Hungarian. Their neighborhoods weren't next to each other. They met at a church that included people from many different backgrounds."

"How else were they different?" Lynne wanted to know.

"When the family is together, they like to play board games and card games but not card games with regular cards. They use Rook cards and Uno cards and even spoons for a lot of games. My family doesn't play games, although when we were kids, my dad taught us checkers and chess. Jerry's family didn't play those while we were there."

"Did they ask you many questions?"

"No. That's another way they're very different from my family. You know my mom can ask a dozen questions in half an hour. The only way they showed that I might be someone special to Jerry was when we were all sitting around one night having dessert and his mother said, 'We're very glad you could come for Thanksgiving. When we saw Jerry cut his hair, we thought there must be someone special in the picture. We've wanted him to cut it for years, but he didn't.'"

"What did you say?"

"I just said I liked long hair on a man as long as he kept it clean but that my parents really thought a person who was going to be a pastor shouldn't look like a hippie. They smiled at that. Then the conversation switched to talking about plans for the other days we'd be out there."

"Did you meet all his family?"

"I met his two older sisters and their husbands. His oldest

sister has twin girls. They're just three and a half years old. I met his younger brother, the only one of them who did not go to Wheaton College, which is less than half a mile from their house, but Dave chose to go to Valparaiso. He's a year older than me and studying for an engineering career. He seems very easygoing. He was the only one who could teach me how to play Rook. Everyone tried, but they got so hyper when I made a mistake that I got tense and made more mistakes. Dave took me aside and in fifteen minutes helped me master the basics."

"He's more easygoing than Jerry?"

"Yes. Jerry and Alice are very competitive in games. Jerry's oldest sister, Nancy, and her husband, Ken, are great and also easygoing, but their twins take a lot of time and attention. Ken is a principal. Nancy is an elementary teacher but busy with the twins right now. They didn't play games the whole evening. Nancy is the oldest, then Alice, then Jerry, then Dave. Alice and her husband, Dick, lived in Hawaii. I think she has a job in Washington, DC, now, and her husband is a commercial pilot."

"Did you meet any of Jerry's other family members, like aunts or uncles?"

"We went to his mother's sister's house one day for a meal, so I met a few aunts and uncles and cousins. After a big meal there, instead of games, the older people sat and talked around the table, and most everyone under thirty watched *Willy Wonka*. They practically have it memorized."

"Did you go to Jerry's church? I mean the church his family attends."

"Yes. And a couple of women came up and said they heard Jerry was bringing a special friend home for Thanksgiving. They asked how we met. I told them I was at a college near the seminary where Jerry was studying. They were surprised that he was going to be a pastor. They said they were lunch ladies in the cafeteria where Jerry went to middle school and that they never would have guessed he'd be a pastor. He was a live wire!"

"Ha, it's good to learn that." Lynne laughed as she said this.

"Yes, I did try to listen and talk to anyone who came up to me."

"Did the family do anything special because you were visiting?"

"I think so, yes. They don't have a lot of money. Jerry's dad works as a manager for a trucking company in Chicago, and his mom works in the office of the Conservative Baptist Missions. They took us all into Chicago to see that new movie *Fiddler on the Roof* on Friday and to the Ice Capades in Chicago on Saturday afternoon. Those were big treats for everyone. I'm sure they did that not only because I was there meeting them. They wanted to give all their children and grandchildren a great holiday."

"What about you two?" Beccy pressed.

I remember pausing. I didn't have much time before I had to go to a Gordon Players rehearsal, but I knew I should tell them. They were my closest friends and really prayed for me.

"I got a marriage proposal."

"What?" Their question was an exclamation in unison.

"We always stayed up later than everyone else. His family doesn't watch television much, but Jerry and I both like Dick Cavett, so while we're watching it, something came up, and Jerry said, 'When we're married . . .' and then something else. I was startled by the when-we're-married part because I haven't even been able to tell him I love him. So I didn't say anything. We watched a little more, and something else came up, and Jerry said it again: 'When we're married . . .' I asked him, 'Do you realize you've said that twice, but you've never proposed to me, and I haven't even been able to say I love you, meaning the kind of forever commitment of love?'"

Lynne gasped.

Beccy asked, "What did he say to that?"

"Nothing. He was quiet. I guess I sounded a bit angry. We didn't talk more, just watched another segment, and when the next set of commercials came on, he turned to me and said, 'Will you marry me?' I looked at him like he had just blasphemed. I said, 'What? You're asking me during a commercial of the *Dick Cavett Show* to marry you?' He said he wanted to be able to talk to me about what he thinks about a future together, and it sounded like I needed him to propose if he was going to be able to do that. I insisted, 'But a proposal on a commercial break?' He said, 'I had planned to take you to Pemaquid in the spring. I was going to propose and give you a ring, but I was waiting until you could commit. I wanted to do a romantic proposal, but it sure seems like I need to ask you now.' I asked, 'You're positive that, with all our differences, I'm the person for you?' He said yes. 'Jerry,' I replied, 'I can't say yes to you at this moment.'"

"I can't believe you didn't say yes," Lynne said softly.

"I can believe it," Beccy affirmed. Her voice held a mix of frustration and sadness.

"So now you two know what you can continue praying about. I have to go to my meeting. We can talk more later."

23

CHRISTMAS, THE NEW YEAR, AND THE FAITH OF FRIENDS

Jerry became a part of my days in early December. It never felt like he needed us to be alone. I couldn't say he pressured me to make a decision. He'd easily spend time with me and talk with my friends. Beccy was trying not to ask me about the final list of my pros and cons. Lynne just shook her head over my process of deciding about love. She said she knew I was in love with Jerry.

Ordination was ahead for Jerry, and we often talked about how difficult it was to choose a denomination. I felt fine identifying as a Christian or even just saying I was a follower of Jesus, but Jerry did not want to work alone as a pastor of small independent churches. He always found strength in a community of believers and explained the plusses of being connected to a denomination. We talked about projects, exams, friends, and our families. We didn't talk about marriage except to agree to pray about that step.

I did not tell Jerry I was not counting on my father's approval, nor did I need it. If Jerry was the man for me to marry, I would not let my father's opinion affect our relationship. My trust in my father's opinions was about nil.

Then came the day to drive to New Jersey for Christmas. We would arrive in Bay Head very late. It could be less than a five-hour drive but not with the holiday traffic that had already started. People who owned houses along the beach also came there for Thanksgiving or Christmas. The background of the ocean made every family gathering more special.

The car trip passed quickly because time with Jerry usually was filled with conversation. He asked so many questions, which was something his friends teased him about. I could tell that he was still nervous about my dad.

We arrived at Andrew's by the Sea at midnight. The porch lights were always on at the guesthouse through the dark hours. The entrance hall and stairs were also lit.

Mom came to the door, and I could see Dad just a step behind her. We had one suitcase each, so it was easy to drop mine and give the expected hug and kiss. Jerry stood a bit awkwardly but did return my mom's hug and shook hands with Dad.

"You two should go to bed," I told my parents. "We don't need anything, and we're going to take a short walk before we come in for the night." I took Jerry's hand to leave the house before there could be more questions and conversation.

It was a brief distance to the corner, then a right turn, and we could see and hear the ocean at the end of two blocks. The wind had picked up, and we didn't talk until we arrived at the boardwalk that connected the end of the street to the beach. It went through a short section of dunes, and Jerry took my hand. We stepped out onto the beach. The wind seemed even stronger and colder, so we hugged each other, our arms around the other's waist, while we looked out at the waves in the December moonlight.

I took a breath to make sure I'd be loud enough to be heard over the waves. "Jerry, I wanted to tell you without Dick Cavett or anyone else as a distraction that I do love you. I have come to believe that God has put you in my life."

That was the short speech I had prepared. Jerry's hug and kiss afterward let me know he'd heard it all. We continued to embrace for a short time in the December ocean air, just long enough for him to repeat his proposal and for me to accept.

When we returned to the house, I told him on the porch before we went in, "Italians expect a ring to be given when the guy asks for permission to marry the daughter, so we don't have to say anything now. I just wanted you to know I love you before you suffer through Christmas with my family."

"We'll come down again in the spring, after I have the ring, and I'll ask permission of your parents then."

"Jerry, since we saw *Fiddler on the Roof*, it made me think that if my parents, or mostly my dad, is not willing to give permission and a blessing, I'd marry you anyway. A big part of why I love you is that you're so different from what he would choose for me in a husband. I respect you more than I respect my father."

Jerry didn't say anything else, but I felt he really hoped for my father's permission. He knew a constant tension existed between my father and me, but I had not given Jerry all the reasons why. I didn't know when I would.

ARRIVING BACK at Gordon the day before the new semester started, I knew soon I'd be sitting in my room facing Beccy and Lynne who would want to know all about Christmas with Jerry and my family. I'd ask them for descriptions of their holidays first. Lynne's father was the head of a national organization for

Christian young people, InterVarsity. Beccy's father was an assistant pastor at the large church my family attended.

I had often looked at their fathers and compared them to my own. I wondered if theirs were as good as they seemed or if they had flaws that their wives and families knew but kept hidden. Lynne and Beccy seemed genuinely appreciative of and comfortable with their dads, moms, and siblings. Their time with family was the focus of their Christmas. They were always open and honest with me.

Because Bay Head was so far south of our families, we spent just Christmas morning there. Jerry seemed amazed that he had multiple gifts under the tree and a stocking by the fireplace also filled with treats. His family tradition for gifts went along with family differences in expressing affection and having lots of food available as a symbol of love. By nine thirty that Christmas Saturday morning, we got into the car to head north to see the rest of the family.

Our first stop was Aunt Philly's house in Nutley. Jerry was shocked when we got there. She greeted us at the side door with a hug and kiss. Then she opened the door to the basement, which was big enough for a dining area, a living room area, and, on the far wall, a bar that her husband had designed. It was nicer than the bar in Uncle Sammy's restaurant but not as big. The noise of a party emerged.

Jerry might have gotten a view of the spaces all decorated as we descended, but before he was at the bottom step, he'd had half a dozen gorgeous young Italian female cousins greeting him. They approached him with hugs and kisses. The male cousins came up too and gave hugs, handshakes, or both. He told me afterward that the experience had been overwhelming. He didn't know what to do. He said never in his life had he been given so much physical affection from people he had just met.

I told him they knew he might be joining the family. No one in my family brought a special someone around unless it was a serious relationship.

When I told Beccy and Lynne about this, they laughed. They said they'd be overwhelmed too by all that hugging and kissing with strangers, good-looking or not. And it wasn't just at Aunt Philly's. We went to Aunt Vee's house next. Since she and Uncle Nunzi lived above his barber shop, it was a reverse experience of going upstairs, opening a door, and again being hugged and kissed by aunts, uncles, cousins, and Grandma, who had not been at Aunt Philly's house.

Before we headed back to Bay Head, we'd visited Uncle Louis's house too, which had been filled with his wife's family. Almost across the street, Uncle Sammy's house had been full with his own children, some cousins, and his wife's family. At the late hour we left Uncle Sammy's, we did not go see Beverly and Pauline. We planned to have lunch with them the next day after church.

"I bet that was a different gathering," Beccy remarked.

"Yes. A quick kiss from Bevy and Pauline for Mark and me. Then a lovely dinner at a formal table but with no wine like the Italians. My aunt Beverly is more of a teetotaler than Grandmere, and Grandmere was a member of the Women's Christian Temperance movement. Grandpere probably had to go out to the barn for an illegal drink, like he does now to smoke his cigars. Grandmere does not approve of any liquor or tobacco."

Lynne frowned.

"Why the frown, Lynne? You don't drink."

"I was just thinking, how will you manage a wedding reception with people who always have liquor when they celebrate, and people who are teetotalers or even upset by the sight of people drinking?"

Beccy and I laughed. "That's a ways off, so there's no sense worrying about it now."

"What did you do for the New Year?" Lynne asked.

"We drove north again. Our church had a New Year's Eve service, with lots of music, refreshments, and games. At eleven forty-five, we all gathered in the sanctuary to pray out the end of the old year and to pray in the new year."

"Beccy, you were there?"

"Yes, Ginny and I have been in the same church since we were teenagers."

"That's right. I remember now you asked to be roommates before you came to college."

"Yes, once we knew we were both accepted at Gordon, it seemed like a good idea to at least be slightly acquainted with the person we'd live with, but you're our next best friend, Lynney babe."

"And Sunday you all drove north again?"

"Yes, but in two cars because Dad was going to stay there. It's amazing how much more relaxed the atmosphere is, even in our car, when my father isn't in it."

"And he doesn't know that Jerry proposed and that you accepted?"

"No. Jerry is going to visit over spring break and ask for my parents' permission and blessing."

"You don't sound very happy about that," Beccy observed accurately.

"I told Jerry that after seeing *Fiddler on the Roof*, I realized I don't need my father's permission concerning who I marry. Traditionally that seems to be important, but it's very old-fashioned. For a permission and blessing to matter to me, I'd have to respect my dad a lot more than I do."

"That makes me feel very sad," Lynne said, speaking softly.

"Dads should make us feel safe and loved and be a kind of model of the man we can look for in our own lives."

"You're very lucky to have had a dad like that, Lynne. I bet most people don't. Beccy, you probably feel the same as Lynne?"

"Yes, and I'm really going to pray that whatever this is with your dad can be resolved and forgiveness can heal the two of you."

"I'll pray with you," Lynne agreed.

I looked at them both. They had a lot more faith than I did.

24

COUNSELING, CHILDCARE, AND
PAINTING DAVY CROCKETT

Although Beccy used every opportunity to talk to me, to ask more about the bitter tension between my father and me, I did not want to tell her all the words and actions that had embittered me. She admired her own father so much, it was hard for her to understand that a Christian man could be despised by his daughter.

She worked to help me see that I needed to forgive him. Forgiveness could be healing for me and for him. Beccy suggested I should ask him for forgiveness for my rotten attitude toward him. I told her some of what had changed about him since the fire but not about his question and not about him slapping Mom.

I had told Jerry about my father's question after the fire and about the many changes in my dad and our family life because of his moods. However, I also had not told Jerry about Dad slapping Mom. I didn't know why that seemed even worse than Dad's question to me, but it did.

Jerry signed us up for premarital counseling with Dr. Ensworth, the professor of psychology and pastoral counseling at the seminary. I thought it would be more difficult to talk about whatever the counselor brought up because the man was a stranger, but since my father was so anticounseling, I said, "Sure."

We talked about childhood experiences during the counseling sessions, and I realized my childhood had been extremely different from Jerry's. Both my mother and my father had done a lot of activities with us and taken us places as often as they could afford to, but they were never farther than a few states away. Jerry's family had traveled much more around the United States. My parents never played games with us. Jerry's family played games every time they were together. Jerry's family had fun together. My nuclear family existed together. Lots of hugs and kisses and food didn't symbolize love in Jerry's family. They were more like my New England relatives.

We talked about friendships and family events and then, surprisingly, we skipped to our teen years and to high school. I never had to talk about the fire with Dr. Ensworth. I didn't say much about high school with the counselor, but I did decide to tell Jerry when we were alone about my father slapping my mother.

"Jerry, I know your family didn't say I love you out loud as much as mine did when we were young, and your family is as reserved as my New England family with affection, but you also said your dad worked a lot and your mother ran things. That wasn't true in my house. It also seems like you felt sure your parents loved you, and you didn't hear them argue a lot. My parents did argue, though mainly because my father was angry. He sulked too. You don't seem like you would ever sulk because you talk things out."

"I don't think anyone in my family sulked."

"How about fighting?"

"You mean wrestling or punching?"

"Either or both."

"I wrestled with my brother, but it was just playing around."

"Mark and Andy did that too. But if they punched or hit, they were punished."

"But your dad spanked all of you as part of his regular discipline."

"Yes."

"Did your mom ever spank you?"

"No. Her family was against hitting. My dad always said that made her and her brother spoiled, but he never said that about her older sister, Beverly."

We rode in silence until I said, "I brought this up because I saw Dad slap my mother when I was a senior in high school. I haven't told anyone but you."

"What happened after he slapped her?"

"She cried and went to her room. Mark wasn't around."

"Did your Dad know you saw him hit her?"

"Yes. I was standing by the knife drawer in the kitchen, and I thought this was how awful things happen in a family. I tried to look at my father in a way that let him know he disgusted me and then I went to my room."

"I'm sorry you had that experience."

"Jerry, if you ever hit or slap me, that will be the end for us. I might still love you, but I would not live with you. It would be as bad as if you committed adultery. I could forgive you for either a hit or unfaithfulness, but I would not ever want to live with you. If that seems like conditional love to you, I'm sorry, but that's what I know about myself."

He took my hand, and we rode quietly back to the college. Even though these conversations did not take place in our premarital counseling, the discussions with the counselor did bring up more for us to discuss together.

Jerry would finish seminary that year, but I was just completing my second year in college. He knew I would move to wherever he got his first church position, and I planned to finish at whatever college was closest to that location. I felt badly that he seemed to have more unconditional love for me than I had for anyone and wondered if that would change in time.

Sometimes he talked about life after we were married and after I had my degree. He said he didn't want to wait a long time to have children. That concerned me. I figured we better talk about that even if the counselor didn't bring it up.

Children seemed even more undesirable to me than getting married. Of people I knew, Christian and non-Christian, even if their marriages had difficulties, it was through children that they had the most trouble and pain. Raising a child seemed an overwhelming responsibility. Fear and grief were magnified over concern for children.

I wondered if Jerry thought it would be easy to raise children. Did he know anything about them from diapers to death? I did not know if Jerry had experience with children other than the time he spent with his cousins.

When the couple he knew from college asked if we could babysit for them, I agreed with enthusiasm. I could watch how Jerry interacted with a baby, and it would be natural to talk about how a child could bring unexpected problems and pain to a family. My plan was to have Jerry do as much as possible with the baby, who was almost a toddler.

The evening gave me even more information than I'd hoped for. Jerry's friends were thrilled to have at least one experienced babysitter able to stay for as late an evening as they wanted. Jerry did really well entertaining their baby. He made her laugh and then said good night to her when I took her upstairs to change her before putting her to bed. As soon as I lifted her, I could smell that she needed a diaper change.

Upstairs, I discovered that she had made a huge stinky mess. Perfect! I called for Jerry and listened to him come up the stairs. With careful staging placement, I stood at one end of the bassinet so that when Jerry entered the room, he'd get the full view of the smelly mess overflowing the diaper. He stopped suddenly and looked from the mess to me.

"I know you want to have children, so I thought I'd see how you do changing diapers."

Without gagging, and with some helpful guidance, Jerry cleaned away what even I with my experience as a nurse's aide saw as a big mess. While he worked, I thought of the worst mess I'd ever had to clean up. It was a mess that made me believe little boys were very different from girls and far more gross.

Mom worked hard to toilet train the boys before they turned a year and a half old. I had heard her tell people that toilet training should happen before children could confidently run around on their own. She was successful because she took them to the bathroom on a regular schedule. One day she stayed outside talking to friends while she thought the boys were still napping.

Andy woke from his nap and realized that he had a load in his pants. Active and uninhibited, he used what he found to start coloring in the light areas of the Davy Crockett wallpaper next to the crib. Mark woke and decided he would help and started coloring in the light areas in the lower part of the wallpaper with Andy's claylike brown excrement.

I heard the boys laughing, but without looking in the room, I went down to the second level to tell Mom they were awake.

She wasn't in sight, so I opened the door that went from the kitchen into the garage. We had a washer and dryer out there and a long counter for folding clothes.

There was still no sign of Mom, so I went back into the house, through the dining room and living room and down the stairs to the first level and our family room. The front door was open, and I could see Mom standing on the porch talking to our neighbor, Mrs. L, who also had two boys. Mrs. L thought her sons never did anything wrong, and she told people that as a fact. I saw her boys in school, so I didn't believe her.

"Mom, Mark and Andy are awake. I heard them laughing."

She said a quick goodbye to Mrs. L and reentered the house. She always tried to take the boys right to the bathroom as soon as they woke up from a nap. We started upstairs slowly, but by the time we stepped onto the third-floor landing, the peals of laughter coming from my brothers' room alerted us to something out of the ordinary.

We rushed to the door, and Mom flung it open. I stood beside her, but I did not scream like she did. I couldn't make a sound. My voice and even my breath stopped.

What the boys had done seemed unbelievable. I thought little brothers were gross creatures. Now they had proved to me that little boys were alien beings. There seemed no limit to their outrageous actions.

Andy had two fists full of his poop. He seemed unfazed by having it on his hands, wrists, and arms as well as the rails of his crib. The whole room smelled of it. He jumped, startled by Mom's scream, which was followed by her silence and stare.

Mark was no better. He stood beside the crib with just as much poop on his hands and arms. The wallpaper once had a cream and white background, soft green hills, woodland trees, blue streams, and purple mountains supporting many of Davy Crockett's adventures battling Indians, hunting bear, and climbing mountains. Now the wallpaper appeared only in brown tones as far as my brothers could reach from baseboard to arm length above Andy's crib.

BY THE TIME these memories had sped through my mind, the baby was clean and in a fresh diaper, and Jerry looked relieved. "You've changed a lot of diapers?"

"Lots, for babies and for adults. Remember, I was a nurse's aide for a couple of years. You did a good job with that mess. I'll put her in the crib, make sure she's settled, and come downstairs."

25

UNWELCOME INTERRUPTION
PROVES CRUCIAL

One beautiful April day, Jerry and I went into Boston. He said he wanted it to be a special date. Finding the famous pond that led to Robert McCloskey's book *Make Way for Ducklings* was fun, since Grandmere had often read that to me when I was little. A relaxing swan boat ride was accompanied by a sky such a beautiful blue it should have a scent. The scattered fluffy clouds of angel white and bright sunshine were not common in Boston in April. I wished the ride would go on for hours.

We walked near the tallest building in Boston, the John Hancock tower, but Jerry said he wanted to continue farther on. Just a few blocks away was a little jewelry store. He wanted some idea of what I liked in diamond rings.

∾

THE TIME ARRIVED for a long weekend in the spring, so Jerry and I planned to make the trip to New Jersey. Since Lynne wasn't going home to Wisconsin, she asked if she could come along too as prayerful support for what she knew would be the time of asking my parents about marriage. We were not concerned about my mom at all. She got married when she was nineteen and had only ever made me promise I wouldn't get married that young. Plus, I felt sure she saw Jerry's good points, especially since he had cut his hair.

Friday evening after supper, Dad went to his easy chair and watched television until he fell asleep. Jerry and I and Lynne talked. Jerry and I would get both of my parents in the living room so that we could speak to them, and Lynne would stay upstairs and pray.

Saturday was gray, not the kind of day people would be rushing out to activities or the beach. Dad didn't do that anyway. When he was in Bay Head, he took it easy unless there were jobs in the house or yard that Mark and I and Mom could not fix.

After a big breakfast, Lynne excused herself to go upstairs. Jerry said that he and I would like to talk and asked if we could move into the living room.

My parents agreed, but they moved slowly. I figured they knew what was coming and also that they knew they did not agree on what the response should be. It was about 10:30 a.m. when we all sat down in the living room.

"Mr. and Mrs. Riposta, I know you realize Virginia and I are serious in our relationship. We know we love each other and would like to marry. Today we want to ask for your permission and blessing."

Mom looked at Dad's frowning face and literally started twisting her hands in nervousness. Dad cleared his throat and said, "Jerry—" Then the doorbell rang.

We didn't rent any rooms or suites from November to May, and this was not a holiday weekend. The neighboring houses were empty. No one should be at the door. The doorbell rang again. Dad got up to answer it, and Mom followed him.

It was a couple their age from our church in Chatham. They said they were just out for the day exploring the shore and felt led to stop and say hello. They were more cheerful than my dad was sour, so he invited them into the living room. Mom went to get some coffee for everyone.

I took Jerry's hand and pulled him through the dining room and into the back hallway.

"I can't believe God let this happen. Lynne is upstairs praying, and these people just randomly show up." My eyes filled with tears. I realized once again how odd it was that I had not cried over Andy's death. Now, except for the troubles and suffering of people I loved and those I encountered in movies and books, tears fill my eyes only when I was angry. And I was furious now.

∾

LATER LESSONS LEARNED: Crying

Crying can happen as a physical response to something in the eye, pain, and pressure. Crying delivers nutrients and washes out toxins or irritating particles.

Crying also happens due to emotions. Some people cry as a release of tension. The emotions leading to tears are strong and with stress hormones and painkillers. A person's tears can stir empathy or sympathy, and crying is considered normal human behavior.

In grief, people often cry. Other people feel grief like a pain behind the eyes, a sneeze that will not happen, or twisted intestines, and yet they do not cry. When a person feels devastated, they may experience an involuntary cutoff from normal emotional expression through tears. *The shock of loss may move grief to a feeling of unreality.*

The American Psychological Association dictionary describes the lack of tears and emotion when one might expect them to appear as absent grief. Psychologists think this lack of emotion and tears is an impaired response to grief. If there is no physical reason for a person to keep from crying in grief, the person may be experiencing denial, a need to avoid the emotional realities connected to the loss. This is labeled complex or complicated grief.

It is possible for a person experiencing complicated grief to cry over nonpersonal sad events, movies, books, spiritual experiences, events that stimulate anger or laughter, or even anticipatory grief, which is grief that can see the loss coming. People who do not cry over their own personal losses may preserve and distract themselves from tears by focusing on the changes and work that must be done after the loss.

26

TENSIONS, WORTH, AND SILENCE

"Your dad was going to say no."

"I know. We expected that, right?"

"I prayed and hoped he would say yes."

"I never thought he would, and I told you I don't care. I don't need his advice or approval for anything in my life."

Jerry gave me a hug even though I didn't want one at that point. "Should we go back and be social?"

"No. We don't have to do that." While I was quiet, we heard Mom offering the guests coffee, which they refused.

The woman said, "We don't plan to stay long, but when we got to Point Pleasant, I said we should go a little farther and say hello to Katherine and Frank."

"Do you know this couple?" Jerry whispered.

"I've seen them at church but don't really know them. They've been in classes and social gatherings with Mom and Dad. We can wait in the kitchen until they leave, and we can hear them from there."

We sat in the kitchen and listened to a conversation that lasted less than an hour. The couple asked who the young man was they'd seen with me when they came into the house. Mom answered.

"That's Jerry. He and Virginia are pretty serious, talking about marriage."

"Really? Is he in college?"

"No. He's finishing seminary. He's going to be a pastor."

"That's wonderful!" the man said. "Our daughter has had us in a panic with the losers she's been dating. One guy doesn't even try to hide that he takes drugs as a method of recreational fun. Said it like a challenge to us when we were talking with him."

"It's been a nightmare," his wife agreed. "Our sons in high school are also giving us stress and nightmares due to their activities. So much of it is because of the friends they have. At a certain age, you just can't control what they do because they're not home much."

"We've prayed through tears and gritted teeth all winter, and this spring hasn't been much better," the man added.

His wife said, "You must be so thankful that Virginia has found a young man who loves the Lord. I would be ecstatic."

"That is definitely something to give thanks to the Lord for," the man affirmed.

Jerry and I looked at each other, wide-eyed. How had this happened? Right at the point when he had asked the big question, these people had interrupted. They couldn't have been a better setup to speak to my father on our behalf than if we had staged it. We heard the four adults pray briefly and then my parents walked them to the door.

When it sounded like Mom and Dad had returned to the living room and we heard them talking softly, we joined them. When we were all seated, Jerry spoke up.

"Mr. Riposta, you were about to say something before your

friends arrived. We really want to hear your answer about giving us your permission and blessing."

My dad knew we'd heard the conversation from the hall or the kitchen. Dad was a lot of things, but he wasn't stupid. "After that visit, what can I possibly say but yes?"

WE never even had to show an engagement ring to my parents. That helped, since we did not pick it up until late May. Lynne was happy through all the following days, as she had been upstairs in the front hall able to hear what was happening and praying for us the whole time. She seemed less surprised than Jerry did by the interruption that proved so crucial, but I knew Jerry, Lynne, and Beccy had been praying for weeks about the meeting with my parents.

The grudging permission to marry had not included any words of blessing, and I was as mad as I was thankful for the couple whose words and experiences changed my father's mind. He had given grudging permission.

We talked about the bad feelings between my dad and me when I was back in the dorm. Beccy and Lynne asked me if I had considered that God might want me not only to forgive my father but also to ask my father to forgive me.

"Forgive me? Why?"

"God had brought you through the fire, through years of having a dysfunctional dad. God still preserved your heart to care about other people in spite of the troubles in your home. God opened your heart again in the summer in Mexico. You got that scholarship that allowed you to come to Gordon, and you didn't even apply for it. Coming here meant you met Jerry. You've healed enough to actually think marriage is not always going to be terrible, but you know we need to forgive others."

"You said I need to ask my father to forgive me."

"Have you done anything mean or rotten toward him?" Beccy knew I had given him plenty of rotten looks. "You told me you tried to get your mother to leave him, that you've let him know by your actions that you hated how he acted."

"And you think I should ask him to forgive me, seriously?"

"If God has brought you to this point, how could you not want to start marriage with the air cleared? You told me if you ever did get married, it would have to be to someone who loved God more than you did, someone who could help you grow in trusting God. Didn't Jerry do that?"

"Yes."

Lynne had been listening quietly. In her soft tone, she asked, "Don't you think Jerry would want you to have all the resentment cleared up between your father and you?"

People had come into my life who accepted love with all its risks. They were also people who understood the power of forgiveness: Beccy, Lynne, Elisabeth Leitch, and many others. Just the previous year, we'd all read and discussed *The Hiding Place*, in which incredible challenges for the power to forgive appeared in Corrie ten Boom's story.[1] Examples scraped against the armor around my heart.

By receiving love from a man who loved God and lived like it, I decided to consider the idea of forgiveness with my father. If I forgave Dad, and he forgave me, wouldn't that be some kind of miracle? I felt a pressure of needing to end my own emotional struggles with fear, anger, and resentment.

"I'll think about it more." I meant it, and for that evening we left the topic alone. Even though it felt miserable, I realized I needed to forgive my dad, but I also needed to ask him to forgive me. If I went into marriage with the weight of anger, resentment, and unforgiveness, it likely could cause problems in my relationship with Jerry. I could hold a grudge, but Jerry never seemed to do that. Grudges in a marriage would be bad.

Later that spring, on a long weekend at home in New Jersey, that Saturday afternoon my dad was the only one home. He was reading the newspaper. I decided to approach him and to ask for forgiveness for my anger and hateful attitude toward him over the years since the fire.

"Dad?" I sat down on a chair across from where he sat on the couch.

"Yes?" He peeked around the edge of the paper at me.

"I wanted to talk to you about something that really has been bothering me."

He put the paper on his lap.

"Dad, I know you could tell I've been angry with you. I lived at home according to your rules, and we didn't talk much. I do believe you want the best for us, but I got angry over how you acted. You were very different after the fire. I resented the way you ran our house, the way you acted when you were angry. Now I know I need to ask for your forgiveness for holding hatred and anger toward you. I forgive you. I want us to have a better relationship. So I'm asking now, will you forgive me?"

Had I made it clear enough? Had I said it right? He stared at me with a frown. Then he slowly lifted the paper until it totally blocked his face and became a wall between us.

I sat for a few seconds, shocked by his reaction. Was he really going to hold that paper up like a shield and not speak to me? All the anger of past hurts from him surged inside of me. When it was clear that paper wall was not coming down, I left the room.

While the anger and hurt I felt stirred up a rage of memories of his past negative actions, I tried to remember that there had been a time when he had been different, a good father.

That didn't work. It seemed like I heard a voice that said, *You are ridiculous. You don't have to forgive him, and he doesn't have to forgive you.*

Forgiveness is a choice. I had made the choice and wanted to stick to it. I knew that. Desmond Tutu said, "Until we can forgive, we remain locked in our pain."[2] If I wanted to be healed, I needed to keep to the path of forgiveness, at least in my head. It might be years before my heart felt the forgiveness I had decided to give.

If Dad would not forgive me, he would have to stay locked in his pain. I would keep my decision to forgive him in my mind and hope that one day I would feel it in my heart. I had done what I could. I could not make him forgive me.

SUMMER FILLED QUICKLY with hours of work. Jerry took five jobs in Massachusetts to try to build a nest egg for us. I worked my two jobs at the shore and tried with scattered phone calls to plan the wedding with Jerry. Though I was never one who dreamed of being a bride, I did love autumn colors and thought I'd like a wedding in the fall. If not the fall, summer colors were rich and varied, so that would work, and if the wedding couldn't be in the summer, then spring had gorgeous blossoms of light and pastel colors. The date that worked best for us was December 16.

My semester would just have ended. Jerry's last final exam was December 14, and we had a housesitting job from December 17 to April 15 in Rockport, Massachusetts. The gorgeous house had a view over Cape Ann and Sandy Bay.

Jerry saw the posting at the seminary, and as we were the first couple to apply and we had some strong recommendations, we got the job, which looked like a honeymoon of months, since

I arranged to have all my classes on Tuesdays and Thursdays. Jerry still had to drive school routes and trips for the bus company near the college, but we felt relieved to have a fully furnished beautiful house to live in while Jerry looked for a job as a pastor and I completed another term. We would have no housing costs.

A temporary glitch came when Jerry arrived in Bay Head to drive me back to Gordon. My father took him aside in what I thought was a ploy to bring a problem into our happiness. "You know you're responsible for her education now."

Jerry looked startled. He'd just entered the front hall, and when my father came to the door, Jerry expected a greeting.

"She's marrying you, so you'll have to assume all the costs for her education, and since she's in year three, she should finish school."

"Yes, I agree. We'll manage," Jerry responded with more confidence than he felt.

I came down the front hall stairs and said, "Since my parents have always had some big expense for this guesthouse and have given me nothing for school, it's not like we're losing their support." My father frowned at me and went back into the living room.

As I hugged Jerry, I spoke in a voice I was sure my father could overhear. "I've managed by saving everything I earn, by working at school, and by receiving a scholarship, and this year I took out a student loan. Only two years of student loans won't be terrible to pay back."

That bit of tension was nothing compared to the differences in ideas between generations and families over wedding plans. When did parents of the bride start believing they should plan the wedding and reception? Does it go back to the fact that tradition calls on them to pay for the wedding?

From the location of the wedding ceremony and reception

to the number of guests, the decorations, music, food and beverages, and seating, all found differences arise between the generations. When the families also include people who are teetotalers and people who love to drink and carouse in celebrations, extra tensions pull on anyone planning the wedding. Jerry's family and the cousins my age on my mom's side of the family did not drink much but saw a champagne toast as appropriate.

Jerry and I knew my parents did not have the money to put on the typical Italian wedding at a gorgeous venue with a sit-down dinner, gift bags, liquor, and band for dancing, but we knew they wanted to do more than the finger sandwiches, cake, and punch at a church hall that often comprised a small-town New Englander's wedding. With differences of opinion on every part of the ceremony, Jerry said we needed a face-to-face conversation that would allow us and my parents to plan what mattered most to them. Though neither they nor we felt comfortable with the divide, we decided that Jerry and I would plan the wedding and my parents could plan the reception.

Cost would be a consideration on everything because my parents were moving again, this time to a small ranch-style house just a couple of miles from the church we attended in Chatham. It would mean that they and Mark would live together again, all week, every week. Because the guesthouse at the shore did not go on the market at the best buying time, my parents knew they'd be paying two mortgages until the Bay Head house was sold.

Mark again qualified for the high school football team, and he got a job as a busboy at a popular restaurant. I felt relieved for him knowing he wouldn't have to be at home a lot. We had moved often, and he knew how to make friends. We also could work on our own when no friends were around. Mark said the atmosphere at home was tense but not miserable and was mainly connected to finances.

Mom wanted the experience of going to a bridal salon with me, even though we couldn't afford any dresses there. When I found out I was the size of the display gowns that people could try on, I asked how much one would cost. They were one-tenth of the actual price. I was thrilled to find a gown on that trip to a fancy salon.

Beccy and her mother had the talent of clothing designers and the skill and machines to make everything from delicate items to coats. As a wedding present, they wanted to make all the bridesmaids' gowns. I had Beccy, Lynne, Kathy, all friends my age; a junior bridesmaid, Uncle Sal's daughter Lesley; and twin flower girls, the daughters of Jerry's sister Nancy and her husband, Ken.

The men would have to have rented tuxedos for the 3:00 p.m. wedding, but because we rented a batch for the groom; Jerry's brother, Dave, who would be his best man; Gordon; Mark; Uncle Sal's son Louis; and a ring bearer, who was the son of longtime friends at the church, a good deal on the tuxedo costs was arranged. When talking over the progress we'd made and the way other wedding needs seemed to fill in easily, we wished we could have planned the reception too, but we decided to be grateful for what we could choose.

Evie Tornquist, the dear sweet singer I'd known from childhood who now was famous in Christian music circles, sang as a wedding present. The church organist and pianist, who had been my friends for years, also played as a wedding present. Al Green, another friend since my childhood in Irvington, took pictures as a wedding present. Since we had a wedding date on the Saturday before Christmas, the church would already be fully and beautifully decorated with holiday flower arrangements, candles, ribbons, and bows. The only venue cost for the wedding in the sanctuary and the reception in the church hall was for the custodian's cleanup for Sunday. Most churches do not require members to pay for use of the facilities.

And the pastor? People usually do pay the pastor. Sometimes it's something the pastor chooses. Sometimes it's an expense set by the church board.

In meeting with our pastor, Leroy Webber, we found that he and Jerry had gone to the same college, Wheaton College. They had also been in the men's Glee Club that sang locally, around the nation, and around the world. This meant they had both survived the club's hazing ritual and were considered brothers. For this reason, Pastor Webber said he didn't want any payment from us.

Jerry asked him, "What do you usually ask for?"

Pastor Webber smiled and said, "I tell the groom, you can give me what marrying her is worth."

∽

In Long Hill Chapel with Pastor Leroy Webber

In the tradition of the Italians, I carried a satin purse as we made the rounds at the reception, talking to all the guests. Every Italian and Jewish family, plus everyone who had ever been to an Italian wedding, put an envelope in the purse. Aunt Beverly and Aunt Pauline were the only New Englanders who followed that custom. Jerry's parents also put an envelope in the satin purse. Jerry's dad worked with so many Italians at the trucking company, he'd heard many times about the wedding gifts they gave.

Of the 520 people who came to the wedding, 230 came to the reception, a buffet dinner. From the people unfamiliar with the Italian custom of giving money as a wedding gift, we received most of the china and crystal we'd hoped for as well as many extra items that were more decorative than practical. Wedding gifts of cash came to a surprising total. Jerry and I had the same idea when we realized what we had received. We decided to reimburse my parents for what they'd spent on the reception.

Although it wasn't a sit-down, waiter-served meal that we'd had with all my father's family weddings, waiters did serve hors d'oeuvres and beverages, and the buffet had everything from lasagna to roast beef. The five-layer wedding cake topped by a bride and groom had luscious white frosting, flowers, and, inside, raspberry, chocolate, and white cake. When my parents got married, Mom had asked Dad not to squash the cake all over her mouth, but he did, so she did the same to him. I asked Jerry to not make a mess on my face when he fed me the cake, and he didn't, nor did I to him. I wondered if Mom noticed the difference while she watched us go through that part of the wedding ritual.

The toasts made people smile and laugh. My parents smiled and laughed too, but behind their smiles I saw tension. This had all cost more than they could afford.

They didn't have to pay for a band, but there was background music that only stopped when the surprise quartet got everyone's attention. They stood up near us at the wedding party table. "Sunrise, Sunset," my favorite song from *Fiddler on the Roof*, was sung by this quartet that included the ring bearer's father, two youth group leaders, and a deacon. They had never sung together, and their voices would not have earned them a place in any choir.

I appreciated that my mom knew I loved the song. She had recruited these men to sing. "Sunrise, Sunset" had made my eyes fill with tears when I heard it in *Fiddler on the Roof*. This quartet's version only made people teary-eyed because they laughed so hard.

The throwing of the bouquet caused more commotion than expected as kids tried to push teenagers and single adult women away from catching the bouquet. Removing the garter became rowdier than anything the New England and Midwest families had seen. Probably because all the Italian men, from my teen cousins to my oldest uncles, had been subtly pouring drinks from bottles they kept under their tables. The long cloths on the reception tables let them lift, pour, and pass bottles so that the teetotalers wouldn't see how many times alcohol filled glasses. There was no way my father's family would celebrate a wedding without liquor. The champagne toasts may as well have been ginger ale.

Jerry and I kissed when the guests tapped their glasses. We were glad the fellowship hall had so many tables that there was no room for dancing, because dad's family had never been to a wedding with no dancing. Lack of space could be the excuse. Mom and Dad didn't want anyone to know they couldn't afford live music.

When it was near time for us to leave the reception, we asked Mom and Dad to join us in a small alcove away from the guests. Jerry and I had looked at enough of the gifts in my satin purse for him to write a check that would cover all they'd spent on the reception. Jerry held the check toward Mom and Dad while I explained briefly that we really wanted to do this because we had received far more in gifts than we had expected.

Mom's eyes immediately filled with tears. She hugged and kissed us both. Dad stood like a statue. Mom, Jerry, and I looked at him. He turned and went back to the reception.

MY FATHER's choice of remoteness and silence added to the anger I felt toward him. I had to deliberately return to mentally choosing forgiveness. I also wondered if my choice of not speaking to my brothers, when I had two of them and knew silence would anger them, was a trait inherited from Dad. I couldn't remember him giving the silent treatment to Mom or us before the fire.

Jerry had taken counseling courses but admitted that my father's reactions bothered him. He affirmed that we should not respond in anger or take it personally. How did I not take it personally? I could see Dad had turmoil and struggles of his own. Since he wouldn't ever go to any kind of counseling, God would have to work out his troubles.

LATER LESSONS LEARNED: The Silent Treatment

In some college psychology courses, I learned that people who feel overwhelmed by emotions like embarrassment, anger, and frustration often choose to physically and verbally pull away. For some it is a power play to affect and control others by making them feel rejected. It has a negative effect on the self-esteem of the one who receives the silent treatment.

Used frequently, the silent treatment becomes a method of emotional abuse. A person receiving the silent treatment feels a lack of control. Using silence as a form of punishment causes it to fall into the category of emotional abuse.

Silence from one expected to speak is a passive-aggressive way to try to control another. The hope is that the person receiving silence will feel badly and be the one to give in to what the silent person wants. The receiver of the silent treatment should show that this behavior will not get what that silent person wants.

27

WELCOME AND UNWELCOME CHANGES AND MESSAGES

I had no idea how many couples have to get up really early the day after they are married to drive to a housesitting job a few states away, but that was our day after the wedding. I put on the going away outfit Beccy and her mom had made as an extra present for me, and Jerry dressed in his regular casual clothes. We both laughed over the many bloopers of our wedding night, and I hugged him and told him that what we gave my parents as we left the reception was one of the reasons why I loved him.

Housesitting in Rockport, Massachusetts, seemed like a four-month honeymoon. Jerry had only his bus driving job and some interviews, and I had arranged to have all my classes on Tuesdays and Thursdays. The house had a great view of the water and of the most picturesque area of Rockport. By April we knew we would move to Ironton, Ohio. Jerry would be the minister of Christian education there and so would assist the head pastor in all ways, but his main responsibilities would be with youth.

Marshall University in Huntington, West Virginia, was just

thirty minutes away, so I could commute and finish my degree there. The tristate experience was interesting to both of us, as we often shopped across the river in Ashland, Kentucky, and lived and worked in Ohio while I finished my bachelor's degree in West Virginia. Ashland was a dry county. I didn't know what that meant at first but soon learned that was why Ironton had as many bars as churches.

Ironton had warmhearted people but a cramped gray atmosphere due to the coal, iron, and chemical plants along the Ohio River. Extreme differences were obvious between the rich and the poor areas of town. The poverty that appeared suited stereotypes of Appalachia.

My first full-time job was at the food stamp office. My second job was as a social worker, and since they were short-staffed, I often had to go alone to visit families. It was a relief when a job teaching language arts at the middle school opened. I signed a contract to teach middle school in Ironton.

A week after I signed that contract, I received a call from the head of a church board in Massachusetts. They were looking for a pastor and had read about Jerry and had talked to people at the seminary. They wanted to know if we could come to Williamstown for a few days to see the area and so that Jerry could speak to and meet with people as a candidate to be their pastor.

I told the man, who was the head of the search committee, that we weren't looking to move and thanked him for calling. Then I worried about how Jerry would react.

When Jerry got home, I told him about the call. He said, "I'm not looking to move to Massachusetts, but I'd talk to them. They're looking for a pastor, and I do want to be a pastor."

"But I just signed a contract to teach here in the fall."

"You could get a teaching job wherever we live, and I'd be a pastor."

"It's so far away. They didn't offer to fly us there."

"The best part of being here has been the people. You and I know that the factories, iron, coal, cement, chemical plants, factory whistles that sound like screams, and county poverty like deep Appalachia gets you down. I can't count the number of times you've said to me, 'If I could just spend a day in a beautiful setting with an art museum, my soul would be totally refreshed.'"

"I have said that, but I did sign a contract."

"I'm sure they'd let you out of it."

"Are you going to call Williamstown back?"

"I think that would be polite. I'll tell them that we've talked and that we'll pray about it."

Before Jerry called the gentleman back, my parents called. Mom was going to need some surgery. She wondered if we could come up for a few days or a week. We could and we told her so. No sooner had we finished the call than Jerry said, "You know, it's only about three and a half hours from your parents' house to Williamstown."

I didn't say anything, but I didn't object to him calling back the man from the Williamstown First Baptist Church pastoral search committee. We drove to New Jersey, and after helping Mom and keeping everything in the household running smoothly, Jerry called Williamstown. We arranged to drive to the Berkshires, which was on the opposite side of the state from Gordon and not a place either of us had visited.

It was an easy and beautiful drive up the Taconic State Parkway. They put us up in a deacon's house. That gentleman and his wife had teens who seemed happy that the church might get a young pastor. For our first activity, the host couple took us out for a tour of Williamstown.

"We thought we'd start on a road not far from our house. One of the best places in town is the Clark Art Institute. It's the largest private art collection in the United States. You could spend days in it, and the grounds around it are as beautiful as the art inside."

I looked at Jerry, and he smiled at me. Almost at that instant, we both knew we would end up moving to Williamstown. It wasn't because everyone we met was interesting and kind. Nor was it the call from my mom that made the drive to Williamstown easier. The words I said often in frustration in Ironton about what would refresh my soul had not been heard only by Jerry.

WILLIAMSTOWN HAD beauty and so much to offer, such as Williams College with its programs that residents could enjoy, an InterVarsity Christian Fellowship, a summer theater festival that brought world-famous people to town, museums, libraries, a quirky movie theater, a deli, restaurants, cafés, buildings that had been on magazine covers, a large parsonage built in 1904, special events every season, and natural beauty. The first autumn had stunning leaves and weather that brings people to enjoy the beauty of the Berkshires. Though the New England way was very different from the warmhearted southern hospitality of Kentucky, I was familiar with it. The church and townspeople were welcoming.

We settled in, and I did not get a teaching job right away because, after almost five years of marriage, I was pregnant. Moving to accept God's leading for timing in marriage had been difficult, but thinking about all the things that could break a heart because of a child bothered me more than I told anyone. Pregnancy, for me, did not have the unpleasantness of nausea that I heard about from so many people.

Jerry and I took Lamaze classes. I wanted to control

bringing a child into the world as much as I could. If I chose natural childbirth, I could know everything that happened. I worried about what I might say if I took any drugs.

We received wonderful encouragement and baby gifts from people in Massachusetts and New Jersey, but I thought of all the terrible things that could happen with a child. I settled on the fact that because I hid so many of my negative judgmental thoughts, my baby would have horrendous defects. Although outwardly I could be kind and pleasant, I knew I judged others and myself harshly. If a person's inner thoughts and emotions could affect the development of a baby, I would be facing serious trouble with the child I carried.

My sleep became irregular, even though my obstetrician said I could have a glass of wine to help me relax in the evening. That at least made me smile. Baptists didn't drink, and Jerry went to the liquor store to buy wine for me. The wine did not help me to rest more easily.

Would it have helped to talk to someone about this? Probably, but I didn't. The baby was due in September. In June we had a reunion with Robin and Jack and the others who had lived in the house in Beverly Farms. Robin was pregnant too, and I wanted to talk to her about my fears, but I didn't.

In July when my parents had their twenty-fifth wedding anniversary and came up to visit us, we surprised them by taking them to the church hall, where it was full of family and friends. They even saw friends from their early years as a couple. Mom was so happy that she cried, smiled, and laughed. From Dad, I witnessed some of the most relaxed smiles I'd seen from him in years. He seemed to talk easily with all the old friends.

In August, one of my bridesmaids was getting married in North Jersey, so we drove down, even though it was just five weeks before my due date. While we were there and after we returned to Williamstown, I had such terrible sleep and thoughts about the baby that I finally told Jerry about my fears. He could hardly believe I'd had these worries for months and not told him. We prayed together. Prayer was his go-to action for anything.

That night I had one of the most vivid dreams ever. I'd had the baby. I was in a hospital room, and a nurse, a beautiful woman in a crisp uniform, came into the room carrying the baby. The child was swaddled in a blanket striped with blue, green, pink, and yellow.

"Take a look at your baby. We know you want to." She gave the baby to me. Its head and face looked perfect. The bright-brown eyes had tiny dark lashes, and the baby waved small pink hands. I could see all the fingers. The baby kicked hard, and the blanket fell away from its legs. I could see the little feet and toes. I cried and asked, "Is everything all right? Is my baby all right?"

"You have a healthy, beautiful baby." She smiled.

I started to turn the blanket back because I wanted to see if I had a boy or girl. As quick as an ocean breeze, the nurse lifted the baby out of my arms. "You'll have to wait for that," she said and left the room.

In the morning I told Jerry about my dream. "It was so real."

"Some cultures value dreams as messages much more than we do. You know how many people in the Bible saw messages in dreams."

From that night on until I went into labor, I slept as well as any nine-month-pregnant woman could have.

When our son was born in mid-September, Jerry was at my side in the delivery room. It was a twenty-seven-hour labor because of breech birth, which meant we knew it was a boy before we knew what he looked like. The doctor laughed when he announced that.

It hit me then that being a parent was a huge responsibility. Tears filled my eyes—tears of happiness, relief, and nervousness. My only unpleasant feeling was jealousy because after all the work I did, Jerry got to hold the baby first!

ANYONE WHO HAS HAD MORE than one child knows how different siblings can be from one another, even though they have the same parents and grow up in the same environment. When our first child was four, we had another baby. Now we had a boy and a girl. I told Jerry that was all the kinds there were, so we should be content with two healthy children. Fortunately for me, he agreed.

Tears of happiness and relief came again as our daughter arrived one morning. It took years for me to climb over a wall of fear regarding parenting. I learned that I had to trust more in God. Crying has come in times of praying for my children and others, more tears than I had cried over the years before becoming a parent. Parenting taught me about being God's child. I couldn't ever see my children question, learn, face difficulties, hurts, choose to disobey, or come in for forgiveness and a hug without thinking of my actions as a child of God.

I also started to think about aspects of parenting in ways I never did before I was a parent. My relationship with my parents continued to be much the same, but I did see the father I remembered from my childhood when Dad talked, played, or read with our children. His voice held a relaxed playfulness that had disappeared after the fire. I wondered if becoming a grandfather might lead to some healing in our relationship.

My mom drove up to Williamstown frequently and often

brought one or more of my aunts with her. Dad remained distant except at holidays. Then we would get together in New Jersey or they would come to Williamstown. His only warmth and animation appeared with his grandchildren. When the children napped or went to bed for the night, Dad walked, read, or watched television. Mom was glad to talk late into the evening.

We'd met many other young couples through our Lamaze classes and local activity groups. The Baptist church sponsored a community-wide Vacation Bible School each year, and we felt settled in the community. The grade school was right across the street from the parsonage. We could watch our eldest on the playground at recess right from our living room.

The Berkshires had some tough winters, my least favorite season, but we had fun making snow forts, snow people, creatures, and igloos with the kids. When spring arrived, we buried away those awful below-zero weeks, but one April weekend we had twenty-six inches of snow. Because one of our children often got pneumonia every winter in one lung or the other, we had talked about moving to a milder climate, but where? The pediatrician said we didn't have to move but thought it reasonable to consider a warmer location. As usual, Jerry's response was that we could pray about moving farther south.

Not a week later, we got a letter from a church in Miami, Florida, looking for a pastor. It was a general letter they'd sent to several candidates, not like the personalized call we'd received from the Williamstown people.

"Jerry, look at this! Miami!"

"Miami? Florida?"

"Yes. I speak Spanish. I could get a teaching job, and the kids would adapt and probably become bilingual."

"I think it's too far south. Do you really want to live in Florida?"

"I don't know."

We didn't respond. Seven years in Williamstown seemed like just a few. Except for the winters, we were happy to stay. It had vibrant options for all ages and diverse people literally from around the world because of the college and its graduate programs. We enjoyed being a host family for foreign students, and they experienced time with a family as they missed their own families.

A couple of weeks later, we received a phone call from a place called Cape May Court House, New Jersey. Though I'd grown up in New Jersey, it always seemed to me that New Jersey ended at Atlantic City. They had the phone call set up for a committee call. They had been looking for a pastor for over two years and had come to a decision that Jerry seemed like the ideal candidate for their next pastor.

Jerry asked why they had been looking for a pastor for so long. They explained they'd had a painful church split a few years back. It took weeks to get a search committee together. Then that committee had given up after searching for a year. Now this second search committee was praying and working as carefully as they could to find the right person to lead them.

I mouthed the words at Jerry, "We don't want to move."

Jerry told them we were not looking to move but thanked them for considering him.

"Are you sure you wouldn't consider a move?" they asked.

I held my breath thinking, *He's going to say we'll pray about it*, but he didn't. He just said, "At this time we really aren't looking to move." That was it.

When we glanced at each other, neither of us saw relief or any evidence of feeling we had made the right decision.

"I feel badly that they were so positive about you and you had to turn them down."

"I didn't have to."

"Why did you?"

"We're warned in seminary that going into a situation after a church split usually will be a short-term transition time while the church tries to stabilize itself. The church will need help to heal from hurt feelings, anger, and resentments. It's guaranteed to be difficult for the pastor and their family. I might do it on my own, but it wouldn't be anything like being here for you and the kids off and on throughout the day."

"You always say we should pray about it, but you didn't this time."

He sat down. "We could, but pray for what? To move so far away from what we have here, into a situation that has not recovered from a church split? God would have to make it incredibly clear."

"We could do what Gideon did."

"Praying by putting out a fleece?"

"Put something in our prayer that could not be a coincidence so we'd know we should consider this move."

"Not that we would definitely move."

"No, just that we'd be open to talking with them more."

"I can't call them, and they can't call me."

"Why not?"

"Protocol. If a church calls and talks seriously to a pastor and they are turned down because the pastor isn't looking to move, they need to respect that. It's just the way things are done in the denominational search for a pastor."

I looked at the clock. It was 6:00 p.m. on a Friday. "Let's pray that in forty-eight hours they will contact us and ask if you wouldn't please reconsider talking more with them about the possibility of moving."

Jerry agreed, so that's what we prayed together.

Sunday was a full, tough day. It was always busy with Sunday school, the church service, students to the house for lunch, and a couple of hours of rest before different evening events and activities. I kept jumping every time the phone rang, but it never was anyone from that New Jersey church.

We had to be at church at six, and we were running late. The parsonage was only a half mile from the church. Jerry had our eldest child by the hand and was at the front door. I was carrying our youngest and was about to join him when the phone in the front hall rang, only ten minutes until the time would have been up.

"It's them." I looked at the clock. Jerry went to get the phone.

He listened for a few minutes and then said, "Yes, yes, I understand. Virginia and I have discussed it further. Yes, we'd be willing to talk more with the church about the possibility."

That was it. He hung up and said, "That was the area minister. That means she oversees all the churches in a certain area. She's worked a lot with the Cape May Court House church because of their struggles. She said they called and told her that I had turned them down. They were very confused because they felt sure they had found the right person. She told them she would pray with them about this but that neither they nor she should try to get me to move since I told them I did not want to. Then she said that all this weekend she has felt compelled to call and ask if we would at least reconsider talking more with the church about the possibility of being their pastor."

"I knew it."

"What?"

"When it was them, a call in the last ten minutes of the forty-eight-hour time limit—I don't know how long it will take, but we're moving there."

$\sim$

LATER LESSONS LEARNED: **Trauma and Grief**

Grief, faced slowly on its own or through sudden traumatic incidents, can cause a variety of mental illnesses, depression, substance abuse, anxiety disorders, phobias, and manic phases. Grief is normal and different in timing and appearance for everyone, with stages people recognize as denial, anger, bargaining, depression, and acceptance. People in stages of grief cry, have difficulty sleeping, experience unusual levels of energy, avoid social situations, have trouble concentrating, question spiritual beliefs and life goals, and feel confused, angry, guilty, lonely, depressed, and sad.

In normal grieving processes, an individual settles into a new pattern and modes of coping after a few months, but triggers can cause a painful revisiting of the earliest grief emotions. Trauma and grief often come with a violent or sudden death, and for adults this can be more intense when the person who died is a child or young adult. Traumatic grief has the extra intensity of debilitating reactions and can last for years, with triggers recognized in posttraumatic stress disorders. People who deny or delay grief can shut off emotions in a stoic depression that lasts until some other traumatic event triggers the emotions of the first grief. Chronic depression arises often from the grief and guilt that a person locks away.

Doctors explain that grief can exist as acute or persistent. Acute grief finds a level of coping usually within a year or two. Persistent grief lasts longer. Men try to resist grieving, but this puts them into categories of greater physical and mental health dangers. Talking about one's loss can help, whether the story is told all at once or in pieces. Sharing one's memories provides an outlet for grief. Without talking about the loss, one locks into an incomplete grief and feelings of being alone.

28

FIRST LOVE AND LONG-LASTING BATTLES

Jerry was pastor of the First Baptist Church in Cape May Court House for twenty years. People were welcoming and helpful to us and our children, but Jerry was right about it taking a lot of his time, far beyond the hours in Williamstown. He often apologized for not being home more, but I knew he needed to do all that he was doing.

The parsonage had been built by men from the church and was surrounded by fourteen acres. The first time I put our daughter in the stroller and had our son walking alongside me to go into town, the roadside was so rough that the wheels fell off the stroller. I started to feel isolated and to get grouchier about Jerry being out for so many meetings and visitations.

When we'd been there just four months, and it was winter, which was never my best season, we had an argument about how irregular our family time was. I was a city girl and now lived surrounded by woods and fields. It felt remote, even lonely.

We didn't pray together on this evening because I was still irritated. Jerry had warned me he'd be out doing much more visiting and attending church meetings, but I had not believed it would be a problem. That night I had another rare and vivid dream. Because of the dream, I felt settled and resolved in accepting the demands on Jerry's time. In the morning I spoke with Jerry about it.

"Last night I had a dream that I was waiting for you at the church. I was standing in the hall near the nursery where the kids were playing. You were in a meeting. I was feeling angry and wishing your meeting was finished. A woman came into the hall where I was. She was absolutely beautiful in a totally natural way. I can't tell you her hair or eye color or what she was wearing, but she glowed with beauty. She said, 'Don't be jealous. You knew when you married him that he loved me first. He committed to me first. I am his priority and you know that.' I was as stunned by her words as I was by the sight or feeling of her. She hugged me. I don't know whether she was the church or the Holy Spirit, but I want to tell you that her hug wrapped me in some kind of security. I'm sorry for being so aggravated by the long hours you're working here. I love you. It will get better. I'm sure."

Our children grew up with easy access to the Atlantic Ocean and the South Jersey woodlands. We had the space and environment to have pets like box turtles and king snakes, a dog, and a pony. We had a small-town atmosphere from October through April and then the area swelled with summer residents.

For the first few years, we often saw my parents, who could drive down from North Jersey even more easily than coming to Williamstown. But when they moved to Maine in retirement and then to Florida after just a few years of living through the Maine winters, my aunt Virginia and uncle Nunzi stepped in to act as substitute grandparents. Other family members visited. Some liked the true South Jersey so much that they even rented or bought property in Cape May County.

When Mom and Dad moved to Maine, we found out from a phone call. They didn't write letters. We saw them just once a year. They did not seem happy. When I heard they were moving from Maine to Florida, I made jokes as much as everyone else about them not being able to take the Maine winters.

WE MADE a trip to visit them in Florida after they had moved from a rental house into a condominium that they bought. Their unit had its own pool and hardly anyone used it, so our children enjoyed full days outside in the water. It didn't take long to see that Dad had lost the remoteness, sarcasm, and avoidance of conversation. Even his posture and body language were more relaxed. He was as welcoming toward Jerry as he could have been to any family member.

What happened? I couldn't ask him, but I asked Mom when he wasn't around.

"I'm not sure, but you know when we settled into the little house in Maine, we couldn't just retire. That's why we bought the small Sears catalog store in Belfast. Running that was work on every level, even though we didn't have a lot of products in the store. The work went from physical to ordering to book-keeping to deliveries. I thought your father was going to have a nervous breakdown because he hates surprises. He needs to have a plan and have everything work out as expected. It sure didn't feel like any kind of retirement business on the side, and winters were worse than I remembered.

"When I saw how upset he was all the time, I said that we should sell the business, sell the house, and move to Florida and that we could find some easy work to do there. He was so relieved that he cried. You know, I think he had as full a collapse as he had after the fire, but he had no medicine. I had to deal with selling the store and the house, but he packed up everything we would bring, and we searched for rentals together."

"I'm sorry you had to be alone with him through all of that."

"Mark and Pam helped as much as they could. And after a while in the rental, we searched out condos, and this one is in a great spot and was a reasonable price. We'll be all right here, even though our social security and retirement checks are small. Your dad got a job as a security guard at the courthouse, and he likes that. It's very flat here, and he's has taken up bike riding. We've already made good friends. He seems more like the man I married."

"And he's really better? I mean in his moods and everything with you?"

She took my hands and looked directly at me when she said, "Your father brings me coffee in bed each morning. We spend a lot of time with friends we've met at church, and some of his nephews and nieces, your cousins, are in Florida now."

I must have still looked skeptical.

"We don't talk about Andy much, but he doesn't flinch the way he did at the mention of Andy's name. He stays in the room if some visitors ask about the pictures we have of three children and when people who knew Andy talk about him. I think your dad will continue to get better while we live here."

Mom had always been a hopeful person, and she continued to keep precious items to herself that Dad was not ready to see. As I helped her clean one day, I pulled a bedspread down from the shelf in her closet. There was the old black suitcase. I wondered how often she still looked at the contents, but I didn't ask her about it.

On one of our last days during that first visit to Florida, Mom was out golfing with friends. Jerry and the kids were swimming. My father was sitting in their second floor sunroom where he could see the pool. *Should I go down and join the swimmers or actually try to have a conversation with him that would show me if he had changed?*

"Dad?"

"Yes?"

"Can we talk?"

He nodded. That was a surprise, and I chose to sit near him. Before I could say anything, he spoke. "I never wanted to talk to you about the ways I hurt you and our family. I can't explain how a heavy cloud smothered me. It didn't lift."

I didn't dare say anything. I just looked at him. He continued slowly, still gazing at the children in the pool, not at me.

"I felt such shame and embarrassment when you talked to me about forgiveness. You're strong. You've come through well. You made a good choice in Jerry. I doubted him for years because—"

"Because he wasn't like anyone you would have picked out for me?"

"That long hair, it took me years to look at him and not see that. When I was a teenager, we used to beat up guys in our neighborhood who had long hair. I probably felt shame for that too. I couldn't find a way to be different. But something happened in Maine, where I knew I would either go crazy or ask God to be merciful and help me. I begged for help so that your mother and I could have a fresh start."

"And you've found it here."

"I'm feeling better, clearer. I've even been able to talk about Andy with your mother and some other people."

"You are different, better."

"I'm proud of you, Virginia. You did well even with no support from me."

"So you do forgive me?"

"I did, long ago. God's in charge, not a twelve-year-old, not a teenager, not me. I couldn't forgive myself for not being able to get into the house to rescue Andy. I couldn't forgive myself for breaking down and existing on medicine, for my angry moods. I couldn't forgive myself for the way I was treating your mother and you kids. I went through the motions of what a man with a family needed to do. I couldn't find my way out of the dark cloud until everything in Maine became too much for me. Then I saw a sliver of light, and my prayers didn't just bounce off the ceiling."

The conversation stopped because his grandchildren clamored loudly for Gramps to watch them dive into the pool, which he did. I waited and watched them too.

We never had another conversation like that one, but it was enough. Visits to Florida improved. Family from the north and cousins living in Florida came to visit. Even Uncle Sal moved to Florida. My parents opened their condo to be a sharing house so that we could bring guests, the children's friends, and the foreign visitors we hosted. The atmosphere was healthier than it had ever been since the fire.

I had found some peace with Dad, but there were still sore, unhealed spots. In our years in Cape May Court House, I taught in their K–12 system. The students loved breaks in routines with field trips, but going distances was expensive. When I taught the elementary grades, popular field trips were to the library and the fire station, both within walking distance from the elementary schools.

Taking classes to the library was a treat. Visiting the fire station thrilled the students more but made my heart clench. I hadn't told Jerry. It was my problem to work out in my mind and soul. I didn't want to be reminded of the fire. At home I had a compulsion to always double check that everything was off before we left the house, and we never used night-lights.

I could talk about Andy and was sure that somehow, some-day, I would change in thinking about fires of any kind. How that would happen, I didn't know, but every presentation at the fire station made me tense. Watching the students pay rapt attention to the firefighters made me pray they would never have to see them in desperate action at their houses.

WITH TWENTY YEARS in South Jersey, Jerry and I could have coasted into retirement by staying at Cape May Court House. In just ten more years, I would have enough time in the school system to retire with full compensation. Jerry would have enough time as a pastor to retire, but our personalities and view of living fully for God did not include coasting. Jerry filled out forms that said he was open to moving. Any church in the denomination had access to lists of pastors who were actively looking to move or who were open to moving.

The timing of the move came when we were fully empty nesters. Our son had graduated from college, married, and he and our daughter-in-law had good jobs. Our daughter gradu-ated college two months before we moved to Holden, Mass-achusetts. She had planned to live at home while looking for a job and told us that she expected to leave the nest, not to have the nest disappear out from under her. Aunt Marie in North Jersey came to the rescue with her spare guest room, and with

New York City so nearby, an unexpected set of options opened for employment.

Jerry and I made a move to Massachusetts with anticipation of challenges and a new phase of life, but it was hard to leave Cape May Court House after twenty years with special friends, experiences, and memories in the southernmost county in New Jersey. I had never lived so long in one place in my entire life. I counted on the friendships we had formed over the twenty years lasting in spite of distance.

Despite my struggles at the start of our years, I had qualified to teach K–12 language arts and English in New Jersey; passed the National Teacher Exam; written curriculum, plays, and scripts used in local schools and in the church; and earned a master's degree in education. Only as we moved away did I see the practical value of how my experiences had equipped me for a variety of teaching job possibilities.

And Jerry could see the same. His work in Ironton, Williamstown, and now Cape May Court House had given him the skills to venture into another small church that needed to grow and change in the twenty-first century. He had gained practical skills for ministry and earned a doctorate in pastoral ministry. Rather than coasting, he had prayed for God to direct us into serving a new church and community.

As empty nesters, we moved to Holden, Massachusetts. Our home was an 1896 house, the parsonage. It was right next door to the church building in the historic district of Holden. Although many people think all priests and pastors live in a house next to or very close to a church building, we never had. The style of the old parsonage included three floors and a full fieldstone basement; it was completely different from the modern parsonage we'd had in New Jersey. There was even a narrow staircase that led from the kitchen to the third floor from a time when servants or children might have needed to use those stairs.

Jerry had full days right away of committees; outreach; visitation in homes, hospitals, and nursing homes; sermon preparation; teaching a Sunday school class; and community involvement. I had more difficulty finding a job in a public school because my eighteen years of teaching in New Jersey put me into a higher pay category with public school teacher union regulations. I tried religious and charter schools, plus long-term subbing in public schools.

A friend suggested I apply for a college adjunct job. She had a full-time position at a college, and in Massachusetts in the early twenty-first century, colleges would hire faculty who had only a master's degree if they had a lot of successful experience in their field. I was hired as an adjunct at a college just five miles from our central location in Holden.

I began teaching in K–12 schools during the day and taught college classes as an adjunct in the evenings. I did not think Jerry and I could be busier, and we both had jobs that were vocations and avocations.

After two years in Holden, we had a good routine of full days. Then one evening when I got home late from teaching a class, Jerry told me he had been honored to be asked to be a chaplain. It would be a part-time job, a volunteer job with no set hours a week. It would vary in responsibilities, but he could do that along with what he did for the Holden First Baptist Church.

"A chaplain? You're a pastor still learning about your church and community. What group wants you to be their chaplain? The senior citizens center?"

"No. The fire department. Apparently, fire departments are recognizing that a chaplain can help the department and the community, especially if someone other than an administrator in the fire department has the role. A chaplain helps the firefighters and people in emergencies who lose everything because . . ."

He stopped talking. My expression showed him something of the shock I felt. I could not have imagined a more unexpected assault on the area I still kept locked away.

"A chaplain for the Holden Fire Department?"

"Yes, their first. You know I want to help the community, and the fire departments do so much. I was really honored to be asked, but if it upsets you too much, I can tell them it won't work right now." He hugged me. "I never thought about how this would affect you. You don't ever talk about the fire."

"Nothing happens by chance. You and I know that."

"I don't have to be the chaplain."

I knew he meant it.

"It's an honor that they asked you. You'll be a wonderful chaplain. I'll be all right with it."

"Are you sure?"

"There's a reason for this, so maybe . . ."

"Maybe what?"

"Maybe never talking about the fire and trying never to think of it is like pus inside my heart. I locked it all away, but that hasn't healed anything. I always felt like God would find a way to help me, but I had no clue how. Maybe you having this chaplaincy will help."

Over the months and years, we both learned that fire department chaplains can have different levels of involvement. Because Jerry was in good physical shape, he could participate in drills and see what the firefighters had to do to train and stay fit. He attended some of their physical trainings and many that were in the department classroom settings. Jerry offered some presentations about marriage and parenting. Firefighters have a job that brings stress to the whole family. After some emergencies, firefighters need counseling beyond debriefing.

Firefighters and any emergency services workers who respond to life-threatening situations have stresses beyond those in other professions. Chaplains do their best to serve them. They visit firefighters who have been injured. They cope with the effects that go along with a line-of-duty death. They travel with departments to the funerals of firefighters who have died in the line of duty. They counsel the depressed and the suicidal.

Then there are the people who have a fire where they live or who are in vehicle accidents, face a group emergency, or have a medical event like a stroke or heart attack, and chaplains help them too. No matter the time of day or the weather, emergency responders have to do their job. There is no way to know how long a fire, accident, or other emergency crisis will last. Firefighters see some of the worst of human tragedies. Chaplains need to give aid to the mind and spirit of firefighters and their families.

Now when the town fire alarm went off at night, Jerry got up to meet them at the fire location. A phone call or pager let Jerry know where he needed to be. Families would need shelter, and Jerry had to arrange that with local auxiliaries or benevolent organizations. Those who were injured, whether they were victims of the fire or the firefighters themselves, needed to be visited at the hospital. If the chaplain is a local clergyperson like Jerry was, they will probably have a rapport already with hospital personnel.

Unruly and hysterical people would also need attention. Chaplains will try to calm and help people. They provide referrals to emergency agencies, counseling centers, and insurance agents. Support and consolation are part of the chaplain's work in emergencies and in days and hours without emergencies.

Counseling, visitation, social gatherings, weddings, and funerals would all be part of the chaplain's job. As the chaplain shows commitment, respect, and dedication for the firefighters and their families, he gains their respect in turn.

Jerry was the chaplain for the next decade that we lived in Holden. I attended some of the fire department socials and fundraisers with him. When I was teaching during the days and evenings, he did his work as pastor and with town committees, the senior center, and the fire department. We always talked about our days when I got home from teaching.

Night calls were the toughest. Sometimes he got calls from the members of the congregation due to health emergencies or a death in the family. He was up in an instant and out into the dark in all kinds of weather, and the Worcester hills around Holden had tough winters of deep snow and ice. I would see him off, pray for him and for the family or person in need, and eventually go back to sleep.

When the night calls were fire department calls, I could see Jerry off, pray for him and everyone involved, but never get back to sleep. In wakefulness and prayer, I wrestled with the last vestiges of anger, guilt, and fear. I have read that in the traditions of fire departments, there was always someone who could act in the role of chaplain, but there was no sight of or word from any chaplain the night of our fire.

29

FINAL STEPS, A CLEARING OUT, AND A CHOICE

The pus of painful memories, guilt, and resentment decreased more with each year. I still had moments when I recognized rancid bits in me, but they were draining away. I enjoyed each day teaching at the college in the full-time position I had been offered.

I started working on a doctoral degree. Because of my background, I could take on several roles at the college. I taught classes to future educators, guided education students completing their master's theses, supervised student teachers, organized the core English classes, taught core classes that prepared students for academic writing, and taught some English literature classes from American Literature to Women's Studies. My name appeared as a faculty member in the humanities and education majors.

In summers, some of the most challenging adventures of my life came when I worked with the nongovernmental organization Amity. Every year they looked for volunteers who would go into remote areas of China. Chinese teachers of English needed no help in writing. They knew more grammar rules than most native English speakers. But they needed help to improve their speaking, listening, and teaching strategies that were necessary for learning English.

My family thought I was crazy to go to China. They worried about me so much that my parents asked me to teach them how to use a computer so that they could email me. Even though I knew electricity and computer access was not guaranteed in all the places where I would be, I bought them their first computer and taught them how to use email.

My father felt like a whole new universe had opened up to him. He did not just email. He went to libraries and museums around the world. He found his favorite preachers and teachers doing online presentations and reveled in this new tool. My mother became jealous of the computer and avoided it. Maybe that's why she so rarely used it.

In the months that I worked in China, a few friends and family members sent encouraging emails. In the earliest of the eight years I worked in China, I did not have a cell phone, and access to the office area with computers was restricted to a few hours a day. All the foreign teachers craved connections to home and would rush to use the computers as soon as they were available.

One person wrote to me every week during the years that I lived and taught in those rural locations, every year that he was alive: my dad. His emails weren't long, but I could tell he enjoyed communicating quickly with someone half a world away. What we'd seen about the future of communications at the World's Fair decades ago had come to fruition.

Dad told me when I got home that he enjoyed figuring out the wording to send messages of faith. He composed them in a way that would not draw negative attention from China's email censors.

.   .   .

Dear Virginia,

I have talked to Father and know that all will be well with you. Light and salt are necessary everywhere. Father will send guidance. You are in my meditation time each day. The words from Father assure us we can have confidence in anything we do for Him.

With love,
Dad

I LOVED my work and the fact that the college was always looking for ways to meet student needs that would equip them for a variety of careers. In the first decade of the twenty-first century, many colleges expanded from traditional liberal arts education to offering courses and programs designed to prepare students for specific professions. The college I worked for added public administration, criminal justice, nursing, health administration, emergency management, counseling, and fire science. Although the professional programs did not have the same number of required courses, making sure students could communicate clearly was important for any field. Every degree required at least one English course.

The professors of English were asked to design and teach courses to help students in the practical specific professional programs. In any specific career-oriented program, students would need professional-level writing skills, the ability to compose presentations for committees and public groups, knowledge of media requirements, and the ability to research and apply for grants. Reading abilities should include identifying trustworthy sources and abilities to summarize and lead in federal, state, and local regulations.

I was asked to teach professional-level writing in the fire

science program. After just a moment of speechless surprise that I tried not to show on my face, I agreed. Firefighters already had my respect and gratitude in a depth they might never understand. If I could help equip current and future firefighters working to complete a college degree, that would be my honor. I also saw it as a grace of final healing.

I was wrong. It was not the last step.

MY FATHER DIED IN 2016. He chose to go to Maine for his last few months. Mark had a large house there full of family. The town had an active and caring hospice agency. Dad had hospice care for five months. In his last days of life on this earth, my mom, sister-in-law, and I slept in chairs in his room to be with him through each night. We and other family members sang to him, prayed with him, and reminded him of all the people he loved who he would see soon, especially Andy. Dad could smile even when he couldn't talk. He had a roomful of family, music, and prayer as he left this life on earth.

Like Andy, Dad had two funerals. One was held in Maine and was attended by family and friends in New England, and one was held in Florida for their friends and family there. He had military honors, music, flowers, and a eulogy for the man he had been when I was a child and for the man who had returned when he and Mom moved to Florida.

When Dad was gone, we all knew Mom could not live alone. She had mild dementia, and though she visited family in Maine and me in Central Virginia, she wanted to stay in Florida. The years there had given her a couple of decades of happiness with the person who had changed and mellowed back into the loving man she had married. She moved into an apartment building for seniors in Jacksonville.

Mom died in July 2020 but not of COVID-19. She had been overwhelmed by dementia. The pandemic rules in the senior apartment facility changed every daily routine. Socializing was prohibited. Isolation pushed her off the cliff of reality and into crippling dementia. In hospice care she curled up into a fetal position and refused to eat or drink. Her death certificate said failure to thrive.

Mom passed away on her wedding anniversary with just the hospice person and my brother present. Those who knew her romantic nature and how much she loved my father saw her passing on that day as fitting. She went to sleep and woke up in the morning of her anniversary perfectly whole, in the presence of all that was love and with the man she had loved for almost seventy years.

Like most funerals in the extreme restrictions of COVID-19 concerns, Mom's service was attended by a small group of family and her closest friends. When her apartment was cleared out, my brother took some items to Maine and dropped off boxes of papers, books, and photo albums for me. I couldn't even bring myself to open them until the fall.

When I did, I read through incomplete journals and letters to her from family and friends. I found Sunday school lessons and books that had belonged to my father. I looked through the photo albums and opened boxes within boxes filled with everything from special issue magazines to books on Mom's interests and souvenirs of trips.

The last box I opened, though large, was not heavy. On top were a couple of her favorite outfits. I took those out wondering where to give them away, and under those I saw a small worn black suitcase.

I could not open the little black suitcase that day. It sat alone on a bed in our unused guestroom. When I did finally choose to open the case, it contained everything I remembered.

Sympathy cards, notes, the funeral guest book, and Andy's clothes—the sweater a lady from church had knit for him, the one that had a hole in the cuff area; a pair of Andy's navy blue pants dress pants with a tear in the knee; a T-shirt with G.I. Joe on it; a blue and white checked shirt; and a pair of blue-, red-, and white-striped swimming trunks that needed a new elastic. I saw the small white envelope and looked into it for the first time. It held the first four baby teeth that Andy lost.

For a long time, I sat holding, looking at, and reading through everything and wondering how many times these items had given comfort to my mother. Was it comfort she felt or a temporary link to the past? A chance to feel like she was touching Andy?

My father did not have comfort for decades. His personality and faith had collapsed into grief and guilt. Could he have been helped by counseling? I think that would have been beneficial to him, Mom, and the family. I did feel thankful he had found comfort in finally seeing that God had forgiven him and had carried him through half a century of isolating grief and blame, waiting for him to see light through the dark cloud.

Some people fall apart in grief. Their foundational beliefs can also shatter when they grieve. Grief has no set pattern or timing. People who do not understand or accept that fact feel frustration and anger, with uncommon patterns and times of grieving. Max Lucado said, "The healing of the heart involves the healing of the past."[1]

Even though Jerry and I later moved to Virginia, I still taught for the Anna Maria College in the online fire science program. Continuing to work with students who are serving people and communities—firefighters, EMTs, police officers, and nurses—gave me peace every time I was able to help them reach their goals. It is an honor to work with them. Every community needs them.

A choice stood before me now. The suitcase and all its contents made me see that I could continue looking inward, looking backward, or seeing and sharing a fuller picture of grace interlaced in my life. The future could include life lessons learned and shared to encourage others. But could I share this? Could I tell the story of how God's grace patiently and finally brought healing to my soul? I could try. And with God's grace over so much time, this is the result of my efforts.

ACKNOWLEDGMENTS

My writing has had encouragement and support from family members, friends, and writers' groups. The primary encourager for all aspects of my life—spiritual, family, career, and writing—is my husband, Rev. Dr. Jerry D. Heslinga, who consistently has encouraged me in more ways than I can name and who has always supported my writing efforts.

More thanks than I can put in a list goes to my friends and spiritual mentors of decades, Beccy Jones and Lynne Drake. Gordon Saunders, Ph.D., a friend of fifty-two years, has been a writing and indie publishing mentor. My own mentor in working with college students, Christine Holmes, helped smooth the transition into undergraduate and graduate teaching, which enriched my life and my skills. Faculty and staff member friends at Anna Maria College and Assumption College encouraged creativity, research, writing, and presentations. Marianne P. Roman and Anne Marie Lauranzon have been wonderful with practical business suggestions. Thanks also to friends who have encouraged me once they knew of my writing plans and goals.

Classmates in writing seminars, conferences, and writing groups like the Flourish Writing Community and the Advancing Writing Endeavors group for consistently providing examples and encouragement. Other writers who have shared important writing tips include Jenny Kochert, Mindy Kiker, Lucinda Bradley, Allen Arnold, Shanae Johnson, Lydia

Scherer, Jane Friedman, Steve Pieper, Stephenia H. McGee, Ingrid Gearhart, Sharon Deming, and Naomi Rawlings.

Over the past three decades, Sandy Kurtz, especially, has consistently prodded and prayed for me in my writing endeavors.

A special thank-you to Tom Parsons, who helped me find the newspaper articles from May 1965, and to Bonnie Parsons for cheering both of us on in our efforts.

To Cindy Bradley go all the kudos a thorough beta reader can receive. Other beta readers who have helped with suggestions, content arrangement, and editing are Minnesota Sparkie, Joy D'Aria, Caryl Saunders, Rev. Kendra Grimes, Carolyn Allard, family counselor Randi Marcinkiewicz, and Jeanne Smith and Dr. I. David Daniels, Ph. D., CSD, VPS, retired fire chief and 30-plus-year veteran of emergency services.

APPENDIX 1: NEWSPAPER ARTICLES

The Herald News
Passaic, NJ
May 11, 1965
Page 11

Union Blaze Fatal to Boy

UNION, N.J. (AP) — A 7-year old boy was burned to death Monday night when a fire that raced through his home caused the roof to collapse.

Two firemen were injured fighting the blaze. Two other children escaped injury.

The body of Andrew Riposta was found in his bed about an hour after the fire started in his home at 1337 Magie Ave., a two-story frame building.

His sister, Virginia, 12, and brother, Mark, 9, fled the house. His parents, Frank and Katherine Riposta were not at home when the fire broke out. They arrived at the scene as firemen played a spotlight at the front door of the house. They had to be restrained by police from trying to enter the building.

The cause of the fire was unknown. Most of the damage was confined to the second floor.

Fireman Michael Pelosi was admitted to St. Elizabeth's Hospital with burned hands. Another fire fighter, Finton Mooney, was treated for smoke inhalation.

Central New Jersey
Home News
New Brunswick, NJ
May 11, 1965
Page 2

Youngster Dies In House Fire

UNION (AP) — A 7-year-old boy died and three other children escaped unharmed last night when a fire raced through the second floor of a house here.

Dead was Andrew Riposta, son of Mr. and Mrs. Frank Riposta, who were returning from a Township Committee meeting when the fire broke out, according to police.

The youngster's body was found in the upper bunk of a bed on the second floor of the house at 1337 Magie Ave.

A 12-year-old daughter, Virginia, another son, Mark, 8, and David Owens, 2, a friend of the family from Elizabeth, managed to flee in time.

The parents returned home as firemen were extinguishing the blaze. They had to be restrained by firemen who put them in an ambulance. The cause of the fire was not known.

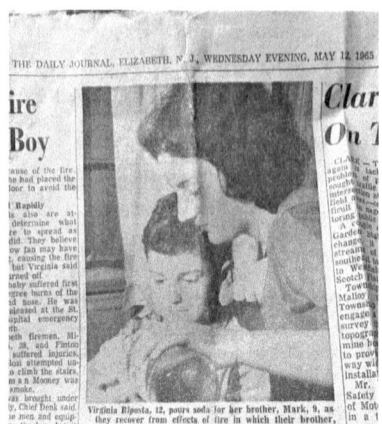

THE DAILY JOURNAL, ELIZABETH, N. J., WEDNESDAY EVENING, MAY 12, 1965

ire Boy

...cause of the fire.
...an had placed the
...loor to avoid the

Rapidly
is also are at-
... determine what
...re to spread as
did. They believe
...ow fan may have
..., causing the fire
... but Virginia said
...urned off.
...baby suffered first
...gree burns of the
...d nose. He was
...leased at the St.
...spital emergency
...th.
...ith firemen. Mi-
..., 38, and Fintan
... suffered injuries.
...toni attempted un-
...o climb the stairs.
...m a n Mooney was
...smoke.
...vas brought under
...y, Chief Denl said.
...e men and equip-
...ng the boy, but it

Clar On ...

CLA... — T...
again ...
... problem ...
... sought ...
... interre...
... field ...
... ficult ...
... toring ...
A C...
... Garde...
... chance...
... stream...
... souther...
... to We...
... Scotch ...
Town...
Malloy ...
... Towns...
... engag...
... survey ...
... topog...
... mine b...
... to prov...
... way wi...
... installa...
Mr. ...
Safety ...
of Mot...
in a t...
... prepa...

Virginia Biposta, 12, pours soda for her brother, Mark, 9, as
they recover from effects of fire in which their brother,
Andrew, 7, died Monday night. Children are staying at

APPENDIX 2: MUSIC ATTRIBUTIONS

Song Credits

- Young, George A. "God Leads Us Along." New York: Warner Chappell Music, 1903.
- Woolston, C. Herbert. "Jesus Loves the Little Children." 1913.
- Barraclough, Henry. "Ivory Palaces." 1915
- Vaughn, John B. "We Shall See the King." 1922.

Songs That Have Been Background Music for This Project

- St. Cyr, Jordan. "Fires." New York: Kobalt Music Group, 2020.
- Hermes, Bernie, Mark Hall, and Matthew West. "Just Be Held." Santa Monica, CA: Universal Music Publishing Group, 2014.
- Lyte, Henry F., and William H. Monk. "Abide with Me." 1847.

- Millard, Bart. "Even If." Brentwood, TN: Fair Trade/Columbia Records, 2017.
- Spafford, Horatio G. "It Is Well with My Soul." In *Gospel Hymns and Sacred Songs.* 1876.
- Tyler, Micah, Matthew West, and Zachary Kale. "I See Grace." Brentwood, TN: Fair Trade Services, 2022.
- Williams, Zach, Jonathan Smith, and Casey Beathard. "There Was Jesus." In *Rescue Story.* Franklin, TN: Provident Music Group, 2019.

APPENDIX 3: QUESTIONS FOR REFLECTION AND DISCUSSION

Parenting

1. Who have you thought about as role models for running a household and building family relationships?

2. How are gender preferences communicated in a family?

3. What have you learned and experienced about sharing, and how do you encourage other people to share?

4. Our family used the phrase "This is a sharing house." What phrase or phrases would describe your household?

5. What kind of leadership exists in your household, and what is this teaching your children?

6. How can children still be made to feel secure and loved when a new baby joins the household?

7. Who have you introduced to your children as safe and important people to contact in an emergency?

8. Have you planned fire drills in your household? Other emergency drills?

9. How would it help a family to talk about and introduce children to the work of first responder/emergency workers?

10. Have you discussed unanswered prayers or unsolvable problems with your children? Why or why not?

11. What teachings from the Bible have been important in your family?

12. If you could change something about your family life, what would it be?

Babysitting

1. How do you introduce a babysitter to key elements of safety in the home?

2. Are there neighbors who people or babysitters in your house could turn to for help in an emergency?

3. Have you explained fire drills and exits in your household to the babysitter? Other kinds of emergency drills?

4. What rules about communication should be clear for a babysitter?

5. How can an organized house help a babysitter to do a good job?

6. What specifics should adults give a babysitter before leaving the household?

7. How can a babysitter be encouraged to ask questions or report issues?

8. Do you know and communicate information about the allergies of children in the household?

9. Do you know if a babysitting course the sitter has taken included unusual hazards, choking, or CPR?

10. What family routines should the babysitter be sure to follow?

11. What expectations about activity and fun should be communicated to the babysitter?

12. What rules and limits should a babysitter follow, since children do best with structure and boundaries?

Fire Safety in the Home

1. Do you have smoke alarms on every level and outside every sleeping area that you test regularly?

2. Is there a carbon monoxide alarm in a central location and by sleeping areas?

3. Is your house number easily readable from the street, even at night?

4. Are all items that could catch fire in your house/apartment kept at least three feet away from space heaters and anything else that gets hot?

5. How have you discussed fire dangers and ways to be safe from fire with other members of your household?

6. Do you turn appliances and portable heaters off when you leave the house?

7. Are flashlights rather than candles accessible when the power goes out? (Never leave burning candles unattended.)

8. Do you make sure to keep wiring and outlets in good condition and replace any frayed extension cords?

9. Do you have a fire escape plan that household members have practiced?

10. How many fire extinguishers do you have, where are they located, and do you and all members of the household know how to use them?

11. Of the main causes of fire in a home, which ones do you see as dangers in yours: heating equipment, smoking, electrical equipment, candles, inadequate wiring, cooking, flammable liquids, Christmas decorations, space heaters, barbecuing, lithium batteries, lint built up in a dryer or hose, aerosol cans, young people who play with matches or fire, combustible construction materials?

12. What should you do if a person's hair or clothing catches fire?

Helping Others through Trauma and PTSD

1. How do you study or have conversations about helping people feel safe and at ease in difficult times?

2. What positive ideas can you share about helping people who have had a family trauma?

3. Sometimes the helpers, as Mr. Rogers called them, find it difficult to talk about tragedy and death. Have you ever had to talk about sad news with someone? How did you choose to present it?

4. What daily life events will a family need help with after a disaster?

5. How well do you allow for spending time without any pressure with someone who has been through trauma?

6. What helps a person to listen and visit without making assumptions about how the traumatized person feels?

7. How can you show that you accept their feelings about what has happened?

8. In what ways do you look for what might trigger effects connected to the trauma?

9. What support do you have for coping and helping someone with trauma and its effects?

10. How can you maintain and encourage a respect for privacy for the person about what has happened to them and what they might have shared with you?

11. Why is it sensible to only give advice if you are asked to?

12. How capable do you feel of recognizing stages of trauma: denial, anger, bargaining, depression, grief, and acceptance?

Forgiveness

1. In forgiving oneself, how are responsibility and worth intertwined?

2. When a person exhibits remorse or shame, what can be affirmed to help them cope with those feelings?

3. Why might understanding the difference between feelings and facts help sort through a situation needing forgiveness?

4. Can a person experience forgiveness if no amends are made?

5. Which compassion and forgiveness-oriented skills do you have: attention, sensitivity, sympathy, distress tolerance, empathy, lack of condemnation?

6. Can you explain why forgiveness matters psychologically, emotionally, spiritually, and physically?

7. How do mercy and grace connect to forgiveness?

8. Does forgiveness require the practice of letting go? Why or why not?

9. Which forgiveness aversion actions do you recognize or have you taken: distancing, unresolved emotion, self-protective boundaries, refusal to forgive as a way to maintain power or control, fear of more victimization, saving face, resistance to understanding the other perspective(s)?

10. Can forgiveness be taught? How?

11. Why has forgiveness been identified as a key part of resilience?

12. What are strong biblical examples of the power of forgiveness for the forgiver and for the ones forgiven?

NOTES

20. Gordon's Gin

1. Elisabeth Elliot, *Through Gates of Splendor* (Tyndale Momentum, 1981).

26. Tensions, Worth, and Silence

1. Corrie ten Boom, *The Hiding Place: The Triumphant True Story of Corrie ten Boom* (Bantom Books, 1974).
2. Desmond Tutu, *The Book of Forgiving* (Harper One, 2014), 16.

29. Final Steps, a Clearing Out, and a Choice

1. Max Lucado, *You'll Get Through This: Hope and Help for Your Turbulent Times* (Thomas Nelson, 2013).

ABOUT THE AUTHOR

Virginia Heslinga, Ed.D., is Associate Professor of Humanities at Anna Maria College in Paxton, MA. She received the Living the Mission Award, which is presented to a member of the faculty who understands and appreciates the great importance of educating the whole student and seizes every opportunity to do so.

Over 45 years, Virginia has taught in a variety of schools, public, private, alternative, homeschools, religious and online. She has worked in this country and in others with every age group. She has articles published in education journals, writes curriculum, and has a novel, *Wounded Dove* based on the amazing true story of a young woman stricken by polio in the early 1900s. Virginia is a child of God, a wife, mother, grandmother, educator, author, and traveler.

www.ingramcontent.com/pod-product-compliance
Lightning Source LLC
Chambersburg PA
CBHW050854150626
46549CB00013B/1618